# Human Rights, the United States, and World Community

# Human Rights, the United States, and World Community

VERNON VAN DYKE
The University of Iowa

New York
OXFORD UNIVERSITY PRESS
London Toronto 1970

Library of Congress Catalogue Card Number: 75-94558



Printed in the United States of America

# Preface

This book concerns policy issues relating to human rights faced by the United States in the United Nations, the Organization of the American States, and other international organizations. Its main purpose is to provide the kind of knowledge that Americans need to make judgments on these issues.

The subject is rapidly increasing in importance. International action on one human right or another has occurred sporadically over a period of several centuries, but it took Dachau and Buchenwald to put the subject on the international agenda on an urgent basis. The UN Charter stresses it, listing the promotion of human rights among the major purposes of the organization. In 1948 the General Assembly adopted the Universal Declaration of Human Rights, and in the ensuing years it has adopted many other more specialized declarations and conventions. In 1966 it adopted, and thus recommended for ratification, two Covenants on human rights, one setting forth civil and political rights and the other economic and social rights. Violations of human rights in Southern Rhodesia have led the Security Council, for the first time in its history, to order the mandatory application of sanctions, and a campaign has been building up for the same kind of action against South Africa. Human rights—above all, those relating to racism and colonialism—are major subjects on the UN agenda. The International Labor Organization, by its very nature, deals extensively with questions in the field of human rights. The Charter of the Organization of the

American States contained provisions on the subject from the first, and they are strengthened by amendments included in the Protocol of Buenos Aires in 1967. The Inter-American Commission on Human Rights is active and aggressive. The Statute of the Council of Europe requires every member to accept the principle that human rights and fundamental freedoms are to be respected, and almost all of the members have ratified a convention spelling out their obligations and arranging for implementation through a Commission and a Court of human rights. The military dictatorship in Greece is currently being held internationally accountable for failing in its obligations; a principle is thus being insisted upon, and a precedent set, that could have far-reaching implications in the future. It is obviously taken to be a matter not merely of domestic but also of international concern that no Hitler shall come to power again.

The United States started out in a position of international leadership in these developments, but Senator Bricker forced an abandonment of this role in the early 1950's. An anachronistic situation thus exists in which a country that champions human rights at home and styles itself as a defender of freedom in the world defaults on its own principles, playing only a secondary and hesitant role in a movement that could contribute much more than it does both to national advantage and to human welfare. Given the default, the movement in the United Nations has come under the very substantial influence, if not the control, of those whose concern for human rights stops with the problems of racism and self-determination and whose ideas about attacking these problems in southern Africa raise the question where the threat to the peace really lies.

In studying these problems and writing this book I have had considerable assistance. The University of Iowa gave me a research appointment for a semester and reduced my teaching load during another semester. The Carnegie Endowment for International Peace provided me with a study in its library for a period of three months. In the Secretariat of the United Nations, Mr. Ilhun Lutem of the Division of Human Rights and Mr. Enuga S. Reddy, Chief, Section for African Questions, both read portions of the manuscript and assisted me with documentary materials. David F. Squire of the U.S. Mission to the UN also read a portion of the manuscript, as did Moses Moskowitz, representing the Consultative Council of Jewish Organizations at the United Nations. Mr. Stephen C. Schott, Deputy Executive Director, President's Commission on the International Human Rights Year (1968), read the whole manuscript. Mrs. Thomas and Mrs. Jones gave me valuable assistance in using UN documents at the Department of State, and Robert Johnston, of the staff of the Inter-American Commission on Human Rights, provided me with documents and gave me information orally. Several colleagues at Iowa have been very helpful, especially Joseph Tanenhaus. And I have learned much from graduate students who have been in my seminars on human rights and who have written theses under my supervision.

The subject is big and complex enough that my treatment of it no doubt still has shortcomings, despite the good help I have had. But I hope that it will be useful nevertheless.

V.V.D.

Iowa City, Iowa
May 1969

# Contents

# I

# Introduction

# 1

# Introduction

The problems to be dealt with in this book fall into three main categories. The first category concerns the question, What are human rights? More particularly, it concerns the question, What are identified as human rights in international discussions and documents, and what are the related issues and controversies? This question leads to others. What intellectual and political considerations influence those who attempt to define human rights, and what are the probable implications and consequences of the definitions advanced? When the United States has faced the problem in international relationships—for example, in the United Nations, in the Organization of the American States, and in the International Labor Organization—how has it responded?

The second category concerns the problem of international obligation. Relationships between individuals and governments have traditionally been, in the main, matters of domestic jurisdiction, and until World War II questions about them rarely arose in international relationships. But since World War II, one of the more prominent questions of foreign policy has been whether and to what extent to make the protection and promotion of human rights a matter of international obligation. What attitudes are taken on this question? What supporting considerations are advanced, and how cogent do they seem to be? What international obligations has the United States in fact accepted, and what additional obligations is it invited to accept?

The third concerns implementation. When international obligations are accepted in the field of human rights, should any special arrangements be made to promote or assure respect for them? What kinds of arrangements—what kinds of measures of implementation or enforcement—have been adopted or suggested? What attitudes have the United States and other states taken toward the various possible measures? How, and how well, have they justified these attitudes?

The problems in all three of these categories fit into a broader context. They concern the age-old question of the relationship of man and the state—the actual and the desirable relationship; at the same time, they concern the relationship of both man and the state, on the one hand, with the international community, on the other. The question is one of emphasis, of priority. Which comes first, the state or the individual? Does the state have untrammeled freedom to treat those under its jurisdiction as it sees fit? What kinds of limitations do states accept having to do with the dignity of man? What kinds of obligations do they have to serve the needs of man? Do these matters belong solely within the domestic jurisdiction of states, or do the people in one state have a proper concern for the freedom and welfare of people in others? To what extent do these matters come up in international organizations, and when they come up what kinds of stands are taken by governments and by those seeking to influence governmental actions? How, and how well, do they justify these stands? If states are, or are to be, legally obligated to respect human rights and fundamental freedoms, what kind of world political order is implied? What happens to sovereignty?

My attack on these questions in this book is not meant to be either personal or polemical; on the contrary, it is meant to be informative, reasoned, and detached. At the same time it is no doubt influenced by values that I held when I began the inquiry and that I still hold—values that are widely shared in the United States and over the world. It is needless and probably futile to attempt to describe them fully, but they can be characterized as liberal and internationalist. They include the assignment of worth to human beings simply because they are human, and they dictate some degree of concern for the fate and welfare of human beings everywhere. The end to be pursued is the creation and preservation, whereever possible, of social conditions that best stimulate and enable individuals to realize their potentialities in a free and responsible way. The state is a means to this end, not an end in itself. Due loyalty is to go to the state, but the arrangements under which other people live, and the international order itself, are also matters of concern. Indifference to the Hitlers and the Stalins of the world is immoral. As the Universal Declaration of Human Rights says, "Everyone is entitled to a social and international order in which the rights and freedoms set forth in this Declaration can be fully realized."

The internationalist aspects of the above position are all the easier to take because they very probably coincide with the requirements of an enlightened nationalism. Human rights are already very largely respected in the United States, and remaining shortcomings are under attack. To promote human rights internationally is thus to promote the extension to other countries of principles to which the United States is already committed. It is to promote the development of a world environment conducive to the achievement of American ideals. Progress is bound to be slow, impeded in many countries by physical circumstance and by deeply rooted tradition and culture. Methods employed might well be ineffective or even counterproductive. But the opportunity exists to serve simultaneously a national and a liberal-humanitarian international interest.

My approach to the problem is mainly empirical. The Charter of the United Nations includes provisions concerning human rights, and so do the constitutions of various other international organizations, for example, the International Labor Organization, the Organization of the American States, and the Council of Europe. Relevant discussions occur in these and other organizations, and in special conferences. The proceedings of these bodies, the recommendations and declarations that they make, and the covenants or conventions that they adopt give voluminous information on the conceptions of human rights that the participants hold. And many other sources, official and unofficial, are available as well.

With respect to the question, what are human rights? (the question to which the chapters of Part II are addressed) we might note that the answers given are neither definitive nor, for the most part, legally binding. For example, in 1966 the General Assembly of the United Nations adopted two Covenants on human rights, one dealing with civil and political rights and the other with economic, social, and cultural rights. But the formal adoption of these Covenants did not mean that they forthwith became binding on the member states, or even on those member states that voted for them; rather, it meant that the General Assembly recommended them to individual states for ratification. The Covenants are to become binding only on those states that ratify, and each state does this in accordance with its own constitutional processes. Similarly, the resolutions and declarations of the General Assembly on human rights are not, as a rule, legally binding. In a few instances, they reflect already existing law, and in other instances they may well constitute steps in the process by which customary law is created. But a two-thirds vote in the General Assembly does not itself mean that law has been enacted. Thus, for the most part, the chapters of Part II deal with recommended definitions of human rights. The extent to which the definitions are already obligatory, or should be accepted as binding, is the subject of Part III. And the problem of bringing about the observance of accepted principles and obligations is the subject of Part IV.

# II

## What Are Human Rights?

# 2

# Civil and Political Rights: Life and Liberty

Spokesmen for all sorts of dictatorships and all sorts of democracies join in the view that men have, or at least should have, civil and political rights; and almost all private parties who address themselves to the question take the same view. Virtually everyone acknowledges a right to life. Virtually everyone endorses liberty—by saying, for example, that the press should be free, that freedom of information should be assured, that arbitrary detention should not occur, and that slavery should be prohibited. Nearly as many say that people have a right to equal and non-discriminatory treatment and that they have a right to participate in government in some way. All agree that people are entitled to the just administration of the law.

But if there is agreement on general ideas and principles, there is sharp disagreement on precise meanings. The American conception of civil and political rights is not universally shared. The effort to spell the principles out reveals different schools of thought, and gives rise to various diplomatic alignments; and as often as not the governments that seek agreement are unable to go beyond general and vague formulas into which each hopes to read the meaning that it prefers. It is with the disagreements, the formulas, and the preferences that this chapter and the next one are concerned.

## THE RIGHT TO LIFE

The statement that virtually everyone acknowledges a right to life means that they acknowledge a right not to be killed—a right to be safeguarded against arbitrary execution or murder. So interpreted, no government openly denies the right, whatever the practices of a few may be. However, when the right to life is interpreted as the right to live, that is, the right to food, medical care, and so on, controversy arises.

In this chapter, on civil and political rights, the first interpretation is assumed. The second interpretation, commonly associated with economic and social rights, will be discussed in Chapter 4.

Though the right not to be killed is generally conceded, basis for marginal controversy exists. When does the right take effect, that is, when does life begin? In general, international declarations and conventions are silent on the subject, leaving the endorsement of the right to life to later interpretation. The draft inter-American convention on human rights is an exception, specifying that the right "shall be protected by law from the moment of conception."[1] The requirement would obviously lead to controversy if pressed, and a number of countries (e.g. Japan) would probably find it unacceptable.[2] Nor would many find it acceptable to time the right to life from a gleam in the eye. The Proclamation of Teheran declares that "parents have a basic human right to determine freely and responsibly the number and spacing of their children."[3] The Proclamation was unanimously adopted in 1968 by delegates attending the official world conference commemorating the twentieth anniversary of the General Assembly's adoption of the Universal Declaration of Human Rights.

Apparently no international conference or agreement has attempted to specify when the right to life ends, that is, when death occurs.

Though the right to life is not construed to forbid capital punishment, the International Covenant on Civil and Political Rights, adopted by the General Assembly in 1966 and thus recommended for ratification, fixes limits on it; for example, according to the Covenant, capital punishment may be imposed only for "the most serious crimes," and may not be imposed on persons below eighteen years of age or carried out on pregnant women. The inter-American draft convention calls for the abolition of capital punishment and specifies that in no case is it to be inflicted for political offenses.[4]

No serious international efforts have yet been made to obtain endorsement of a right not to be required to kill, though some individual countries provide in their domestic law for conscientious objectors.

Since World War II, since Hitler's effort to achieve a "final solution" of what he called the Jewish question, an effort has been made to extend the right to life from individuals to groups, through the prohibition of "genocide," which came to be defined in the Genocide Convention as "any of the following acts committed with the intent to destroy, in whole or in part, a national, ethnical, racial, or religious group, as such:

a. Killing members of the group;
b. Causing serious bodily or mental harm to members of the group;
c. Deliberately inflicting on the group conditions of life calculated to bring about its physical destruction in whole or in part;
b. Causing serious bodily or mental harm to members of the group;
e. Forcibly transferring children of the group to another group."

The Convention giving this definition goes on to declare that not only shall genocide itself be punishable, but also conspiracy to commit it, incitement to commit it, the attempt to commit it, and complicity in it. The Convention binds the parties to enact the necessary enforcement legislation, and it alludes to the possibility that parties might in the future permit the trial of accused persons by an international tribunal on which they would confer the necessary jurisdiction.

Over seventy states have ratified the Genocide Convention. In the United States, President Truman recommended ratification, but the Senate Foreign Relations Committee has refused to permit it, for reasons that we will discuss more fully in Chapter 7. The convention is open to criticism both because of possible domestic complications to which it might lead and because of questions about its potential effectiveness. Especially since the convention speaks of an intent to destroy a group "in part," what is to differentiate genocide from homicide? Might a single murder be genocide? What is accomplished by forbidding genocide that is not already accomplished by forbidding murder? What is to be included under the heading "mental harm"? What would constitute "complicity" in genocide, and what is the relation between "incitement" to genocide, and the right to freedom of speech and press? How would ratification of the convention by the United States affect the constitutional division of powers between the federal and the state governments? Since genocide in the sense of killing of very substantial numbers of people could scarcely occur unless the government was somehow involved, would national legislation provide an adequate basis for enforcement?[5] The vagueness of the definition of genocide and the possibility of abusing the conception are suggested by the fact that a number of African delegates in the United Nations claim that South Africa is guilty of genocide because of its policies of apartheid.[6]

## LIBERTY

Endorsements of a right to liberty are as widespread as endorsements of a right to life, but interpretations differ. We will discuss the right in terms of free speech and press, freedom of religion, and miscellaneous other rights of liberty.

### *Freedom of Speech and Press*

The General Assembly at its very first session adopted a resolution declaring that "freedom of information is a fundamental human right and is the touchstone of all the freedoms to which the United Nations is consecrated."[7] At its third session, in Article 19 of the Universal Declaration of Human Rights, it asserted that

> Everyone has the right to freedom of opinion and expression; this right includes freedom to hold opinions without interference and to seek, receive and impart information and ideas through any media regardless of frontiers.

Two years later it condemned the jamming of international radio broadcasts on the ground that this was "a denial of the right of all persons to be fully informed concerning news, opinions and ideas regardless of frontiers."[8]

On the basis of the views above the General Assembly called a Conference on Freedom of Information which convened in 1948: protection of free speech and press was to become not simply a matter of domestic policy and international exhortation, but of obligation as well. But differences of interpretation quickly appeared. The conference managed to draft three conventions, of which the General Assembly adopted one in 1952—on the International Right of Correction—and ten years later enough states (six) had ratified it to bring it into effect among them. The other two conventions can perhaps best be described as a basis for subsequent steps. The Third Committee of the General Assembly has approved a draft Declaration on Freedom of Information, recommended to it by the Economic and Social Council, and has done considerable work on a potential convention on the subject, but the General Assembly has not found the time to act on either document. Even if a convention on the subject is sometime adopted, the prospect is remote that it will be ratified by any considerable number of states. The reasons for this judgment are not far to seek.

The term "freedom of the press" reflects a reification and is misleading. In a literal sense "the press" cannot be free; it is not an entity that can make choices. The question is by whom it is or should be controlled, and on the basis of what kinds of principles. The question applies to speech as well, at least where mass media are involved. It thus relates broadly to freedom of information and the alleged right to know.

By universal consent, government must play a role in controlling the press and all mass media. Everyone agrees that their power for good and evil is so great that control must not be left entirely in private hands. But the question of the desirable nature and extent of governmental control gives rise to sharp disagreement, producing a virtual impasse in international negotiations. The United States puts the emphasis on control by private parties, that is, on highly decentralized control, and on minimizing legal limitations. The Soviet Union takes the opposite view, insisting on centralized control—on the view that government must see to it that the mass media serve only those purposes judged to be socially desirable. And a considerable portion of the smaller and developing countries, though perhaps willing to leave ownership of the mass media in private hands, want much more extensive governmental regulations and control than the American tradition permits.[9]

In the American tradition—and, for that matter, in the tradition of Western Europe and the English-speaking world—freedom of speech and press exists when private parties and organizations may say and print what they like without advance censorship. It includes freedom to criticize all agencies and acts of government, and to do it in unbridled terms; those in office are supposed to respect and protect the freedom even of their severest critics. It includes freedom to advocate war, revolution, atheism, racial discrimination, fascism, communism, or pacifism. There is no legal requirement that what is said be fair, true, balanced, or objective, and no requirement that it promote purposes that are socially desirable.

The practices cited above rest on the belief that the existence of diverse channels of expression and diverse sources of information is vital to freedom and progress—the surest basis for promoting the good and the right. Put conversely, the fear is that monopoly control, whether in governmental or other hands, might be used to protect error or evil or both.

Government itself is held to need the scrutiny and criticism that freedom of speech and press permit, lest it abuse or misuse its authority and power and go unchecked in doing so.[10] And the people are held to need freedom of speech and press—freedom of communication—if they are to govern themselves effectively in a democratic way. In truth, the common assumption is that the extension of such freedom over the world is a necessary corollary, if not a precondition, of the extension of liberal democracy itself.

At the same time, though the emphasis is on freedom in the sense of decentralized control, some governmental restrictions are accepted. For example, the law prohibits direct incitement to immediate violence and other illegal acts; it prohibits libel and slander; it protects military secrets; and it includes certain other prohibitions, about some of which there is great controversy.

Western European attitudes and practices on the subject are suggested by Article 10 of the European Convention on Human Rights:

> 1. Everyone has the right to freedom of expression. This right shall include freedom to hold opinions and to receive and impart information and ideas without interference by public authority and regardless of frontiers. This Article shall not prevent States from requiring the licensing of broadcasting, television or cinema enterprises.
>
> 2. The exercise of these freedoms, since it carries with it duties and responsibilities, may be subject to such formalities, conditions, restrictions or penalties as are prescribed by law and are necessary in a democratic society, in the interests of national security, territorial integrity or public safety, for the prevention of disorder or crime, for the protection of health or morals, for the protection of the reputation or rights of others, for preventing the disclosure of information received in confidence, or for maintaining the authority and impartiality of the judiciary.

Article 17 of the European Convention is also in point; it specifies that nothing in the convention may be interpreted as implying "any right to engage in any activity or perform any act aimed at the destruction of any of the rights and freedoms set forth herein." West Germany outlaws the Communist party, and defends the action on the basis of this article; moreover, the European Commission of Human Rights has upheld its position. Presumably the article might also be used to defend some kinds of limits on free speech and press—and so could the comparable articles in the Universal Declaration and in the Covenants.

The Soviet Union, as indicated, takes a view opposite to the one accepted in the United States and Western Europe. In the capitalist world, according to the Soviets, the freedom that exists is essentially freedom for the bourgeoisie. Freedom of the press is freedom for those who own the press. If a bourgeois democracy grants free speech and press to revolutionaries, it allegedly does so only on a contingent basis, withdrawing the freedom when and if revolution comes to be really threatening. The bourgeoisie, it is claimed, uses its freedom to promote its own class interests, which in crucial respects are held to be hostile to the interests of the masses of people within the country and over the world. In Moscow's eyes, the free press of the West is thus one of the instruments of exploitation and oppression and one of the supporters of imperialism and war.

This line of thought does not lead the Soviet Union to reject freedom of speech and press. On the contrary, the Soviet constitution guarantees it; and in fact different agencies and organizations in the Soviet Union publish newspapers and have immediate control over other channels and sources of information. According to the constitution, freedom of speech and press "are ensured by placing at the disposal of the working people and their organizations printing presses, stocks of paper, public buildings . . . and other material requisites" for its exercise. But the constitution specifies in effect that the freedom that is granted must be used "in conformity with the interests of the working people, and in order to strengthen the socialist system"; and since the government itself is the agency that formally decides what is in the interest of the working people and what will strengthen the socialist system, control by the government is the dominant fact. According to communist theory, this means control by the people, exercised through the government that speaks for them.

In international negotiations on freedom of speech and press, the Soviet line understandably reflects the conceptions sketched above. Soviet delegates contend that "real freedom of information, and therefore freedom of the Press, can be guaranteed only if the Press is free from pressure and dictation by private publishing monopolies, trusts, and syndicates."[11] Conversely, they hold "that complete freedom of the Press and information can only be assured if the wider masses of the population and their organizations are given the material resources necessary for publishing organs of the Press and for operating other channels of information."[12] They consider it intolerable that freedom should be accorded to "persons engaging in any form of fascist propaganda." They insist that the press "shall not be used for war propaganda"; rather, among its tasks is the "decisive and unremitting unmasking of warmongers."[13] They think it "urgently essential to establish by law strict responsibility for the dissemination of mendacious and libelous information about other peoples and States."[14] They propose that states bind themselves to "take all the necessary steps, including legislative steps, to promote the dissemination of truth and objective information"[15] aimed at strengthening international peace and security. They want a ban on "the dissemination of racial, religious, or national hatred."[16] The Soviet Union took all of these positions in the early years of United Nations negotiations on the subject, and it holds steadfastly to them.

Many of the smaller and developing countries take an in-between view, not asking for government control in the Soviet style but seeking rather drastic modifications of the American pattern of decentralized private control. The outlook is suggested by a statement of a Colombian delegate that the press of his country was free, though "prohibited from publishing anything detrimental to the reputations of individuals, the social order or public tranquillity,"[17] and by a statement of a Spanish delegate that freedom of information "had always been recognized in Spain as one of the inalienable natural rights of the individual. . . . The only restrictions on freedom were those required for the security of the state and the protection of society."[18] The notion that government should protect people from what it regards as evil or error—should assure that the mass media confine themselves to what is true and objective—is widely entertained. One of the motives, at least in many instances, is, obviously, to protect the government from unfavorable publicity and criticism, but other motives also operate. The Western assumption of an abundance of channels of information does not always hold true. Decentralization cannot always be effective, above all in the case of news services and in connection with radio and television. And, assuming that control is inevitably going to be in the hands of a relatively small number of persons, some of whom may be foreign, it is not surprising that some governments decide to exercise the control themselves. Moreover, problems vary. The professional and ethical standards of journalists are not everywhere on a high plane, nor are levels of education and sophistication; and the dangers of domestic disunity and disruption are sometimes acute. Some of these considerations are reflected in the statement of a Malayan delegate at the United Nations that "the influence of any propaganda on a population that was still comparatively unsophisticated was considerable and in an underdeveloped or developing country the task of the information media was not only one of information but also one of education."[19] At the Dakar Seminar on Human Rights in Developing Countries in 1966, a number of speakers sought to explain or justify restrictions on freedom of the press by appealing to "the need to establish and maintain a strong and stable state," or by pointing to "the fragile structure of the African nations" and to the duty of governments not to allow "the disintegration of the nation."[20] In the eyes of many, support for racial discrimination or war is such an obvious evil that it ought to be prohibited, and they get support for their views from precedents set long ago, for example, from the 1936 Geneva Convention Concerning the Use of Broadcasting in the Cause of Peace, in which the parties undertook to prohibit broadcasts inciting to war or to other acts incompatible with international order. In some parts of the world the basic problem is not so much freedom of information as the development of the requisite conditions of a program of mass communication—for example, the training of personnel, obtaining the necessary equipment and material, the development of low-cost techniques, and so on.[21]

One of the principal demands of the smaller and developing countries is aimed essentially at the larger countries with powerful newspapers and other highly developed communication media. It is for action to assure that they will get the same kinds of protection abroad as they get at home from what they regard as the false and the distorted. As a Brazilian delegate once said,

> The more powerful newspapers, which were those of the large countries, were able to have more correspondents abroad. Those correspondents often transmitted inaccurate information, which gave the public a false picture of the country in question and influenced policy with regard to it. A small country could not defend itself against the influence exerted by a newspaper with a circulation of millions.[22]

In seeking to justify demands for action on behalf of accuracy and objectivity, spokesmen for the smaller countries use illustrations that in general are not likely to impress those who accept the American tradition. For example, the Jordanian delegate, referring to Zionist pressures on the American press, once asked that the dissemination of "malicious misinformation" be expressly prohibited.[23] A Nigerian delegate bewailed the foreign correspondent who was more impressed by the number of lizards he saw than by Nigerian streets and schools; and he wanted international action "to ensure respect for the dignity of peoples."[24] An Afghan delegate, arguing for international insistence on "adequate standards of accuracy," complained of American correspondents who reported that Afghanistan was in danger of becoming a Soviet satellite and that the Afghan government was a military dictatorship.[25] A delegate from Ceylon complained that "at the time of the recent elections, all the newspapers in the country had published with the support of international press agencies, false or distorted news about certain members of the Government." In his view, what was needed "was not so much to ensure the freedom of the Press as to make journalists aware of their responsibilities." And he recalled that "in *The Road to Mandalay*, which gave the impression that civilization stopped at Suez, Kipling . . . had alluded to Buddha in insulting terms."[26] A Cuban delegate denounced "repeated slanders concerning the Cuban Chief of State and attempts to conceal the truth about the Cuban revolution."[27] And so on. A considerable portion of the governments in the part of the world stretching from Latin America through Africa and across Asia seem to be smarting because of what they regard as inaccurate, distorted, and unbalanced reporting in the European and American press. They want control (whether decentralized or centralized) managed in such a way as to provide safeguards against such abuses and misuses of the power of the press.

The contrasting views described above made it inevitable that international negotiations would not go well, particularly in view of the fact that so many of the votes in the General Assembly and its committees come from the developing and the communist parts of the world. Of course, much of what the General Assembly has recommended or seems likely to recommend fits with the American tradition, but sharp differences appear in crucial areas.

As already suggested, no great problem has developed about the endorsement of freedom of speech and press in principle. For example, Article 1 of the Draft Convention on Freedom of Information, as approved by the Third Committee of the General Assembly, requires the contracting parties "to respect and protect the right of every person to have at his disposal diverse sources of information." So worded, the requirement is as acceptable to the Soviet Union as to the United States. The article goes on to require, after the pattern of the European Convention on Human Rights, that there be freedom "to gather, receive, and impart" information "regardless of frontiers." A considerable struggle occurred in connection with the choice of the word *gather*, many preferring the word *seek* and contending that those who objected to *seek* were attacking the freedom of correspondents to ferret out the news.[28] Moreover, the article must be read in conjunction with the next one, on permissible restrictions. It asserts that the exercise of freedom "carries with it duties and responsibilities," and is subject

> to such necessary restrictions as are clearly defined by law and applied in accordance with the law in respect of: national security and public order (*ordre public*); systematic dissemination of false reports harmful to friendly relations among nations and of expressions inciting to war or to national, racial or religious hatred; attacks on founders of religions; incitement to violence or crime; public health and morals; the rights, honor and reputation of others; and the fair administration of justice.[29]

These restrictions are more extensive than those provided for in the European Convention and in American law. They are simply permitted, and not made mandatory; but it would not be difficult to read the article as authorizing them, or to interpret the terms in such a way as to modify severely the traditional American conception of freedom. Pressures that led to the inclusion of the article reinforce a conclusion reached by a spokesman for the United States a number of years earlier: "that when it came to the issue of freedom of information, countries were separated by fundamental differences in their political philosophy, governmental practice, and confidence in the intelligence and judgment of human beings."[30]

Other proposed international instruments call for obligatory restrictions. We have already noted that the Genocide Convention bans "incitement" to genocide. The International Covenant on Civil and Political Rights goes much farther in Article 20:

> 1. Any propaganda for war shall be prohibited by law.
> 2. Any advocacy of national, racial or religious hatred that constitutes incitement to discrimination, hostility or violence shall be prohibited by law.

Obvious problems are involved here. In several respects it runs counter to the American tradition and to the requirements of the first amendment. Moreover, what would constitute "propaganda for war," and what would be the test for determining whether "hatred" was advocated and whether it constituted an incitement to hostility? Presumably designed mainly to limit certain types of domestic propaganda, how likely is it that the article would exacerbate international tensions by adding a basis for denunciations and diplomatic protests?

In a somewhat similar vein, the International Convention on the Elimination of All Forms of Racial Discrimination includes Article 4.[31] In it the parties "condemn all propaganda and all organizations which are based on ideas or theories of superiority of one race or group of persons of one color or ethnic origin, or which attempt to justify or promote racial hatred and discrimination in any form." The acceptance of such an obligation—to "condemn"—involves little or no problem, but the article goes on:

> States Parties . . . undertake to adopt immediate and positive measures designed to eradicate all incitement to, or acts of, such discrimination and . . . *inter alia:*
>
> a. Shall declare an offense punishable by law all dissemination of ideas based on racial superiority or hatred, incitement to racial discrimination, as well as all acts of violence or incitement to such acts against any race or group of persons of another color or ethnic origin, and also the provisions of any assistance to racist activities, including the financing thereof;
>
> b. Shall declare illegal and prohibit organizations, and also organized and all other propaganda activities, which promote and incite racial discrimination, and shall recognize participation in such organizations or activities as an offense punishable by law;
>
> c. Shall not permit public authorities or public institutions, national or local, to promote or incite racial discrimination.

The above is to be done "with due regard to the principles embodied in the Universal Declaration of Human Rights," a statement that creates ambiguity about the relation between the requirements quoted and the right of freedom of expression. Ambassador Goldberg chose to interpret the requirements in such a way as to make them compatible with traditional American conceptions. He said that "article 4 does not obligate a state to take action that would prohibit its citizens from freely and fully expressing their views on any subject no matter how obnoxious they may be. . . . We believe that a government should only act where speech is associated with, or threatens imminently to lead to, action against which the public has a right to be protected." He thought it unnecessary "to weaken freedom of speech to defeat racial discrimination. . . . To allow the expression of obnoxious ideas is one of the most effective ways to assure their ultimate rejection." Similarly, he held that "organizations cannot be declared illegal if they merely attempt to win acceptance of their beliefs by speech alone."[32] His statements are in accord with American conceptions, but the interpretation of Article 4 is controversial.[33]

Again problems are obvious, and no good solution is in sight. On the one hand, desires and political pressures within the United States are very strong for the preservation of freedom of speech and press as traditionally conceived. The very persons and groups who are most hostile to war and racism are by and large also the persons and groups who are committed to freedom; and the commitment to freedom reinforces tendencies, evident in Goldberg's statement, to believe that action against the advocacy of war and racism need not include new legal restrictions. Moreover, some on the political Right do not want such advocacy restricted in any case. On the other hand, obvious disadvantages exist in appearing to defend propaganda for war and for racial discrimination. As we will have occasion repeatedly to note, a great many members of the United Nations—above all those from the part of Africa north of the Zambesi—have very strong feelings about racial discrimination and adamantly insist on action against it. The more they are rebuffed the more embittered and alienated they are likely to become. Concrete consequences of this are uncertain, but surely they will not be good either for the United Nations or for the United States.

In any event, the optimism that inspired the policy of the United States in the early post World War II years is long since gone. The stand now is that a treaty is not likely to be an adequate or effective means of promoting freedom of information—a stand that Britain, France, and a number of other countries share. Such hope as exists for helpful international action rests mainly on educational activities (for example, seminars on freedom of information arranged through the United Nations) and on technical aid designed to contribute to the extension and improvement of communication facilities.

### *Freedom of Religion*

The right to freedom of religion is generally conceded in principle, but still raises questions. Article 18 of the Universal Declaration of Human Rights specifies that

> Everyone has the right to freedom of thought, conscience and religion; this right includes freedom to change his religion or belief, and freedom, either alone or in community with others and in public or

> private, to manifest his religion or belief in teaching, practice, worship and observance.

When the Covenant on Civil and Political Rights was formulated, criticisms from the Saudi Arabian delegate led to the deletion of the reference to freedom to change one's religion; instead the Covenant asserts that everyone is free "to have or adopt" a religion or belief of his choice. The change was a concession to classical Islamic law denying a right of apostasy.[34]

In connection with the drafting of the convention on racial discrimination, the original plan was to have it cover religious discrimination as well, but Arab-Israeli difficulties made this impossible (if anti-Semitism was to be condemned, the Arabs wanted Zionism condemned as well); and the proposed separate Convention on the Elimination of All Forms of Religious Intolerance, which includes a special condemnation of anti-Semitism, remains to be adopted by the General Assembly.[35]

Some religions have features that raise serious questions of public policy. When respect for the right to freedom of religion means respect for practices that violate other human rights, what is to be done? The caste system associated with Hinduism contradicts the principle of equality that we will be discussing in a moment. Governments in Islamic countries face a number of problems—in addition to the one concerning a right to change one's religion—because of the requirements of classical Islamic law.[36] Several speakers at the 1966 Dakar Seminar on Human Rights in the Developing Countries spoke of the hold that religions, or at least customs based on religions, have on some peoples of the African continent, and on the wide variety of prescriptions and limitations that are involved. "To hold in check traditions that [run] counter to public order," one speaker claimed, "the State [is] obliged to set limits to the freedom to practice certain beliefs."[37] The draft convention on the elimination of all forms of religious intolerance proposes sweeping obligations.

> States parties shall take effective measures to prevent and eliminate discrimination on the ground of religion or belief, including the enactment or abrogation of laws or regulations where necessary to prohibit such discrimination by any person, group, or organization.

The convention also provides that "any incitement to hatred likely to result in acts of violence" against the adherents of any religion shall be made punishable.

### *Other Rights of Liberty*

The Covenant on Civil and Political Rights specifies that "the right of peaceful assembly shall be recognized" and that "everyone shall have the right to freedom of association with others, including the right to form and join trade unions for the protection of his interests." And then the Covenant adds qualifications. No restrictions are to be placed on the rights "other than those which are prescribed by law and which are necessary in a democratic society in the interests of national security or public safety, public order (*ordre public*), the protection of public health or morals or the protection of the rights and freedom of others." The Universal Declaration includes a comparable affirmative provision.

Apart from trade union rights, which we will discuss in Chapter 4, the principal question raised by the right of assembly and association concerns opposition political parties. *Prima facie*, the terms quoted seem to call for freedom to organize such parties, and it might be that sometime they will be so interpreted; but obviously many of the governments voting for them did not intend this meaning, and the qualifications are vague and general enough to permit a claim that the outlawry of opposition parties is permissible. The subject will come up again below in connection with the question of the right to participate in government.

A number of the rights of liberty relate to arrest and due process of law. Governments readily acquiesce in vague and general principles to the effect that no one is to be subjected to arbitrary arrest or detention and that those who are deprived of their liberty are entitled to court proceedings within a reasonable time. At the same time, a number of countries provide in their law for preventive detention[38] and for the deprivation of liberty through purely administrative action. Moreover, the justice that the courts mete out is not always impartial. Judicial murder occurs. Especially in times of domestic crisis, and above all in revolutionary situations, trials may well be summary. The United States has denounced Castro's Cuba in this connection, just as, after World War II, it accused Bulgaria, Hungary, and Rumania in connection with their treatment of political leaders who were more or less friendly to the West.[39]

The Universal Declaration of Human Rights asserts that "everyone has the right to freedom of movement and residence within the borders of each state." The Covenant on Civil and Political Rights includes a similar provision, but then goes on to admit gargantuan exceptions: the right is not to be "subject to any restrictions except those which are provided by law, are necessary to protect national security, public order (*ordre public*), public health or morals or the rights and freedoms of others. . . ." Interpretations remain to be worked out. The provision is obviously relevant to restrictions on freedom of movement and residence in South Africa and Southern Rhodesia. The exception pertaining to national security seems to permit such actions as that of the United States in removing those of Japanese extraction from the West Coast during World War II. Whether it would permit such relocations of population groups as occurred in Hungary and Yugoslavia after World War II is less certain. Neither is it clear what the relationship is between the requirements of the article and such exchanges of populations by international agreement as occurred between Greece and Turkey after World War I and between Hungary and Czechoslovakia after World War II.

The Universal Declaration likewise asserts the right of everyone "to leave any country, including his own, and to return to his country." The principle became an issue especially in 1949 as a result of the refusal of the Soviet Union to allow Russian women to leave the country to be with foreigners whom they had married. A complaint lodged by Chile led the General Assembly in 1949 to condemn the Soviet practice, and some years later the Soviet Union modified its policy. It would be too much to say, however, that the Soviet Union fully accepted the principle. And, as the Berlin Wall indicates, East Germany rejects it completely.

The Universal Declaration also asserts that "everyone has the right to seek and to enjoy in other countries asylum from persecution." The Covenant on Civil and Political Rights lacks a comparable provision. In 1967 the General Assembly unanimously approved a declaration on the subject that is relatively innocuous. One of the articles specifies that no person entitled to seek asylum is to be rejected at the frontier or expelled or made to return to the state from which he fled. The article is relevant to an agreement that Communist China forced on the Portuguese at Macao, obliging them to take the very actions that the Declaration enjoins. But the Declaration goes on, inevitably, to grant the possibility of exceptions "for overriding reasons of national security or in order to safeguard the population, as in the case of a mass influx of persons." Another article specifies that the right to seek and enjoy asylum "may not be invoked by any person with respect to whom there are serious reasons for considering that he has committed a crime against peace, a war crime or a crime against humanity. . . ."[40] Within the country that grants asylum refugees are of course entitled to human rights, though the fact that they are non-nationals commonly carries disabilities with it; and when they have fled without passports and without means of support many additional problems arise. To help with some of these problems the United Nations maintains the office of the High Commissioner for Refugees.

According to the Universal Declaration, "men and women of full age, without any limitation due to race, nationality or religion, have the right to marry and to found a family. They are entitled to equal rights as to marriage, during marriage and at its dissolution." The Covenant on Civil and Political Rights contains a comparable provision, and the Declaration on the Elimination of Discrimination Against Women, which the General Assembly adopted in 1967, spells out the principle of equal rights for women much more fully.[41] South Africa forbids intercourse and intermarriage between persons who differ in race. In the United States, the Supreme Court has only recently struck down state laws prohibiting interracial marriages.

The Universal Declaration specifies that "no one shall be held in slavery or servitude; slavery and the slave trade shall be prohibited in all their forms." The Covenant on Civil and Political Rights repeats the provision and goes on to prohibit forced labor. A number of other international instruments have dealt with one or another aspect of the subject over the last two centuries. Currently most relevant, perhaps, are the Slavery Convention of 1926, the Supplementary Convention on the Abolition of Slavery, the Slave Trade, and Institutions and Practices Similar to Slavery of 1956, and the Convention on the Abolition of Forced Labor, all of which have been ratified by a number of states on the recommendation of the International Labor Organization. The problem area is more important than most Americans are likely to realize. Ethiopia outlawed slavery only in 1942, Kuwait in 1949, Quatar in 1952. Both Yemen and Saudi Arabia refuse to report to the United Nations concerning the question of slavery in their territories.[42] Apparently some two to four million people still live in slavery or involuntary servitude.[43] Some are plain chattel slaves. Some are serfs, doomed to remain in that status for life. Some are in debt bondage. Some are, in a formal sense, adopted children. Some are wives, bought by their husbands and classified as property.[44] Forced labor also persists, though the numbers of people involved have been drastically reduced by reforms in the Soviet Union since the death of Stalin.

# 3

# Civil and Political Rights:

## Equality and Participation in Government

The Charter of the United Nations asserts in its preamble that "we the peoples" have faith "in the equal rights of men and women," and many other pronouncements go along the same line. The subject of equality and discrimination, above all in relation to race, has generated far more interest and emotion during and since World War II than any other subject in the field of human rights. Struggle concerning it is in progress, involving ominous problems.

The Universal Declaration and other documents speak also of the right to participate in government and in genuine, free elections. Though rights in this category have so far received less attention in the United Nations and in other international organizations, and though different governments assign them very different meanings, they are potentially of great importance.

### ASSERTIONS OF THE RIGHT TO EQUALITY

Formal statements of the right to equality appear in numerous treaties, declarations, and draft documents. In addition to the reference to the subject in the preamble of the Charter, Articles 55 and 56 bind members of the United Nations to cooperate with it in promoting human rights "without distinction as to race, sex, language, or religion." The General Assembly passed a resolution on the subject at its first session (along with the one on freedom of information), declaring that "it is in the higher interests of humanity to put an immediate end to religious and so-called racial persecution."[1] The Universal Declaration of Human Rights asserts that "all human beings are born free and equal in dignity and rights" and that "everyone is entitled to all the rights and freedoms set forth in this Declaration, without distinction of any kind, such as race, colour, sex, language, religion, political or other opinion, national or social origin, property, birth or other status." It further asserts,

> All are equal before the law and are entitled without any discrimination to equal protection of the law. All are entitled to equal protection against any discrimination in violation of this Declaration and against any incitement to such discrimination.

The Covenant on Civil and Political Rights asserts very similar principles. In 1958 the International Labor Organization proposed its "Discrimination (Employment and Occupation) Convention," binding the parties "to declare and pursue a national policy designed to promote, by methods appropriate to national conditions and practice, equality of opportunity and treatment in respect of employment and occupation, with a view to eliminating any discrimination in respect thereof." Note that the obligation is to "promote," implying that progressive realization rather than immediate implementation of the principles is anticipated.[2] In 1960 UNESCO adopted a Convention Against Discrimination in Education. In 1963 the General Assembly adopted a Declaration on the Elimination of All Forms of Racial Discrimination[3] and in 1965 it approved and invited states to ratify an international convention on the subject. In 1967 it adopted a Declaration on the Elimination of Discrimination against Women.[4]

We have already quoted from Article 4 of the Convention on the Elimination of All Forms of Racial Discrimination, calling for the outlawry of organizations and propaganda activities that promote racial discrimination. The preamble to the convention asserts, among other things, "that any doctrine of superiority based on racial differentiation is scientifically false, morally condemnable, socially unjust and dangerous and that there is no justification for racial discrimination, in theory or in practice, anywhere." Article 2 obliges the parties to "undertake to pursue by all appropriate means and without delay a policy of eliminating racial discrimination in all its forms." To this end, they ensure that all public authorities, national and local, will refrain from racial discrimination; and they undertake to amend laws as necessary where the laws have the effect of creating or perpetuating racial discrimination. Further, according to the convention, "each State Party shall prohibit and bring to an end, by all appropriate means, including legislation as required by circumstances, racial discrimination by any persons, group or organization." The obligations proposed are obviously severe, though reservations are possible.[5] The convention came into force in March 1969, having been ratified by thirty-one states and signed by forty others. The United States has signed but not ratified. Only the ratifying states are formally bound, but regardless of this a considerable number of governments—especially those controlled by non-whites—will be pressing for the observance of its terms.

## THE MEANING OF EQUALITY

Human beings differ. They differ in a myriad of ways—in race, sex, language, religion, political beliefs, age, national extraction, nationality, talent, skills, education, interests, achievements, culture, wealth, etc., etc. Even the most ardent advocate of equality does not contend that all differences should be ignored. On the contrary, all believers in equality also believe in discrimination. But which differences are acceptable as bases for discrimination, and which are not? What sort of discrimination is acceptable? How far may the discrimination be carried? Most of the struggle over equality is over the appropriate answers to these questions.

Many centuries ago Aristotle suggested what is now the most widely accepted step toward answers. He favored the reasonable classification of people on the basis of significant differences and discriminating among them accordingly. Equality would prevail within the categories, but not among them. Without such discrimination, injustice would surely be done. With it, justice might be achieved, provided differences in treatment were proportionate to the degrees of difference between the categories.[6]

In effect, Aristotle's ideas concerning classification are accepted in American constitutional practice. The principle that no one is to be deprived of the equal protection of the laws is not interpreted to forbid classification and related discrimination. What it forbids is the arbitrary and the unreasonable.

But what is arbitrary and unreasonable? Answers vary in different parts of the world, and they change. The fact is evident within the United

States alone, most notoriously in connection with discrimination based on race. In 1896 the Supreme Court found it reasonable for states to follow the "separate but equal" doctrine in treating Negroes, but before the middle of the 1950's it had repudiated the doctrine completely; through the whole period, and even yet, intelligent people inspired by what they regard as high moral principle and obviously seeking to promote what they regard as the good of all take different views on the issue.

Historically, agitation for equality has been directed against successive sorts of discrimination deemed arbitrary and unreasonable. In some times and places the preoccupation has been with the arbitrary and the unreasonable in the administration of justice, for example, with prohibiting bills of attainder and providing for writs of habeas corpus. In other times and places the preoccupation has been with discrimination based on birth, for example, with the privileges once accorded to those of noble birth in France and with the implications of caste in India. In still other times and places the preoccupation has been with discrimination directed against certain religious groups or national minorities, or with discrimination based on sex. The bases for discrimination that are acceptable or unacceptable have varied in different countries at different times depending on the outcome of the struggles. By the end of World War II the states represented at the San Francisco conference were ready, as indicated above, to pledge the promotion of human rights "without distinction as to race, sex, language, or religion." In the Universal Declaration they subscribed to a longer list of prohibited bases for distinction; "everyone" was said to be entitled to human rights "without distinction of any kind, such as race, colour, sex, language, religion, political or other opinion, national or social origin, property, birth or other status."

The words "without distinction" and "no distinction" are strong. At the very least, the paragraphs quoted seem to say that any distinction based on the factors named will be considered arbitrary and unreasonable and therefore unacceptable. They seem thus to contribute significantly toward defining the arbitrary and unreasonable; and, of course, they do. At the same time, the terms can easily create illusions. The very fact that they are stated in such extreme language suggests that they are not to be taken literally. The prohibition of distinctions based on sex, for example, would seem to apply to draft laws: to draft men without drafting women would be to discriminate unacceptably against men, denying them equality. But apparently no one expects such a literal construction of the terms.

The prohibition of distinctions based on sex is apparently not absolute, but is subject to the rule of reason! If so, then perhaps distinctions based on the other factors named are also subject to the same rule.

The words "without distinction" and "no distinction" are qualified in another way too. By general consent, "without distinction" means "without *adverse* distinction," and the same rule holds with regard to discrimination. A measure is discriminatory not when it confers a special benefit but only when it "has the purpose or effect of nullifying or impairing the recognition, enjoyment or exercise, on an equal footing, of human rights and fundamental freedoms. . . ."[7] Thus an agreement once made between Greece and Turkey concerning the allocation of governmental positions in Cyprus between Greek and Turkish elements in the population there was not considered discriminatory, even though it made distinctions based on national or social origins.[8]

A very different sort of qualification of the rule against discrimination is stated in the Covenant on Economic, Social and Cultural Rights; in effect it authorizes "developing countries" to deny to non-nationals the economic rights named in the Covenant. It thus permits action against whites and other foreigners whose activities in the developing country date from colonial days. Kenya has illustrated the implications of the principle. At the end of 1967 it put into effect an immigration act requiring all residents of European and Asian origin who had not become citizens but who wished to continue working in Kenya to apply for entry-work permits. The permits were to be granted, for a fee, only when no suitably qualified Kenyan citizen was available for the employment in question, and only for a year at a time, with five years as the maximum. Beginning in 1968 Kenya added another discriminatory measure: it began permitting non-citizens to carry on business only in Nairobi and other main towns. The result was embarrassment for Britain. On granting independence to Kenya, it had permitted Indians there to choose British citizenship. Facing the squeeze in Kenya, many of them started to migrate to Britain, only to intensify racial tensions there. The upshot was the adoption in Britain of legislation providing that holders of British passports who had no substantial connection of birth, descent or residence with Britain could enter the country only if they obtained an employment voucher, no more than 1500 of which would be issued per year. The effect was racial discrimination among British nationals, achieved by indirect means.

Discrimination against non-nationals, it might be noted, is not confined to developing countries. A number of countries regulate or prohibit ownership by aliens of certain kinds of resources, such as land and coal deposits. Similarly, governments sometimes require that leading officers of corporations shall not be foreigners.

## THE SOUTH AFRICAN CHALLENGE: APARTHEID

The sharpest challenge to the principle of equality and the rule against racial discrimination comes from South Africa. The total population of the country is approximately 18,300,000, divided as follows: whites, 3,500,000; coloreds, 1,800,000; Asians, 500,000; Africans, 12,500,000. The whites thus comprise less than 20 percent of the population. Nevertheless, except in restricted areas and to a minor extent in connection with local affairs, they monopolize government, denying suffrage and other forms of political participation to the non-whites, who comprise more than 80 per cent of the population. Moreover, in exercising their political control the whites insist on a policy of apartheid, or, as they prefer, "separate development." From their point of view, the distinctions drawn "do not proceed from any oppressive intent . . . but are, broadly speaking, designed to ensure peaceful development towards the preservation of racial and cultural identities by differentiation and by separation into different areas and different groups, within which each race can develop in its own way and work out its own destiny, with a minimum of racial friction."[9] The Afrikaans-speaking element in the white population takes the lead in this policy and is in general more extreme in its outlook, but even within the English-speaking element support for the principles of equality and non-discrimination is far from general.

It is difficult to describe apartheid and its rationale objectively, for the very words used are at least suggestive of a judgment. Dispute exists even over the question whether the whites should be thought of primarily as racists or primarily as nationalists. By one set of standards they are the benign tutors of less developed peoples who happen to be black, guiding and promoting their social, economic, and cultural development beyond levels so far achieved by the blacks in other parts of Africa. By another set of standards, they are evil masters of peoples whom they hold in colonial-like subjection, gaining both psychological and material rewards from their imperial overlordship and determined to use literally any means that may be necessary to maintain the gratifying position that they enjoy.

Certainly racism plays a very large part in the policies of the South African government and in the thinking of the white portion of the population—especially in the thinking of the Afrikaners. The whole history of race relationships in South Africa bears this out. It is suggested by the traditional practice of the whites to count only themselves among "the people of South Africa."[10] An old constitution of the Boer Republic of the Transvaal included a stipulation that "the people will permit no equality between whites and colored inhabitants, either in Church or State."[11] The language of the relevant legislation in South Africa is mainly in terms of race or color. The Population Registration Act of 1950 provided for the classification of every person as white, native, or colored—a native being "a person who in fact is, or is generally accepted as, a member of any aboriginal race or tribe of Africa," and a colored person being anyone who is neither white nor native. Japanese are classified as white.

Under other legislation the whole territory of the country is divided on a racial basis. Some 13 per cent is reserved for natives, and the areas involved are eventually to be organized into so-called Bantustans—more or less autonomous "homelands" for the natives; only one, the Transkei, has so far been established. According to the 1960 census, 4.6 million natives lived in the reserves, approximately 40 per cent of the total. The rest of the country is considered white or European even though the whites are outnumbered in it by almost two to one. Since it includes so many non-whites, legislation permits the designation within it of "group areas"—reserved for occupation and ownership by a single racial group; in contrast to the reserves, group areas are not expected to be a part of the Bantustan system or to achieve autonomy. Outside the reserves and the group areas, segregation also occurs by the designation of locations where natives must live.

Outside the reserves, non-whites suffer restrictions and disabilities in almost every conceivable respect. In effect, they are regarded as foreign migrants in another man's country even though they may have been born there and lived there for years. Educational and job opportunities open to them are markedly different from those open to whites. Rights of residence and movement differ. The requirement that everyone must carry a passbook and show it on police demand is administered in a way that the natives find especially onerous and humiliating; failure to produce the passbook is a criminal offense. A non-white in a "white" area who becomes unemployed may be ordered out of the area, i.e. relegated to the reserves.

As indicated in Chapter 2, sexual intercourse, and of course marriage, between persons who differ in race is forbidden.[12]

Even those who contend that South Africa should be thought of primarily as multi-national rather than multi-racial do not get away from race or color: the dominant nation is white, and one can be a member of it only by being white. It is not a matter of culture or attitude or education or psychological identification or place of birth. Prime Minister Verwoerd, even while stressing the national idea, also spoke in terms of race and color. "We want to keep South Africa White," he said. " 'Keeping it White' can only mean one thing, namely, White domination, not 'leadership,' not 'guidance,' but 'control,' 'supremacy.' "[13] Seeing the emphasis in the United Nations and elsewhere on equality and non-discrimination, he contended that the world was sick, and that South Africa should not allow itself to be dragged into the sick bed.

> It is White South Africa's duty to ensure her survival. . . . The tragedy of the present time is that . . . the white race is not playing the role which it is called upon to play and which only the white race is competent to fulfill. If the Whites of America and of Europe and of South Africa were dissolved in the stream of the black masses, what would become of the future of the world and of the human race? What would become of its science, its knowledge, its form of civilization . . . ?[14]

"It is the White man," Prime Minister Verwoerd declared on another occasion, "to whom all the progress must be ascribed of which people all over the world at present boast and in which all participate, White and non-White, and from which the freedom of all of them has sprung."[15] Dissolution into "the stream of the black masses" was thus to be avoided at all costs; the whites of South Africa must preserve their civilization and whatever racial purity they yet retained. The thoughts, needless to say, were not unique to Prime Minister Verwoerd. One of the crucial documents on which the policy of apartheid is based is the Tomlinson report of 1955. According to it "the dominant fact in the South African situation" was the unwillingness of the whites "to sacrifice their right of existence as a separate national and racial entity."[16] Both Verwoerd and the Tomlinson report thus took the view that integration—in fact, anything other than apartheid—was unacceptable.

The contrast with contemporaneous developments in the United States is obvious. So, for that matter, is the contrast with the proclaimed goal of all of the American republics, many of which contain indigenous populations that are culturally very distinct; they declare that their goal is "to develop a policy tending toward complete integration of all elements of their citizenry, without distinction of any nature based on racial origin."[17]

As just indicated, an emphasis on national differences goes along with the emphasis on racial differences. Whatever the motives of an emphasis on the nation, its advantages in terms of propaganda and political strategy are obvious. A stress on individuals and their race naturally invokes the principles of equality and non-discrimination, and leads quickly to a condemnation of apartheid. In contrast a stress on nations invokes the principle of national equality and self-determination, and at least suggests the question whether apartheid should not be blessed.

"We South Africans of European descent," the South African Foreign Minister told the General Assembly in 1964, "are a nation in our own right. . . . And, like any other nation, we, too, are entitled to insist upon our right to self-determination."[18] Actually, some question exists whether the whites constitute one nation. Douglas Brown speaks of two separate white communities, and of the voluntary apartheid that they maintain vis-à-vis each other; he suggests that the voluntary apartheid of the white communities "provides a useful model for white-black relations in a free society."[19] C. A. W. Manning speaks not of the nationalism of the whites but of the nationalism of the Afrikaner *volk* and of the difficulties of integrating even the whites.[20] But it is the Afrikaners who are in a majority and who exercise political control—through the National party.

Appealing to self-determination in their own behalf, the Afrikaners profess a willingness to concede a form of it to others. They do not, they contend, uphold the idea of "perpetual domination by one section of the population over the others."[21] They claim that their policy "is not based on any concept of superiority or inferiority, but on the fact that people differ particularly in their group associations, loyalties, cultures, outlook, modes of life and standards of development."[22] They say that "in claiming for ourselves a distinctive destiny of our own, we do not deny to the emerging Bantu nations their right to achieve destinies of their own—each in his own homeland with its culture, heritage, language and concept of nationhood."[23] Or, as Prime Minister Verwoerd once put it, "We do not seek to apply a form of discrimination which denies these [non-white] people human dignity and human rights. We apply a policy which is in fact intended to give them dignity and rights in the highest form, namely through self-government and self-determination."[24]

According to Verwoerd, the non-whites join the whites in wanting separate development. The coloreds "insist on the natural process of separation of the racial groups; the Zulu of Natal also insists on it."[25] More generally, the non-whites allegedly "want to be left alone—i.e., to develop separately. . . . If the masses desire anything, it certainly is not a mixed form of government. . . . The Bantu wants his own areas in which he will have all the opportunities for employment and will govern alone."[26] Verwoerd did not say how he knew this, or claim that the conclusion stemmed from consultation with representative non-whites. Others deny the conclusion, indicating that what the black African leaders want is to be incorporated into South African society, not excluded from it.[27]

As Verwoerd saw it, the policies of apartheid reflected a mutual desire and interest which the whites should promote. He spoke of a policy "by which we on the one hand can retain for the white man full control in his areas, but by which we are giving the Bantu as our wards every opportunity in their areas to move along a road of development by which they can progress in accordance with their ability."[28] Even more, "We must uplift those people and educate them and teach them to be self-reliant in all spheres. . . . We are busy with the process of uplift."[29]

Prime Minister Verwoerd did not have a precise blueprint for the future, or a precise timetable. The object was a division of the country into distinct political entities—the white area completely controlled by whites, and various Bantustans each controlled by the Bantu "nation" inhabiting it. The object was "to build up a South Africa in which the Bantu and the White man can live next to one another as good neighbors and not as people who are continually quarreling over supremacy."[30] The Bantustans would at first have limited powers and would go through a period of tutelage and guardianship. Verwoerd was critical of Britain and other imperial powers which, in his view, had given self-government and independence to black peoples who were not yet ready for it. But increasing power and autonomy would be granted. Perhaps the end point would be a relationship within South Africa analogous to that among the members of the British Commonwealth, perhaps the Bantustans would become independent. These were decisions to be made in the future, depending on the situation that then prevailed. Federation would be unacceptable, for that would imply some degree of subordination of the whites to a federal authority in which the Bantus shared control.

Some of the aspects of the Afrikaner appeal to nationalism and self-determination will be discussed in Chapter 5. Here it is vital to recognize quickly that apartheid in the sense of the territorial separation of people by color or nation simply will not work. After all, the problem has developed to a considerable extent because the whites needed the labor of the non-whites, and because the non-whites saw advantage in offering that labor—wherever the whites were. The result is that whites and non-whites are geographically interspersed through most of the country and the situation is not expected to change significantly. Prime Minister Verwoerd himself accepted and shared the expectation of the Tomlinson commission that at least six million out of some twenty million natives would be permanently resident in the white area in the year 2000 and thereafter, the whites remaining a minority.[31]

From the fact of interspersal arise practices that violate the principles of equality and non-discrimination. Verwoerd talked very sketchily (and no one can know how seriously) of equality among the "nations" of South Africa in a vague future, but he never suggested the possibility of equality for individual human beings within what he thought of as the white area. Here the legislation described earlier would presumably continue in force, with its many provisions for inequality and discrimination. The official line is that in the end all of the Bantus in the white area will be affiliated with a Bantustan. "They will even have the right, while they are in the White area, to take part in the Government of their Bantu homeland, of their ethnic unit."[32] But this would obviously give small satisfaction to those residing for years, if not all their lives, in the same area with the whites.

Afrikaner spokesmen point out that their policies include reverse discrimination, for example, restrictions on property ownership by whites in areas reserved for natives. Moreover, they claim that their Bantus are better off in terms of education, health, and scales of living than are the people of the black African states to the north, and that the Bantu peoples "as a whole are contented."[33] Others also report economic and social progress for the Bantus, and credit the whites with substantial achievements against considerable odds.[34] Regardless of this, the fact of inequality and racial discrimination is egregious. The Bantus who live among the whites and work for them are subservient and oppressed in a psychological, social, and political sense, whether or not they are economically exploited. And it is quite understandable that black African leaders within and outside South Africa—as well as a great many whites—should speak with considerable outrage of the humiliation and degradation in which the nonwhites live. The black Africans and many of the colored peoples of the world are especially aroused about the problem, for the subjection of colored people by whites suggests an inferiority of status which many of them recently shared; and their psychological emancipation cannot be complete as long as vestiges of the old system endure.

### THE WORLD COMMUNITY AND APARTHEID

Through the United Nations and in other ways the world community leaves no doubt that in its view South Africa is violating its international obligations. On few other contemporary issues are so many governments agreed. By the end of 1968 the General Assembly had adopted some thirty-five resolutions on the subject, shifting in more recent years to increasingly condemnatory language. Its early concern was mainly with the treatment of people of Indian origin in South Africa, and the object was to promote negotiations on the subject between South Africa and India. In 1952 it adopted a resolution declaring that

> in a multi-racial society harmony and respect for human rights and freedoms and the peaceful development of a unified community are best assured when patterns of legislation and practice are directed towards ensuring equality before the law of all persons regardless of race, creed or colour, and when economic, social, cultural and political participation of all racial groups is on a basis of equality.

In the same resolution it also affirmed that "governmental policies of Member States which are not directed towards these goals, but which are designed to perpetuate or increase discrimination, are inconsistent with the pledges of the Members under Article 56 of the Charter."[35] The General Assembly has repeated this stand again and again, and no point would be served in citing every instance. In 1961 it affirmed that "the racial policies being pursued by the Government of the Union of South Africa are a flagrant violation of the Charter of the United Nations and the Universal Declaration of Human Rights and are inconsistent with the obligations of a Member State."[36] In 1965, with specific reference to the territory of South-West Africa, it began calling the policies of apartheid a "crime against humanity."[37] The Security Council has not endorsed the use of this language, but in connection with efforts to bring about enforcement action against South Africa (to be discussed below) it has taken the same stand as the General Assembly on the point that the policies of apartheid violate the requirements of the Charter.

It is perhaps needless to add that the Organization of African Unity condemns policies of apartheid as contrary to the requirements of international law. Similarly, a number of the specialized agencies associated with the United Nations, such as the International Labor Organization and the World Health Organization, have condemned those policies directly or indirectly.

The government of Portugal—itself under attack for denying self-determination in Angola and other African territories—is the only one that votes with South Africa on matters pertaining to race, though for varying reasons others sometimes abstain from voting at all. The white regime in Southern Rhodesia (whose policies will be discussed below) aligns itself in spirit with the white regime in South Africa, but is not a member of the United Nations.

Racism and discrimination obviously exist in many parts of the world in addition to southern Africa. Consciousness of color and of differences in culture are endemic to mankind. Claims or tacit assumptions about superiority and inferiority are not restricted to whites. Black African tribes display racial or ethnic hatreds as strong as any in the world, fighting and massacring each other on a scale that certainly would lead to charges of genocide if whites were involved. In Nigeria tribal hostilities disrupt the state. Mortal enmities in the area of Rwanda and Burundi have led thousands of Watutsis to be massacred and tens of thousands to become refugees. The Sudan has similar problems, and the Congo has fought a civil war. It might be that the black African governments could accomplish more in the field of human rights by concentrating on the problems that exist within their own borders instead of on those that exist in southern Africa. Similarly, India, which has complained bitterly through the years about the treatment of people of Indian origin in South Africa, faces enormous problems of discrimination at home. Communal tensions are so great in Mauritius that a considerable portion of the small population refused to join in celebrating the achievement of "national" independence. There are notable differences in these situations, of course. Outside South Africa and Southern Rhodesia racism and discrimination are in the main the work of private parties, condemned by governments. No other governments in the world have so openly flaunted racism and discrimination as have these two; and if they lead in practices that the world condemns, it is at least not surprising that the brunt of the attack should go against them.

From the first South Africa has pled innocent. Apart from the justifications already mentioned, it contends that the Charter requires equality and non-discrimination only with respect to "fundamental" human rights, and that "until fundamental human rights have been defined and have received recognition in a binding form, the provisions of the Charter cannot be said to extend to human rights other than those which are today in international law accepted as being so fundamental that they are not merely of domestic importance but the concern of the society of nations."[38] South Africa also appeals to Article 2(7), specifying that nothing in the Charter authorizes the United Nations to intervene in matters which are essentially within the domestic jurisdiction of any state. Both of these contentions will be discussed in a later chapter. In seeming conformity with the general view that "without distinction" means "without adverse distinction," South Africa also contends that "the Charter did not purport to establish any obligation not to differentiate between members of various groups, but was concerned merely to prevent oppression and unfair discrimination."[39] But South Africa insists on judging whether a policy is oppressive or unfair in terms of its effect on groups as a whole rather than in terms of its effect on specific individuals. Defending its policies in South-West Africa, originally received as a mandated territory under the League of Nations, South Africa claims that "groups which are in substantially different stages of development" need to be treated differently if their best interests are to be served.

> Where, owing to fundamental differences in socio-cultural orientation, stages of general development and ethnic classification, the differences between the groups concerned are of so profound a nature that they cannot be wiped out, a policy of integration is unrealistic, unsound and undesirable, and cannot but result in continual social discrimination, discontent and frustration, friction and violence—a climate in which no socio-economic progress can be expected to take place.[40]

Apartheid, South Africa concedes, means that the "more gifted or developed individuals may to a certain extent be limited by the stage of development of their group," but it alleges that in South-West Africa such individuals constitute a very small minority. In any case it holds that the "slight limitations" suffered by such individuals should be "weighted in the context of the merits and demerits to be considered in making a choice between a policy of attempted integration on the one hand, and a policy of separate development on the other hand."[41] And it cites the experience of a number of other countries where attempted integration has been associated with tension, hostility, and even civil war.

Believing that their point of view and their policies are sound and commendable, white South African spokesmen complain of the injustice being done to them. As early as 1946 Jan Smuts reported "a solid mass of prejudice [in the United Nations] against the color policies of South Africa."[42] Foreign Minister Louw told the General Assembly in 1962 that his country had been "singled out for calumny and vilification, in many cases by delegations whose own Governments are guilty of discriminatory practices and of oppression of large sections of their populations."[43] Far from acknowledging any guilt, and far from promising to work in the direction of the principles of equality and non-discrimination as understood elsewhere, the white spokesmen take pride in their policy. The alternative to it that they see is the "handing over our fatherland to the non-Whites, eventually to the Bantu and to the Bantu dictator—as the result of which the Coloureds and the Indians will suffer together with the Whites."[44]

Uys Kirge, described as a "prominent Afrikaans poet and writer," is reported to comment as follows—obviously with non-whites in mind:

> A man would in time forgive almost anything. But one thing he will not forgive you.
>
> And that is that you wound him in his pride, that you offend him in his dignity, that you damage him in his sense of worth as a man.
>
> Just keep on doing it, just keep on doing it for long enough and he, perhaps the meekest and mildest of men, will in the end kill you for it.[45]

## PARTICIPATION IN GOVERNMENT

Political systems have traditionally not been matters of international obligation. The accepted rule is that the sovereign state may have whatever form of government it pleases—that its freedom of choice is unrestricted. But a contradictory rule has also developed: that a human right exists to participate somehow in government. The rule supplements those pertaining to equality and non-discrimination, under which participation might be denied equally to all.

In part, at least, insistence on a right of participation (like much else in connection with international activity in the field of human rights) stems from experience with Hitler and Mussolini, for their behavior called the traditionally accepted rule into question. Franklin D. Roosevelt suggested this in 1940 when he said:

> Of course, the peoples of other nations have the right to choose their own form of government. But we in this Nation still believe that such choice should be predicated on certain freedoms which we think are essential everywhere. We know that we ourselves will never be wholly safe at home unless other governments recognize such freedoms.[46]

The states in the Council of Europe have gone beyond others in acting along lines intimated by the above. A number of the articles of the European Convention on Human Rights are relevant, including the one on freedom of expression, cited in the preceding chapter. The states ratifying the first protocol of the Convention went farther, however, undertaking "to hold free elections at reasonable intervals by secret ballot, under conditions which will ensure the free expression of the opinion of the people in the choice of the legislature." The words do not provide explicitly for opposition parties or for a right of such parties to compete in elections, and it is still uncertain what interpretations will be championed. The issue arose in connection with Greece after the military *coup d'état* of 1967. The military dictatorship pled the existence of a "public emergency threatening the life of the nation," entitling it to derogate from its obligations under the European Convention on Human Rights. On this basis it suppressed parliament and political parties, and suspended a number of human rights. The European Parliament forthwith declared itself profoundly disturbed by the suspension of democratic and parliamentary life in Greece and urged its rapid restoration.[47] Presumably this was a call for free, competitive elections in the Western sense. The European Commission of Human Rights was also seized of the matter, as we will note in the chapter on implementation through persuasion.

The Universal Declaration also includes an article on participation in government, and so does the Covenant on Civil and Political Rights. In the latter the article reads as follows:

> Every citizen shall have the right and the opportunity, without any of the distinctions mentioned in article 2 [i.e., "without distinction of any kind, such as race, color, sex, language, religion, political or other opinion, national or social origin, property, birth or other status"] and without unreasonable restrictions;
>
> a. To take part in the conduct of public affairs, directly or through freely chosen representatives;
>
> b. To vote and to be elected at genuine periodic elections which shall be by universal and equal suffrage and shall be held by secret ballot, guaranteeing the free expression of the will of the electors;
>
> c. To have access, on general terms of equality, to public service in his country.

We will discuss the requirement of "equal suffrage" below. As to other aspects of paragraphs a and b, it should not be assumed that they require competitive elections. In fact, when the Third Committee of the General Assembly discussed the topic, delegates from both the Soviet Union and Spain welcomed the article, obviously taking the view that its terms permit a single-party system and the outlawry of organized opposition.[48] Many other governments voted for the article—presumably in good faith—even though they permit only one party to operate. Those who restrict the press and still claim that it is free, as noted in the preceding chapter, can with more or less consistency also restrict organized political activity and still claim that the expression of the will of the electors is free: electors are free to express their will, if they wish to do so, within the framework of the single official party; and they are free to join the party or not. Non-communist justifications of such attitudes are suggested by the following excerpt from the report on the 1966 Dakar Seminar on Human Rights in the Developing Countries.

> Several speakers maintained that, in their countries, the maintenance of [a multi-party system] would have had the dangerous effect of sharpening dissensions among the different elements of the population, dissipating the efforts of the people, and impeding the Government's economic development activities. Some speakers considered that the existence of several political parties in Africa was mainly a reflection of regional or tribal particularism, or of the conflict between the selfish interests of certain economic groupings. Furthermore, lacking a strongly developed ideology, some parties had a tendency to borrow their doctrines from abroad, thus opening the way to foreign influences that were undesirable in African political

> life. For all those reasons, it was essential in the national interest that all the energies of the people should be mobilized and channelled towards a single mass party.[49]

Though some persons and governments take the view that elections need not be competitive in order to be free, the contrary view is also held. It is obviously held in countries with multi-party systems. And the Subcommission on Prevention of Discrimination and Protection of Minorities (a subcommission of the UN Commission on Human Rights) endorses the view; in a statement of "General Principles on Freedom and Non-Discrimination in the Matter of Political Rights" it asserts that "genuine" elections require "full freedom . . . for the peaceful expression of political opposition, and also for the organization and free functioning of political parties and the right to present candidates for election."[50]

Paragraph c of the article of the Covenant quoted above, especially when read in conjunction with the rule against discrimination because of "political or other opinion," suggests the interesting thought that the President of the United States should not take party considerations into account in selecting his cabinet, and that the disloyal and the subversive are as much entitled as others to positions in the CIA, but numerous assertions are recorded that this meaning is not accepted or intended.[51]

The Organization of the American States (OAS) has long concerned itself with the question of the right to participate in government. The Inter-American Conference of 1948 approved the American Declaration of the Rights and Duties of Man, which includes the assertion that

> Every person having legal capacity is entitled to participate in the government of his country, directly or through his representatives, and to take part in popular elections, which shall be by secret ballot, and shall be honest, periodic, and free.[52]

In 1951 the American Ministers of Foreign Affairs declared "that the solidarity of the American Republics requires the effective exercise of representative democracy."[53] The Declaration of Santiago, issued in 1959, asserts that "harmony among the American republics can be effective only insofar as human rights and fundamental freedoms and the exercise of representative democracy are a reality within each one of them," and that "the existence of anti-democratic regimes constitutes a violation of the principles on which the OAS is founded, and a danger to united and peaceful relationships in the hemisphere." It goes on to describe some of the familiar principles and attributes of Western democracy, asserting among other things that "perpetuation in power, or the exercise of power without a fixed term and with the manifest intent of perpetuation, is incompatible with the effective exercise of democracy."[54] In 1962 the Ministers of Foreign Affairs resolved "to recommend that the governments of the American states whose structure or acts are incompatible with the effective exercise of representative democracy hold free elections in their respective countries."[55] Individual statesmen have made comparable pronouncements. For example, President Prado of Peru in 1961 associated the principle of free elections with self-determination:

> Self-determination of peoples means . . . the right of each nation to conduct its own affairs in its own way in the exercise of its own sovereignty—and it is indispensable to this principle that the will of the people must be able to express itself through free elections periodically held.[56]

And President Johnson declared in 1966:

> The United States maintains its commitment to government by consent of the governed, a consent to be granted in free and honest elections. It does not seek to impose on others any form of government. But let us stand determined on this principle: Despots are not welcome in this hemisphere.[57]

The significance of such pronouncements is difficult to assess. The presence of so many non-democratic regimes in Latin America suggests that some scoffing is justified.[58] Obviously the OAS has not brought about the observance of the principles that it proclaims. The statements quoted are declaratory and hortatory only, having no binding effect. OAS agencies have refused to adopt the rule that undemocratic regimes are not to be recognized. In fact, its Juridical Committee in 1960 came close to deriding a proposal to enforce respect for democracy in the hemisphere, asking who could tell where democracy ends and autocracy begins and who would enforce a judgment if it were made.[59] Moreover, it recalled a resolution of the Ninth International Conference of the American States indicating that "it is up to the American states, not collectively but individually 'to adopt, within their respective territories and in accordance with their respective constitutional provisions,' the measures necessary to provide for the protection of their democratic institutions." Divergent views thus coexist, and chronic differences appear—reflecting both differing degrees of dedication to democracy and differing conceptions of the feasible. Moreover, efforts to bring about joint action in support of democracy run athwart strong commitments to the principle of non-intervention.

Nevertheless, proposals for some kind of implementing action continue to be made. In 1965 the Rio Conference recommended an exchange of views on the perennial question of the recognition of de facto governments, intimating that assurances concerning the holding of free elections and respect for human rights might be relevant to decisions about recognition.[60] Moreover, as we will note in chapter 8, the Inter-American Commission on Human Rights has concerned itself quite actively with the problem of assuring respect for human rights—including electoral rights and the right to representative government—in Latin American countries.

The same Foreign Ministers who in 1962 recommended the holding of elections also ruled that the Castro regime in Cuba had "voluntarily placed itself outside the inter-American system," but they did not base the ruling on requirements pertaining directly to democracy. Rather, they held "that adherence by any member of the OAS to Marxism-Leninism is incompatible with the inter-American system."[61] This permitted the exclusion of the Castro regime without affecting the standing of, for example, Duvalier.

The most striking fact about international action concerning participation in government is simply that the question is being considered, especially in Europe and Latin America. Quick solutions to long-standing problems and quick changes in traditional practices are not to be expected; it is at least possible, however, that the development of international pressures may have long-term effects and that the international endorsement of principles may strengthen domestic forces supporting them.

## EQUAL SUFFRAGE

The two preceding sections relate implicitly to the principle of equal suffrage. If governments are to hold elections, they must provide for suffrage, and if they are to avoid discrimination on the grounds listed, equal suffrage follows.

Issues pertaining to equal suffrage are currently most acute in connection with South Africa and Southern Rhodesia, but before dealing with them it is instructive to note that it is not long since many states were violating what is now asserted as a human right.

Of the bases for discrimination under international attack, sex and race have played the most prominent roles. In the United States discrimination based on sex did not end until the nineteenth amendment was enacted in 1920. It did not end in Britain until 1928, or in France until 1944.[62] When the United Nations was established, about half the states of the world still discriminated against women in connection with the vote.[63] Now such discrimination has substantially disappeared. It exists in Jordan, Kuwait, Liechtenstein, the northern region of Nigeria, and Switzerland (except that in Switzerland women may vote in some of the cantonal and municipal elections). Women may not vote in Saudi Arabia or Yemen—but neither can men, for no elections are held.[64]

Discrimination based on race is familiar in the United States, though in connection with voting it has been and is being accomplished indirectly. The laws have not discriminated explicitly on the basis of race or color as such. Instead it has been a question of the grandfather clause, the poll tax, literacy tests, and so on—plus private persuasion and intimidation. Moreover, the general economic and educational level at which a high proportion of the Negroes have been allowed to languish has militated against participation in political affairs. The indirect methods of accomplishing discrimination are under attack and are gradually being eliminated.

Similar methods are found abroad. For example, while Kenya was still under Britain a system prevailed that gave a man one, two, or three votes depending on the qualifications he met, and the qualifications were such as to favor the white voters.[65] Latent or active discrimination occurs elsewhere too. In some societies indigenous peoples simply remain outside the political system as a matter of circumstance and tradition, in which case it may or may not be reasonable to speak of discrimination. In Canada, the Indians and Eskimos have gained the right to vote only in recent years.[66] In trust territories, the Trusteeship Council has endorsed "the introduction of methods of suffrage leading eventually to elections by universal adult suffrage."[67]

What has already been said indicates that South Africa does not provide equal suffrage. In the so-called white area only whites may vote and be elected, even though they constitute a minority. Moreover, since the whites monopolize the legislative process, they alone can constitutionally change the rules; and they show no disposition to do so. According to Verwoerd,

> This so-called multi-racial or non-racial policy is not one which provides justice for all races. It leads to Black domination where it is applied, where there are several population groups and only numbers are made to count. If we in South Africa wish to preserve ourselves, which is a right we have, then this policy . . . would be fatal.[68]

Or as a South African author put it, "Anything savouring of an allocation of political power between Whites and non-Whites on the basis of a counting of heads is seen by [the white electorate] as opening a flood-gate which they wish to keep firmly bolted."[69] The non-whites may vote, however, in the Transkei—the one Bantustan so far established—and in certain other restricted areas and circumstances where no authority over whites is involved.

As we will see shortly, the General Assembly has endorsed the principle of one man, one vote and majority rule for Southern Rhodesia. Presumably the same principle should under the Charter apply to South Africa, though insistence on this has not been explicit. A group of experts reporting to the Secretary-General of the United Nations in 1964 on the problem of resolving the situation in South Africa satisfied itself with the assertion of "the first and basic principle that all the people of South Africa should be brought into consultation [through] a national convention fully representative of the whole population,"[70] a position which the Security Council later endorsed.[71] Official declarations by spokesmen for the United States have likewise avoided an explicit statement that the resolution of the South African problem requires the acceptance of the principle of one man, one vote. With respect to Portuguese territories in Africa, the United States endorses the principle, but does not demand its implementation "tomorrow."[72] African spokesmen, however, show no sign of patience on the matter.[73]

H. F. Oppenheimer of South Africa suggests the hypothesis that one result of the adoption of the one man, one vote rule would be the end of the multi-party system.

> Where you are dealing with an electorate which is largely illiterate and quite inexperienced in the working of a parliamentary system of government, the acceptance of the "one man, one vote" principle will, in most cases make it necessary and desirable to adopt a one-party system. The reason is that in a primitive country where literacy is low and tribal loyalty strong, the mass of the people cannot be ex-

> pected to grasp that an appeal to the electorate by an opposition party to turn out the government is not the same thing as an attempt to subvert the constitution. In such circumstances, free elections, far from ensuring stable government, are quite likely to lead to civil war.[74]

Another reason why the one man, one vote rule might end the multi-party system in some countries such as South Africa is to prevent those enfranchised from bringing about changes that the minority opposes.

The problem of equal suffrage is also acute in connection with Southern Rhodesia, which illegally declared its independence from Britain in 1965. Suffrage was the crucial issue. Britain insisted on arrangements looking toward majority rule, which in effect means non-white rule, for out of the total population of about 4.3 million only some 220,000 or 5 per cent are white. In a sense the whites of Southern Rhodesia are not as extreme in their racism as the whites of South Africa. They do not insist on apartheid, nor do they deny anyone the vote explicitly on the basis of race or color. But traditionally they have used various devices (for example, property, income, and educational qualifications) to keep the number of non-white voters very low. The constitution of 1961 left the way open for the non-whites to gain a majority, predictions about when this would happen ranging from fifteen to "upwards of fifty" years.[75] For the time being, however, the constitution in effect allocated 50 of the 65 seats in parliament to the whites, and as it turned out the arrangement was unacceptable to important elements on both sides. Black African leaders rejected the discrimination involved, and many whites wanted guarantees that the discrimination would endure. In the 1962 elections the more racist whites defeated those who had found the constitution acceptable, and three years later (led by Ian Smith) they declared the country's independence.

Already in 1962 the General Assembly adopted a resolution "deploring the denial of equal political rights to the vast majority of the people of Southern Rhodesia" and requesting Britain to lead in the formulation of a new constitution "which would ensure the rights of the majority of the people, on the basis of 'one man, one vote.' . . ."[76] In the fall of 1965, reacting to reports that the white regime in Southern Rhodesia might declare independence, the General Assembly adopted another resolution warning Britain "that the United Nations will oppose any declaration of independence which is not based on universal adult suffrage," and it went on to assert that Southern Rhodesia's policies of racial discrimination and segregation constituted "a crime against humanity."[77] When it came, then, the declaration of independence was a challenge not only to Britain but to the United Nations as well, and the problem was not so much to determine the principles that were applicable as to enforce them. The Security Council soon became involved, finally resolving that "the present situation in Southern Rhodesia constitutes a threat to international peace and security," and ordering enforcement action under Chapter VII of the Charter; we will take up this aspect of the problem in chapter 9. Suffice it to say here that the General Assembly continues to insist on the principle of equal suffrage; its resolution of November 1968 called upon Britain "to use force in order to put an immediate end to the illegal regime in Southern Rhodesia" and "to transfer power, based on free elections by universal adult suffrage and on majority rule, to the people of Zimbabwe."[78] Eighty-six members voted for the resolution and nine (including the United States) voted against; nineteen abstained.

In terms of votes, then, the General Assembly is committed to equal suffrage—to the principle of one man, one vote. But questions of timing and meaning remain. In case of Southern Rhodesia, the demand is for the application of the principle without delay, but the exigencies of politics might still necessitate a compromise looking toward the full application of the principle at a future time. The chief questions of meaning relate to voting qualifications and the possibility of indirect restrictions, and with respect to both South Africa and Southern Rhodesia they offer a considerable range of choice.

Age qualifications for voting are universal, and cause no problem internationally. Citizenship is also a universal qualification, but has caused international difficulties in the past and might do so again. One of the complaints against the Orange Free State leading up to the Boer War concerned the residence requirement for the acquisition of citizenship, and a comparable problem might develop between India and Ceylon, where most Indians cannot vote because they are not citizens.[79] Literacy tests for voting have also been common, and do not seem to be barred by any of the major declarations or conventions on human rights; they are barred, however, in a statement of general principles approved by a subcommission of the UN Commission on Human Rights.[80] Since the Universal Declaration of Human Rights and other instruments bar language as a basis for distinction, literacy in any language would presumably have to be accepted. The Universal Declaration likewise rules out distinctions based on property, a term which might or might not be interpreted to cover income. Nothing is said in international instruments about the kind of discrimination that is effected through gerrymandering, through establishing voting districts that are grossly uneven in size or population, or through inscribing voters on different rolls and granting disproportionate representation to the different rolls.

Questions of the meaning of accepted principles relating to suffrage will no doubt be resolved in some instances by appeals to reason and even by reference to courts; but in many other instances the decisive factor is sure to be the will and the interests of the winner in political struggle.

## QUALIFIERS ON RIGHTS

We have already had occasion to note that in international instruments qualifications are commonly attached to the assertion of rights. The fact deserves emphasis and elaboration.

A very general qualification attaches to all of the rights asserted in the Universal Declaration, namely, that they are set forth "as a common standard of achievement for all peoples and all nations." Where practice falls short of the indicated standard, governments are thus expected to take steps designed to improve the situation. What they are called upon to do is to try to make progress toward the implementation of the rights, not necessarily to achieve the goal immediately and fully. Furthermore, Article 29 contains a qualifier that in words looks very sweeping. It permits "such limitations as are determined by law solely for the purpose of securing due recognition and respect for the rights and freedoms of others and of meeting the just requirements of morality, public order and the general welfare in a democratic society." Actually, the article is not likely to be much invoked. When and if a government chooses to explain or justify its measures, the likelihood is that it will simply contend that it is respecting the rights and freedoms of the Declaration rather than limiting them. Nevertheless, any communist government—given communist definitions of the crucial words in Article 29—could claim to be acting within its terms; and so, perhaps, could the white regimes of South Africa and Southern Rhodesia.

The Covenant on Civil and Political Rights does not repeat the above qualifiers, but instead includes a provision similar to one found in the European Convention on Human Rights. It specifies that "in time of public emergency which threatens the life of the nation and the existence of which is officially proclaimed," the parties may take measures derogating from a limited number of their obligations—in which case they are to inform the other parties. A measure of international accountability is thus maintained; and in any event it seems improbable that states would resort lightly or often to actions implying the kind of emergency indicated.

We should note again an article from the Universal Declaration already quoted in connection with the discussion of free speech and free press. Similar articles appear in both Covenants.

> Nothing in this Declaration may be interpreted as implying for any State, group or person any right to engage in any activity or to perform any act aimed at the destruction of any of the rights and freedoms set forth herein.

In other words, so far as these instruments are concerned, it is all right if a government chooses to deny rights and freedoms to advocates of totalitarian doctrines.[81]

Apart from the qualifiers just named, a number of the rights and freedoms discussed above are stated in declarations and draft treaties that are not legally binding. The question of accepting international obligations with respect to them will be discussed in Part II, and the problem of promoting the implementation of obligations assumed will be discussed in Part III. Meantime attention will be given to economic and social rights and to the right of self-determination.

# 4

# Economic, Social, and Cultural Rights

> Thou shalt not kill, but needst not strive
> Officiously to keep alive.

This couplet is suggestive of the conception of rights that has been dominant in the Anglo-American tradition. Under it the right to life is the right to the protection of a policeman, but not to the services of a doctor. If the government assures such services, it is a matter of benign policy, not a recognition of a claim of right.

A different view appears in Pope John's encyclical *Pacem in Terris.*

> Man has the right to live. He has the right to bodily integrity and to the means necessary for the proper development of life, particularly food, clothing, shelter, medical care, rest, and, finally, the necessary social services. In consequence, he has the right to be looked after in the event of ill-health; disability stemming from his work; widowhood; old-age; enforced unemployment; or whenever through no fault of his own he is deprived of the means of livelihood.

Put in broader terms, the traditional Anglo-American view is that men are entitled to rights in the civil and political realm but not in the economic, social, and cultural realm. But this point of view is rejected in most of the world, and in some countries it comes close to being reversed.

What we will do now is to identify and appraise attitudes on this issue. And then we will examine the various alleged economic, social, and cultural rights, and the controversies that attend international action concerning them.

## ECONOMIC, SOCIAL, AND CULTURAL "RIGHTS": DO THEY EXIST?

John Locke once spoke of "that equal right that every man hath to his natural freedom, without being subjected to the will or authority of any other men."[1] The statement suggests a definition, and it is the definition that concerns us here. According to the definition, a right is something that exists when it is not taken away; men have rights unless they are deprived of them. The definition fits with the idea of an original state of nature in which, in principle, rights (liberties) were boundless; at least no government was there to take them away, whatever other individual men might do. And the definition fits with the great pronouncements of the American and French revolutions. According to the Declaration of Independence, men are "endowed by their Creator" with certain inalienable rights; and according to the French Declaration of the Rights of Man and Citizen, "the aim of every political association is the preservation of the natural and imprescriptible rights of man."[2]

The common law tradition reflects the above view. Under it men's rights and liberties are presumed to exist already, so there is no need to confer them or even to spell them out. "The common law has . . . concerned itself not with the formulation and attribution of rights but with the grant of remedies and the diminution of arbitrary power."[3] If "arbitrary power" —whether of government or of private persons—were suitably limited, rights would survive. Thus rights were assured by prohibitions, not by positive actions arranging for their enjoyment. Claims were justified when they were of a negative sort—when the object was to impose limits on what others could legitimately do. If a governmental agency or a private person overstepped the limits and infringed on rights, the victim could seek a remedy in court. Judicial enforceability was, in a sense, a test of the existence of a right. If it could not be enforced by a court, it was not a right.

A lucid British scholar, Maurice Cranston, responds to the question *What Are Human Rights?* in accordance with the common law tradition. He thinks that rights are civil and political, not economic, social, or cultural. He deplores the fact that a contrary view prevails in the United Nations, indicating that the abandonment of the traditional conception muddies, obscures, and debilitates a philosophically respectable concept.[4] In his view the Universal Declaration of Human Rights is "overloaded with affirmations of so-called human rights which are not human rights at all," and the effect is "to push *all* talk of human rights out of the clear realm of the morally compelling into the twilight world of utopian aspiration." He is appalled by the fact that the General Assembly proclaimed the Declaration as "a common standard of achievement," saying that this "brands the Declaration as an attempt to translate rights into ideals. And however else one might choose to define moral rights, they are plainly *not* ideals or aspirations."

> An ideal is something one can aim at, but cannot by definition immediately realize. A right, on the contrary, is something that can, and from the moral point of view, *must* be respected here and now.[5]

Richard Wollheim takes a similar stand, deriding the notion that a right can be "partially infringed." "There are degrees of frustration, degrees of satisfaction of a desire: a right is either safeguarded or infringed."[6] The attitude obviously excludes the idea of a right to education or a right to social security.

American thought and practice on the subject is mixed. The Bill of Rights is essentially a Bill of Prohibitions against governmental encroachments and not an assurance of governmental initiatives to provide the substance of any affirmative expectation or claim. The American tradition is individualistic. We have already noted that the right to life is defined negatively, as the right not to be killed. Similarly, the right to liberty is not the right to the presence of anything but to the absence of certain kinds of restraints. And the third of the rights named in the Declaration of Independence is not the right to happiness, but to its pursuit.

But the negative view of rights is challenged. Especially since the Great Depression and the New Deal the federal government has been promoting a whole series of economic and social goals, some viewing this as a matter of desirable policy and others as a response to claims of moral right. One of Roosevelt's Four Freedoms was freedom from want. The National Resources Planning Board in its Report for 1943 suggested "A New Bill of Rights"; and in 1944 Roosevelt included in his State of the Union message what he called "a second Bill of Rights." Both the New Bill and the second Bill put the stress on economic and social rights—among them the right to work, the right to medical care, the right to social security, and the right to education. The United Nations Charter and United Nations activities in the field of human rights soon came along to reinforce domestic demands for action in the economic and social realm, and controversy became intense, especially in the late 1940's and early 1950's, when a committee of the American Bar Association and Senator Bricker went into action. The chairman of the committee was Frank E. Holman, who had previously served as President of the ABA. He opposed every aspect of the movement for an international bill of rights, his opposition being intensified because of the fact that the Universal Declaration and later the draft covenants included social, economic, and cultural rights. All this, he said, was "predicated on the un-American theory that basic rights can be created by legislative action."[7] Senator Bricker was outraged by the inclusion of economic and social rights. His view was that they "are not rights or freedoms in any true sense. . . . They are not constitutional rights. . . . Our constitution was designed in the belief that mankind's aspirations can best be achieved through individual initiative."[8] The movement for an international bill of rights was a movement for "socialism by treaty." Claims were not justified if they called for positive governmental action on behalf of welfare.

The issue came up in Congress in even more clear-cut fashion in 1952 when the draft Puerto Rican constitution was submitted for approval. Section 20 of Article 2 recognized a list of economic, social, and cultural rights similar to those spelled out in the Universal Declaration—the right to free elementary and secondary education, the right to obtain work, the right to a standard of living adequate for health and well-being, and so forth. A clause of the section acknowledged that such rights were not immediately realizable, or the type that could ever be realized through court order:

> The rights set forth in this section are closely connected with the progressive development of the economy of the Commonwealth, and require, for their full effectiveness, sufficient resources and an agricultural and industrial development not yet attained by the Puerto Rican community. . . .

The chairman of the Committee on Human Rights of the Puerto Rican constitutional convention testified before a U.S. Senate committee on behalf of Section 20. In his view it stated "basic goals which the people of Puerto Rico recognize and wish to recognize as objectives for which to strive." It had "an educational purpose." "We wanted to tie together these benefits with the need for a greater activity, a greater economic development, a greater agricultural and industrial effort by all of the people of Puerto Rico."[9] But Congress was not persuaded. Representative Halleck assumed that if Congress approved, this would mean a judgment that the constitution was a good one; and he feared the implications for the United States itself. "If you vote for some of these things, you had better get ready to vote for them back home."[10] Representative Crawford feared that Section 20 would impair the credit standing of Puerto Rico with American bankers.[11] Representative Bolton feared that the section would create expectations that could not be fulfilled and that democracy would then seem to have failed.[12] Representative Judd held that "rights are what a government cannot do, not what a government must do."[13] A report of the Senate committee gave a fuller statement.

> To constitute an effective right there must be a well-founded and enforceable claim with a correlative and enforceable duty upon others to satisfy it. Corresponding enforceable duties to the rights asserted cannot be determined and fixed under Section 20, and therefore it is unrealistic, confusing, and misleading to assert such rights in a constitution which is intended to be a fundamental and clear statement of matters which are enforceable and of the limitations on the exercise of power.
>
> . . .
>
> We do not believe it advisable to approve the proposed section of a basic charter for government containing these obvious defects.[14]

The upshot was that Congress required the deletion of the section from the constitution.

To the extent that opposition to the acknowledgment of economic and social rights rests on a definition, it is obviously tenuous. Respect for the established meaning of a word is likely to promote clarity of thought and communication, but this consideration does not necessarily override others. When a high proportion of the governments of the world endorse domestic and international documents including economic, social, and cultural rights among human rights, it is quixotic to appeal to the dictionary against what they do. Humpty Dumpty's stand when Alice objected to his definition of *glory* ("a nice knock-down argument") was more tenable:

> "When I use a word," Humpty Dumpty said, in rather a scornful tone, "it means just what I choose it to mean—neither more nor less."
>
> "The question is," said Alice, "whether you *can* make words mean so many different things."

"The question is," said Humpty Dumpty, "which is to be the master —that's all."

Lest the above appear unduly arbitrary, let it be noted that the word *right* has several meanings and shades of meaning in common usage. Reformers and idealists have long been asserting that men have certain rights without meaning that they were immediately enforceable by court order. Their object has often been to get the rights enforced or recognized in law at some point in the future. The statement that a man has a right to freedom may be either descriptive or normative; it may either reflect the factual situation or assert what ought to be. Claims of right may be morally justified regardless of the question whether they are legally enforceable.

Obviously, those who appeal to the dictionary are also making a policy judgment, and perhaps this is what they are doing primarily. And, conversely, those who advocate that economic and social rights be accepted as human rights are also making a policy judgment. The genuine issue lies in this realm, and has various aspects.

One aspect is moral or normative—whether it is desirable to make the well-being of people a matter of social concern and to assure people that government assumes relevant responsibilities. Of course, the answer has always been in the affirmative in some degree. The question is how far to go and with precisely what kinds of commitments and implementing measures. The moral ideas inherited from the eighteenth century began to change long ago, even within the realm of civil and political rights. In the United States, slavery is gone. "Separate but equal" is at least outlawed. The franchise has been extended in very marked degree, especially with the outlawing of property qualifications, the poll tax, and discrimination based on sex. And governmental programs in the economic, social, and cultural fields have been very greatly extended.

> Ideas of what is due as a matter of moral necessity for human personality vary from one age to another and from one society to another. In general, material and moral progress produces a continuous expansion of the conception of needs. It is therefore to be expected that a twentieth-century declaration of rights should include more than an eighteenth-century declaration, and what is thought to be a luxury today may be regarded as a necessity tomorrow.[15]

The point is illustrated by the fact that "in California creditors in a bankruptcy case can no longer place an attachment on the family television set, which is now recognized as a necessity."[16] And the fact that ideas of what is normatively desirable change is illustrated even better by the construction that Pope John put on the right to life in the statement from *Pacem in Terris,* quoted at the beginning of this chapter. Pope John obviously did not follow the traditional rule that anything qualifying as a right had to be immediately realizable, or enforceable by court order.

Apart from the moral aspects of the issue there are political aspects that we will be examining at various points. Suffice it to note here that sometimes moral judgments have political implications. For many people over the world it probably does not make a whit of difference whether economic, social, and cultural goals are classified as human rights. But for many others it might well make a significant difference. In many situations, pressures for the promotion of goals, and the sense of an obligation to promote them, are made stronger if they are called rights; and, conversely, in these situations it is easier to resist them, or to do little or nothing about them, if they are not called rights. It is perhaps for this reason that progressive liberals are generally inclined to treat economic, social, and cultural goals as rights, whereas those whose views are more conservative generally incline in the other direction.

Attitudes over much of the world outside the United States are suggested by the fact that the members of the Council of Europe, also steeped in the tradition of the rights of man, have formulated a Social Charter in which they recognize economic and social *rights* and manifestly take the view that it is appropriate to make the promotion of these rights a matter of treaty obligation. The Organization of the American States, against the negative vote of the United States, in 1948 adopted an Inter-American Charter of Social Guarantees. Further, far from denying the existence of economic, social, and cultural rights, a considerable portion of the members of the United Nations regard them as more fundamental and urgent than civil and political rights. Charles Malik epitomized developing attitudes many years ago when he was Chairman of the Commission on Human Rights; he spoke of "a quiet revolution" that occurred in the Commission during the early years of its work:

> There were three logical steps to this transition. The first is to say, the civil, political and personal is primary, but the economic, social and cultural also has its place. The second is to move insensibly from this position to the view that both types of rights are equally important. And the third obviously is to say, what is the use of the civil, political,

and personal if the economic and social is not first guaranteed? Therefore, the social and economic is primary and more important.[17]

## THE RIGHT TO WORK

The Charter of the United Nations itself requires members to pursue economic, social, and cultural goals that have come to be treated very commonly as human rights. Among the goals is full employment.

Article 55 is the prime statement of the obligation. Hitherto in quoting it we have focused only on the portion that specifically refers to human rights, but now additional portions deserve attention. The entire article reads as follows:

> With a view to the creation of conditions of stability and well-being which are necessary for peaceful and friendly relations among nations based on respect for the principles of equal rights and self-determination of peoples, the United Nations shall promote:
> a. higher standards of living, full employment, and conditions of economic and social progress and development;
> b. solutions of international economic, social, health, and related problems; and international cultural and educational cooperation; and
> c. universal respect for, and observance of, human rights and fundamental freedoms for all without distinction as to race, sex, language, or religion.

Article 56 then pledges the members "to take joint and separate action in cooperation with the Organization for the achievement of the purposes set forth in Article 55."

The article does not resolve the question whether it is appropriate to speak of economic, social, and cultural "rights." They are treated as goals to be promoted, and the fact that they are mentioned in a and b, separate from c, intimates that there was no intention to group them with human rights. The practice of the United Nations, however, is to ignore the distinction and to treat a and b as if they spelled out some of the meaning of c.

For present purposes, it is paragraph a that is important, especially the reference to "full employment." Members are to take joint and separate action to promote full employment. This, of course, is not the same as guaranteeing individuals a right to work, and the distinction is significant.

Still the actual achievement of full employment would mean work for all who want it. The article imposes an international obligation, a fact reflected in a General Assembly resolution in 1949 recommending "that each Government consider, as a matter of urgency, its international responsibility under Article 55 and 56 of the Charter to take action, as the need arises, designed to promote and maintain full and productive employment. . . ."[18]

Many other international documents deal in one way or another with the problem of full employment and the right to work. A General Conference of the International Labor Organization, meeting in 1944, adopted the Declaration of Philadelphia, stating aims for the ILO that came to be endorsed in its constitution. The Declaration asserts that

> all human beings, irrespective of race, creed or sex, have the right to pursue both their material well-being and their spiritual development in conditions of freedom and dignity, of economic security and equal opportunity.

Moreover, the Declaration goes on to say that

> the attainment of conditions in which this shall be possible must constitute the central aim of national and international policy.

Further, the Declaration recognizes the obligation of the ILO to promote "full employment and the raising of standards of living."

Inter-American documents also deal with full employment and the right to work. The American Declaration of the Rights and Duties of Man, adopted at Bogotá in 1948, contains a ludicrous equivocation: "every person has the right to work . . . insofar as existing conditions of employment permit." The Charter of the OAS is also cautious, though less equivocal. In the Charter, members of the OAS, including the United States, "agree upon the desirability of developing their social legislation on the following bases: . . . work is a right."

The relevant provision of the Universal Declaration of Human Rights is that "everyone has the right to work, to free choice of employment, to just and favorable conditions of work and to protection against unemployment" (Article 23, paragraph 1.). The Soviet Union sought adoption of the added statement that "the state and society shall guarantee this right by measures calculated to provide everyone with the broadest opportunities for useful work, and to prevent unemployment," but the words *guarantee* and *prevent* were too strong to be acceptable to other states. The corresponding provision of the Covenant on Economic, Social, and Cultural Rights (Article 6) specifies that the parties "recognize the right to work, which inclues the right of everyone to the opportunity to gain his living by work which he freely chooses or accepts, and will take appropriate steps to safeguard this right." The same article goes on to say that

> the steps to be taken . . . to achieve the full realization of this right shall include technical and vocational guidance and training programs, policies and techniques to achieve steady economic, social and cultural development and full and productive employment under conditions safeguarding fundamental political and economic freedoms to the individual.

The European Social Charter contains a somewhat similar article. In it the parties, "with a view to ensuring the effective exercise of the right to work," undertake "to accept as one of their primary aims and responsibilities the achievement and maintenance of as high and stable a level of employment as possible, with a view to the attainment of full employment." The parties also undertake to protect the right of the worker to "earn his living in an occupation freely entered upon" and to maintain employment services and provide vocational guidance and training.[19]

Though the stress above is on the fact that the right to work, however hedged about, is commonly included among the economic, social, and cultural rights, we should also note the broader context in which the right is asserted. The United Nations Charter calls upon members to promote not only full employment but also higher standards of living and conditions of economic and social progress. The Declaration of Philadelphia, and consequently the constitution of the ILO, also put the stress on a broad concern for human welfare: the goals are to be well-being, spiritual development, and conditions making for freedom, dignity, security, and equal opportunity. Similarly, the Charter of the OAS declares that the right to work is to be accompanied by respect for the dignity of the worker, and goes on to say that work "is to be performed under conditions that ensure life, health, and a decent standard of living, both during the working years and during old age, or when any circumstance deprives the individual of the possibility of working." The Universal Declaration, after asserting the right to work, goes on to say that "everyone who works has the right to just and favorable remuneration ensuring for himself and his family an existence worthy of human dignity, and supplemented, if necessary by other means of social protection." The Covenant on Economic, Social, and Cultural Rights spells out even more fully the context within which the right to work is to be safeguarded, and the European Social Charter contains not only the article on the right to work, cited above, but also articles on the right to just conditions of work, the right to safe and healthy working conditions, and the right to a fair remuneration.

It goes without saying that private persons and organizations have long championed the kinds of principles cited above from international declarations and treaties. Marxist political parties have been especially prominent in this connection, and so have a number of progressive and liberal parties of a non-Marxist sort. As already noted, Franklin D. Roosevelt set out what he described as "a second Bill of Rights" in his message on the State of the Union in January 1944, beginning with "the right to a useful and remunerative job" and "the right to earn enough to provide adequate food and clothing and recreation." Congress itself declared in the Employment Act of 1946 that "it is the continuing policy and responsibility of the Federal Government" to create and maintain useful employment opportunities for those who seek work, and to promote "maximum employment." President Johnson, addressing himself to the problem of "hard-core unemployment" in 1968, told Congress that the task was "to give reality to the right to earn a living."

Political parties are not the only private organizations to champion such principles. Religious bodies have done so as well. The provision already quoted from *Pacem in Terris* is in point, and other provisions from the same encyclical might be cited. One of them asserts that "a man has the inherent right not only to be given the opportunity to work, but also to be allowed the exercise of personal initiative in the work he does." According to another,

> A further consequence of man's personal dignity is his right to engage in economic activities suited to his degree of responsibility. The worker is likewise entitled to a wage that is determined in accordance with the precepts of justice. This needs stressing. The amount a worker receives must be sufficient, in proportion to available funds, to allow him and his family a standard of living consistent with human dignity.

Obviously the right to work differs in ways already indicated from the right to free speech or the right to non-discriminatory treatment at the hands of government. More broadly, most economic, social, and cultural rights differ from civil and political rights in the manner in which they can be implemented. They are non-justiciable or program rights—rights whose realization depends not upon a court order but upon a set of policies and activities, perhaps carried out over a considerable period of time. Thus they are much less likely than the civil and political rights to be flatly guaranteed or ensured. Furthermore, especially where it is a question of the availability not simply of some kind of work but of a suitable kind, the problem is magnified. And it is this more ambitious goal toward which the Declaration of Philadelphia points, calling for "the employment of workers in the occupations in which they can have the satisfaction of giving the fullest measure of their skill and attainments and make their greatest contribution to the common well-being."

As indicated above, Maurice Cranston attacks the definition of human rights developed in the course of the work of the United Nations. Among the assertions that he picks upon is one contained in both the Universal Declaration and in the Covenant, that men are entitled to "periodic holidays with pay." It is utterly impossible, he correctly says, and will be for a long time yet, to implement this right for everyone in the world; and in his view nothing can appropriately be called a human right if it is impracticable.[20]

The basic problem here is the problem of definition. If something is a right only when it is practicable (meaning immediately realizable?), then holidays with pay are not a right for most of the people of the world; and neither are many of the other economic, social, and cultural "rights." The "right" that Cranston picks on is scarcely even relevant to the circumstances of a substantial portion of the world's population. But still, if the definition of *right* is made to encompass not only what is immediately realizable but what it ought to be a goal of policy to promote, then the naming of rights becomes a political matter, and many influencing factors come into operation in addition to theory and logic.

## TRADE UNION RIGHTS

As in the case of the right to work, a number of international documents assert the existence of trade union rights and, more broadly, of a right to freedom of association. In this respect the contrast with domestic American practice is not so great, for state and federal laws recognize and protect these same rights. Here our main object is to note the extent to which the rights have been recognized internationally and the extent to which their promotion and protection has become an international commitment.

The Declaration of Philadelphia, cited above, asserts the principle that freedom of association is essential and that the war against want calls for an international effort in which representatives of both workers and employers take part. The Declaration also endorses the right of collective bargaining. All members of the ILO subscribe to this declaration. Moreover, the General Assembly endorsed it in 1947, adopting a resolution so specifying and going on to speak of "the inalienable right of trade union freedom of association."[21]

The General Assembly has also endorsed trade union rights in the Universal Declaration and in the Covenant on Economic, Social, and Cultural Rights. The Universal Declaration asserts that freedom of association is a right of everyone, and that "everyone has the right to form and join trade unions for the protection of his interests." The Covenant spells the right out more fully. It specifies that everyone has the right to form trade unions and to join the union of his choice, that trade unions themselves have a right to establish national federations which in turn may form or join international trade union organizations, and that parties are to ensure the right to strike. It remains to be seen, however, how various qualifications will be interpreted. The rights are to be "subject to no limitations other than those prescribed by law and which are necessary in a democratic society in the interests of national security or public order or for the protection of the rights and freedoms of others"; and the right to strike must be "exercised in conformity with the laws."

The International Labor Organization is naturally concerned with trade union rights. It has recommended for ratification both the "Freedom of Association and Protection of the Right to Organize Convention, 1948" and the "Right to Organize and Collective Bargaining Convention, 1949." By 1967 the first had been ratified by 73 states and the second by 81.[22] The purpose of the conventions is to safeguard trade union rights against interference by the state and by the employer, respectively.[23] The Right to Organize Convention recognizes the right of both workers and employers, "without distinction whatsoever" and without previous authorization, to form and join organizations of their own choosing; it further stipulates that "workers' and employers' organizations shall have the right to draw up their constitutions and rules, to elect their representatives in full freedom, to organize their administration and activities, and to formulate their programs," and that "the public authorities shall refrain from any interference which would restrict this right or impede the lawful exercise thereof."[24] Correspondingly, the Collective Bargaining Convention is designed to safeguard workers against discrimination by management because of trade union membership or activities. The rights and prohibitions are roughly those of the Wagner Act, which Congress enacted during the New Deal.[25]

One of the perennial questions concerning these agreements is the extent to which the Soviet Union and other communist countries are abiding by their terms: can and does genuine trade union freedom exist in one-party totalitarian systems? A committee of the ILO which considered the question in the mid-1950's concluded that "the organizations of workers in their hierarchy are all able to look after themselves and are not likely to be subject to domination and control by the government"; the committee did not say, however, "how far both the government and the trade unions themselves are subject to the domination of the Communist Party."[26]

Finally, various regional declarations are in point. Both the American Declaration on the Rights and Duties of Man and the Inter-American Charter of Social Guarantees assert the right of association, and the latter asserts the right to strike. And the European Social Charter includes articles on the right to organize and to bargain collectively. The parties undertake "that national law shall not be such as to impair, nor shall it be so applied as to impair" the freedom of workers and employers to form local, national, or international organizations and to join those organizations. In connection with the right to collective bargaining, they agree to promote consultation between workers and employers, and machinery for negotiation, conciliation, and voluntary arbitration; and they recognize "the right of workers and employers to collective action," including the right to strike.

### THE RIGHT TO EDUCATION

The Covenant on Economic, Social, and Cultural Rights specifies that its parties "recognize the right of everyone to education." Moreover,

> they agree that education shall be directed to the full development of the human personality and the sense of its dignity, and shall strengthen the respect for human rights and fundamental freedoms.

> They further agree that education shall enable all persons to participate effectively in a free society, promote understanding, tolerance and friendship among all nations and all racial, ethnic or religious groups, and further the activities of the United Nations for the maintenance of peace.

Primary education, according to the Covenant, "shall be compulsory and available free to all." Secondary education (including technical and vocational secondary education) "shall be made generally available and accessible to all by every appropriate means"; one of the appropriate means is "the progressive introduction of free education." Similarly, higher education is to be made "equally accessible to all, on the basis of capacity, by every appropriate means"; and again one of the appropriate means is progressive action to make higher education free. For adults who did not obtain or complete a primary education, "fundamental education" is to be encouraged. The school system itself is to be developed at all levels, an "adequate fellowship system" is to be established, and "the material conditions of the teaching staff [are to be] continuously improved." Finally, parties to the Covenant undertake to respect "the liberty of parents . . . to choose for their children schools other than those established by the public authorities" so long as these schools meet minimum standards; the object is to make it possible for parents "to ensure the religious and moral education of their children in conformity with their own convictions."

The Universal Declaration, the American Declaration of the Rights and Duties of Man, and the OAS Charter all contain similar, though briefer, articles. In the OAS Charter the member states agree to promote the right to education "in accordance with their constitutional provisions and their material resources." The states in the Council of Europe included an article on the right to education in a protocol supplementing the European Convention. The article stipulates that "no person shall be denied the right to education," and then goes on to reserve the right of parents to ensure the education of their children "in conformity with their own religious and philosophical convictions." Four states attached reservations to their acceptance of the latter clause, reflecting problems about its meaning and applicability. Implications of the reference to "philosophical convictions" are especially uncertain.[27]

In the United States, education is left primarily to the states, and all of them provide for it in their constitutions and laws. The constitution of North Carolina describes education as a right: "the people have a right to the privilege of education, and it is the duty of the State to guard and maintain that right." With a few exceptions, the states admitted to the Union since 1876 have been required by Congress to provide for public schools "by ordinance irrevocable without the consent of the United States."[28] Whether or not this means that individuals have a right to education, the states involved are bound to make it available. In contrast, the constitution of Alabama, after declaring that it is the policy of the state to foster and promote the education of its citizens, specifies that "nothing in this constitution shall be construed as creating or recognizing any right to education or training at public expense." In the struggle over integration it has been established that if a community chooses to maintain schools it may not legally discriminate among children on the basis of race; but it has also been established—at least for states that became part of the Union prior to 1876—that if a community prefers simply to close down the public schools rather than admit Negroes, the federal constitution and laws permit it to do so; and thus the way is open to a violation of the standards endorsed in the Universal Declaration of Human Rights and other international instruments.

## THE RIGHT TO SOCIAL SECURITY

Social security, broadly defined, is regularly included among the economic, social, and cultural rights. The Declaration of Philadelphia called for "the extension of social security measures to provide a basic income to all in need of such protection and comprehensive medical care." According to the American Declaration of the Rights and Duties of Man," "every person has the right to social security which will protect him from the consequences of unemployment, old age, and any disabilities arising from causes beyond his control that make it physically or mentally impossible for him to earn a living." The Universal Declaration of Human Rights declares in Article 22 that

> everyone, as a member of society, has the right to social security and is entitled to realization, through national effort and international cooperation and in accordance with the organization and resources of each State, of the economic, social, and cultural rights indispensable for his dignity and the free development of his personality.

Article 25 adds to the statement of the right:

> 1. Everyone has the right to a standard of living adequate for the health and well being of himself and of his family, including food, clothing, housing and medical care and necessary social services, and the right to security in the event of unemployment, sickness, disability, widowhood, old age or other lack of livelihood in circumstances beyond his control.
> 2. Motherhood and childhood are entitled to special care and assistance. All children, whether born in or out of wedlock, shall enjoy the same social protection.

The Covenant on Economic, Social, and Cultural Rights is even fuller in its exposition of rights in the field of social security. Among other things, it speaks of "the fundamental right of everyone to be free from hunger" and names some of the kinds of measures that parties are to take in respect of that right—for example, to improve methods of producing and distributing foods, to develop or reform agrarian systems, and to disseminate knowledge of the principles of nutrition. It also speaks of "the right of everyone to the enjoyment of the highest attainable standard of physical and mental health," and again names some of the kinds of steps to be taken to give effect to the right.

The International Labor Organization has been especially active in promoting social security. Among other things, after formulating a number of individual conventions in earlier years dealing with various aspects of the subject, it developed a comprehensive convention in 1952—the Social Security (Minimum Standards) Convention—covering nine different branches of social security: medical care, sickness benefit, unemployment benefit, old age benefit, employment injury benefit, family benefit, maternity benefit, invalidity benefit, and survivors' benefit.[29] As of 1960, ten countries had ratified the convention, not including the United States. Especially in view of the fact that some of the branches of social security covered fall within the sphere of state action, the President has not recommended ratification.[30]

The European Social Charter includes an article specifying the kinds of actions that parties are to take to ensure "the effective exercise of the right to social security." They are a minimum to meet the standards fixed in the ILO convention just cited and are to endeavor to go progressively to higher levels. Further, so as to minimize obstacles to the mobility of labor among the Council of Europe states, they are to treat non-nationals as well as nationals.

### THE RIGHTS OF WOMEN AND CHILDREN

A number of international declarations and conventions are designed to identify and promote the rights of women and children. The Charter of the United Nations itself, in obligating members to promote human rights, lists sex as one of the prohibited bases for discrimination, and a great many other international instruments assert the same rule. The rights set forth in the Universal Declaration are for "all" and for "everyone," and when something is forbidden it is to be done to "no one." Both of the Covenants on human rights prohibit discrimination based on sex, and then repeat the point in a separate article in which the parties "undertake to ensure the equal right of men and women to the enjoyment" of all the rights set forth.

The extent of the historic discrimination against women is suggested by the fact that it is built into our language—as when we speak of *mankind* and as when the American republics formulated a Declaration of the Rights and Duties of *Man*. United Nations agencies, in contrast, run into protests when they use the term *man* as if it naturally encompasses women as well. The reference must be to both men and women, or to human beings.

The American Declaration on the Rights and Duties of *Man* in fact prescribes equality before the law without distinction as to sex, and includes an article calling for special protection for women during pregnancy and the nursing period, and for children. Similarly, the Inter-American Charter of Social Guarantees calls for special protections for women and children. In 1949 the General Assembly approved a Convention for the Suppression of the Traffic in Persons and of the Exploitation of the Prostitution of Others, consolidating and extending the scope of several earlier conventions.[31] The ILO sponsors both the Convention on Equal Remuneration for Men and Women Workers of Equal Value, 1951, and the Discrimination (Employment and Occupation) Convention, 1958. There is a Convention on the Nationality of Married Women, 1957; and a Convention on Consent to Marriage, Minimum Age for Marriage and Registration of Marriages, 1962, and a General Assembly recommendation on the same subject.[32] In 1967 the General Assembly adopted a Declaration on the Elimination of Discrimination against Women, repeating some of the principles already cited and adding others.[33] The Declaration urges states to take all appropriate measures to ensure the principle of equality of status of the husband and wife; in particular, women are to have "the same right as men to free choice of a spouse and to enter into marriage only with their free and full consent" and are to have "equal rights with men during marriage and at its dissolution." Child marriage and the betrothal of young girls before puberty is to be prohibited. Girls and women, married or unmarried, are to have equal rights with men in education at all levels—a principle also set forth in UNESCO's Convention and Recommendation against Discrimination in Education, 1960. They are to have equal rights with men in economic and social life—with respect to vocational training, choice of profession and employment, and advancement; with respect to social security; and with respect to the receipt of family allowances. Measures are to be taken "to prevent the dismissal of women in the event of marriage or maternity and to provide paid maternity leave, with the guarantee of returning to former employment, and to provide the necessary social services, including child-care facilities."

The principle that married women should have equal rights with their husbands raises objections, especially in connection with property rights. In the Third Committee of the General Assembly, for example, the Ecuadorian delegate held that to assert this principle was "to ignore the system which had been established by the majority of legal systems and which was based on the principle of authority in the family, as in society. . . . Marriage established community of property between husband and wife . . . and it was the duty of the husband to administer the wife's property."[34] Similarly, the delegate from the Sudan objected that some of the applications of the principle of equal rights were "prejudicial to the family." Nevertheless, in the General Assembly the vote for the resolution was unanimous, which reflects the fact that no formal and strict obligation is imposed.

The General Assembly in 1959 adopted a Declaration of the Rights of the Child.[35] The declaration repeats the usual ban on discrimination. It asserts that "the child shall be entitled from his birth to a name and a nationality." He is to enjoy the benefits of social security, and to have a right to adequate nutrition, housing, recreation and medical services. "He shall, wherever possible, grow up in the care and under the responsibility of his parents, and, in any case, in an atmosphere of affection and of moral and material security." He is entitled to an education "which will promote his general culture, and enable him, on a basis of equal opportunity, to develop his abilities, his individual judgement, and his sense of moral and social responsibility, and to become a useful member of society." He is not to be "admitted to employment before an appropriate minimum age; he shall in no case be caused or permitted to engage in any occupation or employment which would prejudice his health or education, or interfere with his physical, mental or moral development."

> He shall be brought up in a spirit of understanding, tolerance, friendship among peoples, peace and universal brotherhood, and in full consciousness that his energy and talents should be devoted to the service of his fellow men.

In 1965 the General Assembly elaborated on this latter point in a Declaration on the Promotion among Youth of the Ideals of Peace, Mutual Respect and Understanding Between Peoples.[36]

It is easy to be cynical about the endorsement of high moral principle. And it is worth noting that the General Assembly, in asserting the rights of the child, was necessarily rather vague in identifying those who are responsible for seeing to it that the rights are observed. Nevertheless it is interesting that so many intelligent men and women in the delegations sent to the United Nations believe it worth while to go through the laborious process of formulating the principles, negotiating to obtain agreement on them, and bringing them to a vote in the plenary meetings of the General Assembly.

## THE RIGHT TO PROPERTY

The Universal Declaration of Human Rights asserts a right to property, but the Covenants on Human Rights do not.

According to the Universal Declaration, "everyone has the right to own property alone as well as in association with others," and "no one shall be arbitrarily deprived of his property."

Though the United States would have been willing simply to repeat those statements in the Covenants, other governments were not entirely satisfied with them. None denied the right to property, in principle, though some questioned whether the right to certain kinds of property—for example, to public utilities or to factories—should be classified as a human right. Moreover, all governments, including that of the United States, insist on a right to take property in certain circumstances; that is, they insist on a right of eminent domain, or a right to nationalize or expropriate. Further associated with the taking of property are various questions relating to compensation. Broadly speaking, the conflict that developed in the effort to formulate an article on the right to property was over the issue of international accountability in the handling of these matters. The United States upheld the principle of accountability. It acknowledged that property rights are subject to limitations, but wanted to specify that the limitations must be "reasonable," that no property was to be taken "arbitrarily," and that "just" compensation must be paid. Others, seeking to minimize international accountability, objected that the words "reasonable" and "just" were subject to different interpretations and might be used as a basis for foreign interference in their affairs; and they objected to the word "arbitrarily" on the ground that it had no commonly accepted meaning—that when a government takes property it would do it "lawfully," and that was reassurance enough.

Basic to the whole issue, quite obviously, were differing value systems, differing conceptions of the national interest, and differing traditions. The Soviet and other communist governments had no desire to endorse a right to property, and governments in many of the newly independent and developing countries had little enthusiasm for it. In many of the African countries, for example, communal ownership of some forms of property is the tradition, and in many of them the rights of private ownership are thought to be entitled to respect only so long as development plans are served.[37] Resentment and hostility toward foreign owners exist in a number of countries, as well as a belief that the property rights of foreign capitalists lack a moral basis. Various factors lead to such attitudes, among them the influence of Marxism, the connection between foreign property rights and imperialism, and the belief that the foreign owner has acquired some or all of his property through an imposed system of exploitation. In any event, enough states shared enough of these views that the outcome in the Commission on Human Rights and later in the General Assembly was an impasse; and the decision was simply to omit any reference to property in the Covenants.[38]

The question of a right to property was also troublesome to those who drafted the European Convention on Human Rights. The solution arrived at—in the first protocol of the Convention—is the following statement:

> Every natural or legal person is entitled to the peaceful enjoyment of his possessions. No one shall be deprived of his possessions except in the public interest and subject to the conditions provided for by law and by the general principles of international law.

The purpose of the reference to the principles of international law was to indicate that, regardless of how a government chose to treat its own citizens, foreign owners were entitled to fair compensation.[39] Following the paragraph quoted just above, the European Convention goes on to acknowledge "the right of a State to enforce such laws as it deems necessary to control the use of property in accordance with the general interest."

## THE POLITICAL IDEOLOGY OF ECONOMIC AND SOCIAL RIGHTS

The economic, social, and cultural goals identified in documents on human rights are naturally humanitarian. Parties of the Center and the Left usually espouse them most ardently, but at the same time, even the most vigorous champions of the Right hesitate to say that the systems that they favor are not designed to provide for work, health, education, and so on.

The Universal Declaration obviously falls far short of an endorsement of socialism. The promotion and achievement of its goals is not charged exclusively or even primarily to the state. A preliminary paragraph of the Declaration urges "every individual and every organ of society" to promote respect for the rights and freedoms named "by teaching and education." Moreover, with reference to the economic, social, and cultural rights, the Declaration says that everyone is entitled to their realization "in accordance with the organization and resources of each state." Different patterns of social organization are thus assumed. On behalf of the United States, Mrs. Eleanor Roosevelt (who served as Chairman of the Commission on Human Rights in its early years) long ago made it clear that the statement of economic, social, and cultural rights in the Declaration did not "imply an obligation on governments to assure the enjoyment of these rights by direct governmental action."[40] She did not claim, of course, that the Declaration is irrelevant to governmental policy. As a minimum, it seeks to impose a moral obligation on governments not to subvert or act contrary to the principles endorsed; and more positively, like the UN Charter itself, it calls on governments to promote the goals indirectly if not directly, for example, by creating and maintaining the kinds of conditions that favor their achievement. But the statement that "everyone" has a certain right does not say who is to see to it that the right is realized or prescribe a method of implementation.[41] The Economic and Social Council once defeated a motion that it appraise the standards by which members of the United Nations defined the meaning of full employment. The fear was that this would lead to an appraisal of "the relative virtues of various national policies," and that this appraisal would be influenced by ideological considerations.[42]

The Covenant on Economic, Social, and Cultural Rights, as contrasted to the Universal Declaration, puts more stress on governmental obligations and actions, but even so it does not give clear-cut support to any one ideology or political movement. In Article 2 each party "undertakes to take steps . . . to the maximum of its available resources, with a view to achieving progressively the full realization of the rights recognized in the present Covenant by all appropriate means, including particularly the adoption of legislative measures." An active role for government is thus explicitly envisaged. In connection with justiciable rights—those subject to enforcement by court order—the obligation of government is clear and strong; for example, the parties undertake to *ensure* that discrimination based on sex will not occur with respect to the rights named, and to *ensure* trade union rights. The Soviet Union proposed somewhat comparable statements in connection with the non-justiciable rights, asking that governments undertake to *guarantee* them, but its view did not prevail.[43] In the Covenant on Economic, Social, and Cultural Rights as finally approved, the usual statement is that the parties *recognize* the various rights and will take the appropriate or the necessary steps to promote their achievement. For example, as noted earlier, the parties "recognize the right of everyone to the enjoyment of the highest attainable standard of physical and mental health"; and the consequent steps to be taken are "those necessary" for the achievement of a series of more specific goals—for example, "the prevention, treatment and control of epidemic, endemic, occupational and other diseases."[44] Thus inactivity is ruled out. Laissez-faire is not enough. The principles endorsed might theoretically limit some conservative parties over the world in the attitudes that they take on social policies, and it is understandable that conservatives in the United States might associate the promotion of economic and social rights with "creeping socialism." Senator Bricker made the association, and so have some of the employer delegates sent by the United States to conferences of the ILO.[45] But the words used in the various documents are vague enough to permit various lines of action. Socialization is obviously not required.

The Inter-American Charter of Social Guarantees is specific in assigning certain duties to the state. The state is to provide vocational and technical training. It is to "sponsor the establishment of popular farms and restaurants and of consumer and credit cooperatives." It should "promote and provide for recreational and welfare centers that can be freely utilized by workers." The presence of such stipulations helps to explain the negative vote of the United States on the Charter and the disclaimer of obligation under it.[46]

## CONCLUDING COMMENTS

As indicated at the outset, the object of this chapter has been to identify economic, social, and cultural rights; and the major ones have been covered. Two brief comments might be added.

On the basis of sample surveys, Hadley Cantril has reported on the concerns of people in a number of countries in different parts of the world. The questions posed were in terms of the hopes and fears of the respondents for themselves and for their country, not in terms of general principles or rights. Nevertheless it is noteworthy that hopes and fears having some bearing on human rights fell much more in the economic and social category than in the civil and political category. Hope for an improved or decent standard of living, for example, is far more prevalent than is fear of a lack of freedom. And within the realm of the political, much more concern appears for honesty, stability, and efficiency in government than for democratic or representative government. At the same time, within the realm of the civil and political, fears and hopes concerning discrimination show up frequently.

The findings are obviously significant, but at the same time need to be interpreted with caution. Cantril himself suggests this, referring to "concerns [which] are seldom mentioned because they are taken for granted, and which are infrequently mentioned simply because they do not exist." Less than 1 per cent of the respondents within the United States, for example, expressed concern for freedom of speech, though surely many more would have done so if they had believed such freedom to be in jeopardy.[47] Further, frequency of mention by a sample of the population may or may not be a reliable indicator of the level of concern within the government. The records of the United Nations suggest that by and large the delegates attending the relevant meetings become emotionally aroused about the right to self-determination and the right to equality and nondiscrimination much more than about the economic, social, and cultural rights described in this chapter.

The second concluding comment is very different. It is that the declarations and agreements mentioned in this chapter mark a minor revolution in international affairs. What once were matters of exclusively domestic jurisdiction, rarely entering the field of international action, are now declared to be of common concern. Common standards of law and practice are being elaborated, and (in varying degrees in different connections) the principle of international accountability for the observance of these standards is being developed and accepted. We will discuss the question of international accountability and the problem of implementation more fully in the chapters of Part III.

# 5

# Self-Determination and Minority Rights

Neither the Charter of the United Nations nor the Universal Declaration of Human Rights suggests that questions about self-determination and minorities should figure importantly in discussions of human rights. The Charter endorses self-determination as a principle, saying that one of the purposes of the United Nations is "to develop friendly relations among nations based on respect for the principle of equal rights and self-determination of peoples"; but it does not suggest that self-determination is among the human rights. And it does not mention minority rights at all. The Universal Declaration says nothing about either subject.

Nevertheless, self-determination has become an emotion-laden term in the field of human rights, a shibboleth that all must pronounce to identify themselves with the virtuous. The idea of minority rights is not equally favored. In fact, most of the champions of self-determination would be happiest if the question of minority rights never came up. But the one idea connotes the other, for self-determination is potentially a right for minorities as well as for others.

Both terms are vague. Who are the "selves" who are entitled to self-determination? What is a minority, and are minorities among the "selves?" Precisely what may the selves determine—what choices are open to them? When or under what conditions? By what process? Whether or not minority groups are entitled to self-determination, should they be accorded some kind of differential status and treatment, or is it enough if the individual members of such groups enjoy human rights?

All of the above questions arouse controversy. In an official sense, as we will see in this chapter, some have been settled by a two-thirds vote in the General Assembly, but in a practical sense they are likely for the indefinite future to remain sources of trouble and conflict.

## SELF-DETERMINATION AS A RIGHT

As indicated above, the Charter speaks of self-determination as a *principle*, a term acceptable to the United States and Britain, among others. But already in 1950—well before the great influx of newly-independent members so sensitive about colonialism—the General Assembly, against the negative votes of the United States and Britain, requested a study of the "ways and means which would ensure the *right* of peoples and nations to self-determination."[1] Within two years the General Assembly went farther, deciding to include an article on the subject in the International Covenant or Covenants on Human Rights then being drafted.[2] In this official sense, then, self-determination became a *human right*. It is set forth in Article 1 of both of the Covenants approved in 1966. Paragraphs 1 and 3 of that article are as follows. Paragraph 2, which concerns "economic self-determination," will be discussed later.

> 1. All peoples have the right of self-determination. By virtue of that right they freely determine their political status and freely pursue their economic, social, and cultural development.
> 3. The States Parties to the present Covenant, including those having responsibility for the administration of Non-Self-Governing and Trust Territories, shall promote the realization of the right of self-determination, and shall respect the right, in conformity with the provisions of the Charter of the United Nations.

In the crucial vote on the question of actually including the above article in the Covenants—a vote taken in 1955—the United States, Britain, France, and, in fact, most of the other members of the Atlantic community voted against. The vote was 33 to 12, with 13 abstentions.[3] Respect for the principle of self-determination appeared on every hand, but so did reluctance to call the principle a right that entailed a legal obligation and that gave the "selves" (whoever they were) a strong basis for a claim. We will discuss the reasons for the conflicting views in a moment. As former colonies achieved independence and joined the United Nations, the demand that self-determination be classified as a right became even stronger.

In 1960, by a vote of 89 to 0, with 9 abstentions, the General Assembly adopted its Declaration on the Granting of Independence to Colonial Countries and Peoples, which, among other things, repeated paragraph 1 of the article slated to go into the covenants, quoted above. This time the United States, Britain, and France abstained.[4] Since then the stand of the United States on the question whether self-determination is a principle or a right has become somewhat unclear. The Assistant Secretary of State for International Organization Affairs said in 1963 that the United States wants the inhabitants of Micronesia "to exercise their inherent and inalienable right of self-determination,"[5] and in the same year the United States voted for a General Assembly resolution reaffirming the "inalienable right of the Angolan people to self-determination and independence."[6] In the 1966 Special Committee on Principles of International Law Concerning Friendly Relations and Cooperation among States, the United States proposed a resolution speaking of the "duty" of states "to respect the principle" of self-determination, and Britain adopted the same language in a resolution that it presented the next year.[7] A review of UN practice leads Rosalyn Higgins to the "inescapable" conclusion that self-determination "has developed into an international legal right," though "the extent and scope of the right is still open to some debate."[8]

## INTERNAL SELF-DETERMINATION

Self-determination is thought of as either internal or external. Internal self-determination relates to sovereign states and has to do with control over their political life, for example, with the question of freedom from foreign intervention and with the question of representative government or majority rule. External self-determination relates to political entities or "peoples" that lack sovereignty, and has to do with their right to get it.

Czechoslovakia in 1966 advanced a definition incorporating elements of both meanings: "All peoples have the right to self-determination, namely the right to choose freely their political, economic and social systems, including the rights to establish an independent national State, to pursue their development and to dispose of their natural wealth and resources."[9] Acknowledging that the term is most commonly applied to external relationships, a spokesman for this definition explained that "even when the process of decolonization was completed, the principle of self-determination would remain fully valid. . . . It would be contrary to the essence of the principle if, once a people had attained its independence, it was deprived of self-determination in the domestic sphere."[10]

Governments generally endorse internal self-determination in the sense of freedom from foreign intervention. None makes an explicit, general claim of a right to intervene in the domestic affairs of other states, and none admits that it is itself the creature of a foreign power. But obviously the principle is sometimes violated. To say the very least, the Soviet Union has put a peculiar and distinctive construction on internal self-determination in relation to the states of eastern and southeastern Europe. It illustrated the fact by its behavior in the area during and after World War II, by its intervention in Hungary in 1956, and again by its intervention in Czechoslovakia in 1968. Following the intervention in Czechoslovakia, Foreign Minister Gromyko spoke of those "who are tempted to try to roll back the socialist commonwealth, to snatch at least one link from it," and he said flatly that the Soviet Union would not allow that to happen.[11] In other words, for the communist countries of eastern and southeastern Europe, internal self-determination is rigidly limited.

The United States too imposes limits on the right of internal self-determination. In a previous chapter we have already noted Roosevelt's statement in 1940—primarily with reference to Nazi Germany—that, though "the peoples of other nations have the right to choose their own form of government, . . . we in this Nation still believe that such choice should be predicated on certain freedoms which we think are essential everywhere." In 1943 he added that "the right of self-determination included in the Atlantic Charter does not carry with it the right of any Government . . . to commit wholesale murder, or the right to make slaves of its own people, or of any other peoples in the world."[12] Much more recently, President Johnson, confronting a crisis in the Dominican Republic, declared that "the American nations cannot, must not, and will not permit the establishment of another Communist government in the Western Hemisphere."[13]

Sometimes the idea of internal self-determination goes beyond the notion of freedom from foreign intervention and extends to the notion of representative government or majority rule. Discussing participation in government in Chapter 3, we have already cited a statement by President Prado of Peru that it is "indispensable" to the principle of self-determination "that the will of the people must be able to express itself through free elections periodically held." In 1962 the Inter-American Peace Committee reported to the American Ministers of Foreign Affairs that Castro's government in Cuba

> impedes the exercise of the right of self-determination, as it is conceived in the inter-American system, that is, as the right of each and all of the citizens to contribute with his vote, given in free elections, to the formation of the government that they may prefer to give themselves.[14]

Along the same line, the report of a symposium on representative democracy held in the Dominican Republic in 1962 includes the following statement:

> Within the regional organization of the Americas, self-determination of peoples signifies not only the right of colonial peoples to independence . . . but also the right of each national community . . . to direct, organize, and develop its national life in accordance with its free and spontaneous will . . . through the exercise of representative democracy.[15]

Rosalyn Higgins even suggests that the right of self-determination should be defined as "the right of a majority . . . to the exercise of power."[16] The case of Southern Rhodesia offers some support for the view, for there the General Assembly demanded that Britain transfer power not to the minority white regime but to "the people of Zimbabwe on the basis of elections conducted according to the principle of 'one man, one vote.' "[17] But the General Assembly has not been consistent in identifying self-determination with majority rule. Too many governments, including some in Africa, would fail the test. And in connection with Southern Rhodesia the concern seemed to be much more with racial discrimination than with self-determination as such.

Portugal has its own special definition of self-determination: "the consent of the people to a certain structure and political organization." And consent is manifested not necessarily in elections or in plebiscites, but "by participation in administration and by participation in political life."[18] What proportion of the population must participate, and in what way and on what basis, is left unclear.

Obviously, for many governments and political leaders, the word *self-determination* has become a weapon, used in political struggles simply because it has appeal, whether or not it is apt. And those who try to derive advantage from the word's appeal are inclined to read into it whatever meaning serves their purposes.

### EXTERNAL SELF-DETERMINATION FOR PEOPLES OF DEPENDENT TERRITORIES

As noted above, virtually all governments endorse external self-determination for colonial peoples, whether calling it a principle or a right. So generally is the idea accepted that we will take it for granted and focus on the qualifications that are attached.

It is common to insist that colonial peoples shall become independent, or exercise their right of self-determination, only when they desire it and when they are in some sense prepared for it. Thus President Truman once said that "all peoples who are prepared for self-government should be permitted to choose their own form of government. . . ."[19] Along the same line, the parties to the Southeast Asia Collective Defense Treaty and the Pacific Charter, in reaffirming their support for the principle of equal rights and self-determination of peoples, declared that they would "earnestly strive . . . to secure the independence of all countries whose peoples desire it and are able to undertake its responsibilities."[20] Secretary of State Dulles once said that "our desire is a world in which peoples who want political independence shall possess it whenever they are capable of sustaining it and discharging its responsibilities in accordance with the accepted standards of civilized nations."[21] The United States representative to the General Assembly in 1963 endorsed self-determination for South-West Africa "as promptly as the expression may be freely and responsibly exercised."[22] In the same year the United States opposed "immediate" independence for Angola "in view of the desperate shortage of educated and trained people."[23] In Congress Senator Ellender of Louisiana took a similar view, listing various prerequisites for independence, including trained people in various categories, an educational system, and resources for a more or less balanced economy. As he saw it, none of the new nations of Africa that he had visited met even a majority of his requirements. He said that he had "yet to see any part of Africa where Africans are ready for self-government."[24] An American spokesman is quoted earlier affirming the "inherent and inalienable right" of the inhabitants of Micronesia to self-determination. He added, however, that the United States did not think the right should be exercised "until these people have acquired a first-hand knowledge of both the benefits and the responsibilities of twentieth-century civilization."[25]

Qualifications and reservations of the above sorts seem to be eminently sensible, but it is obvious that they could be used in bad faith, as an excuse for delay. Consideration of the latter possibility led the General Assembly to include in its Declaration on the Granting of Independence to Colonial Countries and Peoples the statement that "inadequacy of political, economic, social or educational preparedness should never serve as a pretext for delaying independence." The wording is indecisive. Of course, it conveys a sense of impatience about decolonization and of suspicion of the motives of the imperial powers; at the same time, the statement that inadequate preparedness should never serve as a pretext may or may not mean that it could never be a genuine reason.

African states themselves usually demand not immediate independence for remaining colonies but immediate steps toward independence, or the promotion of independence as a goal. Among their concerns is the question whether independence really goes to "the people"; more crudely put, the concern is that independence should not go to white minority regimes that practice racial discrimination. This is the central issue in the case of Southern Rhodesia, where whites who constitute only 4 per cent of the population control the government that declared independence. It is also a problem in connection with South-West Africa and the African territories of Portugal. One of the formulas used by the General Assembly is that "the wishes of the people" should be "ascertained through plebiscites or other recognized democratic means, preferably under the auspices of the United Nations."[26] Obviously "the people" include the whole population, not just the whites. No one can say to what extent the concern of the champions of decolonization in Africa is with majority rule and to what extent it is with racial matters; in any event they do not want white power to survive independence.

Britain faced a comparable problem about the conditions of decolonization in British Guiana, where a withdrawal in 1953 would probably have meant power for a party with strong totalitarian inclinations. As Maurice Cranston says,

> In the event, British "colonialism" remained as a bulwark against totalitarianism, remained as the true guardian of the people's rights and liberties; far from "promoting freedom" by quitting British Guiana, the British would in fact have been extending the range of oppression in the world. They did so when they left Ghana to the mercies of the native dictator, Dr. Nkrumah.[27]

Does self-determination necessarily mean independence? A document already cited intimates that it does. It asserts the right of self-determination, but is entitled a "Declaration on the Granting of Independence . . . ," and at several points in the text the assumption is that the outcome of self-determination is "complete independence and freedom." The Declaration ignores the possibility that people might choose a status other than independence, as Puerto Rico has done. When the Cook Islanders did so in 1965, the General Assembly was incredulous. The issue in the elections in the Cook Islands was a new constitution which provided for self-government but which left New Zealand responsible for the islands' foreign relations and defense. The party favoring the constitution won 14 out of 22 seats in the parliament. In response, the General Assembly was willing to acknowledge that the Cook Islands had attained full internal self-government, but it refused to say that they had "exercised their right of self-determination." Instead it promised "to assist the people of the Cook Islands in the eventual achievement of full independence, if they so wish, at a future date."[28] Even the Security Council has demanded recognition of the right of peoples to "self-determination and independence," as if the one almost automatically means the other.[29] At the same time, the possibility that people might voluntarily choose something other than independence is acknowledged. A delegate from Sierra Leone once described the African attitude as follows:

> At no time have the African representatives said that self-determination is not self-determination unless it leads to independence. What we have always said is that it seems most unlikely to us that any African people given the right fully to determine their political future would prefer to remain Portuguese, or for that matter British or French. But should they so freely choose, their choice will and must be respected by all.[30]

From the point of view of the United States the crucial goal is not independence but self-government. The United States made this clear in a resolution submitted to the 1966 Special Committee on Principles of International Law Concerning Friendly Relations and Cooperation Among States, and it went on to say that the achievement of self-government might take any of three forms: emergence as a sovereign and independent state; free association with an independent state; or integration with an independent state. Moreover, according to the resolution, the principle of self-determination should be presumed to be satisfied wherever a sovereign state exists "possessing a representative Government, effectively functioning as such to all distinct peoples within its territory."[31] Britain incorporated the same principles in a similar resolution that it introduced in 1967.[32]

As the reference to the Cook Islands suggests, the exercise of self-determination contributes to the problem of mini-states. Something like 73 political entities (states, or territories readily indentifiable as potential states) have populations under one million. Fifteen of them are already members of the United Nations, leaving some 58 additional prospective members. Sixty of the 73 have populations under 300,000.[33] A few deserve to be called advanced, but most are in the category described as "developing" and some should be called primitive. The representative of the United States no doubt had the problems of some of these potential mini-states in mind in explaining his abstention from the vote on the Declaration on the Granting of Independence to Colonial Countries and Peoples. He questioned the wisdom of espousing principles that would result in "unnecessary political fragmentation" and that would "fly in the face of political and economic realities." "Full democratic self-government within a larger and stable political system," he said, "is sometimes a more worthy immediate objective than full political independence."[34] Everyone acknowledges that a proliferation of sovereign mini-states will involve great problems, both for many of them individually and for the United Nations as an institution. But where colonial entities are concerned the champions of self-determination have found no acceptable stopping point: the right belongs to all, even to the smallest, the weakest, and the most backward.

## SELF-DETERMINATION FOR MINORITIES

The story is very different where minorities are concerned—or, to put it more broadly, where the question is whether portions of the population of the metropolitan state also have a right to self-determination. It is one thing to take the view that dependent territories may secede from an empire, and another thing to say that population groups within the homeland have the same right. The rule is that states want to preserve their territorial integrity, and exceptions to that rule are very rare. The United States itself fought a revolutionary war for secession from the British Empire and then a civil war to prevent secession from the Union.

The problem is extremely troublesome and might well become explosive.

The idea of self-determination became a powerful force in world affairs mainly as a result of the speeches of Woodrow Wilson, and he advanced it in circumstances suggesting that it was applicable to the component nationalities of sovereign states and to minority groups.[35] Views expressed in the United Nations by Western European representatives go along Wilsonian lines. Thus the British representative opposing the idea that self-determination is a right, once declared that the concept "could not be whittled down to exclude minorities or groups wishing to secede," and he wondered whether the members of the United Nations "were indeed prepared to face the consequences of assuming a legal obligation to promote the right of self-determination within their borders."[36] Similarly, the representative of Denmark took the view that a national group desiring self-determination "was just as likely to be found in the border province of an independent State as in a colonial territory."[37] A Belgian representative considered that an endorsement of the right of self-determination "was tantamount to an incitement to insurrection and separatism." He found it a "startling internal contradiction" to claim that the right was inapplicable to minorities."[38] And a representative from New Zealand held that "the principle of self-determination knew no frontiers. . . . The establishment of a right of self-determination would detract from national sovereignty and involve a right of secession."[39] Needless to say, those construing self-determination along the above lines opposed the unqualified assertion that self-determination is a right.

Most champions of self-determination construe the term differently. The fact is evident in the Declaration on the Granting of Independence to Colonial Countries and Peoples. In the first place, the very title suggests that self-determination is for political entities that are in a colonial status. In the second place, the Declaration, after asserting the right of "all peoples" to self-determination, goes on to assert that

> any attempt aimed at the partial or total disruption of the national unity and the territorial integrity of a country is incompatible with the purposes and principles of the Charter of the United Nations.

The Charter of the Organization of African Unity goes along parallel lines. The parties adhere to the principle of "absolute dedication to the total emancipation of the African territories which are still dependent" and at the same time to the principle of "respect for the sovereignty and territorial integrity of each state." Moreover, they express "unreserved condemnation" of subversive activities by one state in the territory of another.[40]

Individual spokesmen for newly independent states take the same line—that self-determination applies to colonies and has no further relevance once the colony becomes independent. Thus Doudou Thiam, writing as the Foreign Minister of Senegal, states as fundamental principles:

> 1. No historical, geographical or ethnic considerations should justify one African state in claiming sovereignty over another African state or territory.
> 2. The frontiers drawn between the various African territories in the colonial era should be regarded as valid and should be maintained.

Thiam thought that two states might unite or federate in accordance with the principle of self-determination, but they were to act as political entities. No secession was to occur, no transfer of territory from one sovereignty to another. Any effort by one state to acquire people and territory from another would constitute imperialism, even if the purpose was to unite members of the same tribe.[41]

Similarly, according to Subandrio, a former Foreign Minister of Indonesia, "The right of self-determination applies . . . to the entire population of a colony as a unit and to the entire territory of a colony as a unit. . . . [It] is not something to be applied to racial, cultural or ethnic groups within a colony."[42] Spokesmen for India take the same position. At a meeting of the Security Council in 1960 the Indian delegate deplored Pakistan's appeal to the idea of self-determination. It was clear to him "that the 'self' contemplated in the enunciation of this democratic principle is not and cannot be a constituent part of any country." He predicted "disastrous consequences" if the principle were "extended" in this way, and he referred to the many countries in Africa and Asia with dissident minorities that might like to set up governments of their own. "The principle of self-determination cannot and must not be applied to bring about the fragmentation of a country or its people. . . . The future of the world depends upon the evolution of multiracial States and nations."[43]

The General Assembly's Special Committee of Twenty-Four (i.e. the Special Committee on the Situation with Regard to the Implementation of the Declaration on the Granting of Independence to Colonial Countries and Peoples) applies the above principle to the colonial territories themselves, prior to independence, insisting that boundary lines be frozen. With special reference to South-West Africa the Special Committee in 1967 reaffirmed "that the partial or total disruption of the national unity and territorial integrity of colonial Territories is incompatible with the purposes and principles of the Charter of the United Nations and of General Assembly Resolution 1514 (XV)"—the latter being the Declaration on the Granting of Independence to Colonial Countries and Peoples.

Implicitly and in effect the Security Council also denies that the right of self-determination is a right of secession. In 1961 it "strongly deprecated" secessionist activities in Katanga, declared that those activities were contrary to Security Council decisions, and authorized action to defeat secessionist efforts.[44] And in 1963 it provided for the establishment of a group of experts "to examine methods of resolving the present situation in South Africa through full, peaceful and orderly application of human rights and fundamental freedoms to all inhabitants of the territory as a whole. . . ." The words "as a whole" were meant to and in fact were interpreted to preclude any examination of the partition of South Africa as a possible solution of its racial problem.[45]

The United States joins the majority in defining self-determination in such a way as to exclude secession. In 1952 Mrs. Eleanor Roosevelt asked a series of questions on the subject and gave what she said was the obvious answer:

> Does self-determination mean the right of secession? Does self-determination constitute a . . . justification for the fragmentation of nations? Does self-determination mean the right of people to sever association with another power regardless of the economic effect upon both parties, regardless of the effect upon their internal stability and their external security, regardless of the effect upon their neighbors or the international community? Obviously not.
>
> . . . Just as the concept of individual human liberty carried to its logical extreme would mean anarchy, so the principle of self-determination of peoples given unrestricted application could result in chaos. Is either principle thereby invalidated? Certainly not.[46]

Similarly, at the time of the Congo crisis the Deputy Assistant Secretary for International Organization Affairs declared:

> There is no absolute principle of self-determination. We fought a civil war to deny it. We have recognized both at home and abroad the dangers of Balkanization. . . . The application of the principle

> in the Congo without any qualification would mean the creation of some 20 tribal states and the disintegration of the whole into disorder and chaos.[47]

Two years later the Assistant Secretary for African Affairs expressed the same view. "Like the question of what constitutes a bargaining unit in labor relations," he said, "the right of self-determination has to be based on a practical historical unit in order to permit fast and sensible results." And citing African attitudes, he described respect for historical frontiers as a "useful and important base and adjunct for our policy of self-determination."[48] At the same time, the United States does not entirely refrain from taking jabs at the Soviet Union by pointing to its practice of denying self-determination to component peoples of the U.S.S.R. regardless of constitutional provisions granting a right of secession.[49]

For its part, the Soviet Union takes a position more or less analogous to that of the United States, championing self-determination in the sense of the right of colonies to independence but at the same time adamantly insisting on the principle that respect must be shown for the territorial integrity of sovereign states.

Some scholars take a similar position. The full version of the definition advanced by Rosalyn Higgins, quoted in part above, is that it "refers to the right of the majority *within a generally accepted political unit* to the exercise of power." (Italics added). She stresses that it is "necessary to start with stable boundaries," and she illustrates her view by saying that "there can be no such thing as self-determination for the Nagas. The Nagas live within the political unit of India, and do not constitute a majority therein."[50] She does not comment on the question why, if the Pakistanis were accorded self-determination, the Nagas cannot enjoy it too.

Actually, it should already be clear that self-determination is a term with a number of meanings. Usage has been varied enough to offer a considerable range of choice. Within the vague and broad limits established by usage, a governmental leader can endorse (or formulate) the meaning that serves his purposes best—that fits best with the values that he postulates. It happens that those hostile to colonialism found it expedient to champion the right of self-determination as the right of colonies to independence. But it also happens that a considerable portion of the colonies, once freed, face great danger of internal disruption if they say that the right of self-determination also means the right of national or tribal groups within their borders to secede. Postulating survival as a value, they find it imperative to limit the meaning of self-determination accordingly. But those who start with a different postulate (for example, that a nation or tribe divided by existing boundaries should be united), come out with a different imperative. They are likely to define "peoples" in terms of shared ethnic or religious or linguistic or other cultural characteristics and then demand self-determination even if it means the re-drawing of the boundary lines of sovereign states. A number of governments are in an ambivalent position on the issue, facing one or more potentially dissident minorities within the state but also looking outward to one or more irredentas across the border. For them the problem of the meaning to assign to self-determination must be especially tantalizing and vexing.

Dangers for the future are indicated by the fact that a number of governments have already felt compelled to take action against domestic groups demanding self-determination. Walker Connor cites instances in which the action took the form of military campaigns: "Present or recent cases in point include Algeria (the Berbers), Burma, Burundi, mainland China (Tibet), the Congo, Cyprus, India (Mizos, Nagas), Indonesia, Iraq, Nigeria, Rwanda, South Vietnam (the 'Montagnards'), and Uganda."[51] Sudan belongs on the list too. India, in addition to her policy toward the Mizos and the Nagas, denied self-determination to Hyderabad, and denies it to Kashmir. Nigeria's effort amounts to a full-scale and very bloody civil war against the Ibos, who have proclaimed the independence of Biafra.[52] Apart from such policies, repressive efforts are sometimes directed against individual dissident leaders, raising questions about respect for their human rights. "Viewing self-determination movements as threats to survival, governments have tended to react violently and to justify the cruelest of treatment accorded to implicated leaders by branding them as rebels or traitors and therefore something worse than criminals."[53] The Somalis have gotten nowhere in an effort to achieve unity at the expense of Kenya and Ethiopia.[54] In several other instances governments have been rebuffed when their pleas for self-determination for given "peoples" involved a threat to the territorial integrity of neighboring states.[55] Austria, though greatly concerned about Italy's treatment of the German-speaking population of South Tyrol, deliberately stopped short of invoking the right of self-determination, acknowledging that "such a solution was not realizable, since any attempt to settle the problem on that basis would seriously disturb democratic Europe and be harmful to the interests of all concerned."[56]

Some of the problems alluded to above continue to exist, and others are bound to arise. A considerable portion of the states of the world have populations that are divided along national, ethnic, linguistic, religious, or other lines. Homogeneity is not the rule. Integration is in process in many countries, to be sure; but consciousness of cultural differences is becoming sharper in many others, including many of those that have stood out as champions of self-determination.[57] They may come to wish that they had been more circumspect, for what was fatal to empires could also be fatal to heterogeneous states.

## SELF-DETERMINATION FOR SOUTH AFRICAN PEOPLES

As indicated in Chapter 3, South Africa is almost universally condemned, in angry terms, as racist. The white government of South Africa, however, pleads innocent, and does so on the basis of an appeal to the ideas of cultural nationality and self-determination. It holds that, though the populations of some other states should be thought of as multi-racial, her own population should not.

> The crucial difference is this—our task in South Africa is not *primarily* that of solving a problem of races; it is a problem of bringing about a situation where peaceful co-existence of the various nations in our country will be possible.

Not integration, then; not assimilation or denationalization; but co-existence. According to the official position, the whites themselves constitute a distinct nation "entitled to insist upon our right to self-determination." And at the same time, the government says that it wants to grant self-determination to the various non-white "nations" of which South Africa is composed. Peaceful co-existence is to be achieved "by the independent development of each people towards the full realization of its separate nationhood and the recognition of the right of each nation to govern itself in accordance with its own national traditions and aspirations."[58] On the basis of this line of thought, the white government has already established a Bantustan or homeland called Transkei, composed of a number of Xhosa-speaking tribal groups, and has given it a measure of autonomy; and it envisages the creation of other such political entities. A South African representative described the policy to the General Assembly as follows:

> South Africa's policy of autonomous development is designed to benefit all the nations of South Africa. The purpose is to maintain

> the self-determination of all her peoples, on a basis of equal human dignity. Wherever serious potential friction is encountered in the world, it can be ascribed to some fear of domination of a certain group by another group. South Africa seeks to avoid this potential source of friction by following an evolutionary process which will enable each population group to achieve self-realization within its own sphere. . . .
>
> The ultimate aim of South Africa's policy is therefore the creation of separate, independent and self-respecting communities which will be free from the more serious prejudices, frictions and struggles which are bound to arise under any policy of attempted forceful integration of the different nations or population groups.
>
> The policy is not based on any concept of superiority or inferiority, but on the fact that people differ particularly in their group associations, loyalties, cultures, outlook, modes of life and standards of development.[59]

The white government of South Africa envisages the application of a comparable policy to South-West Africa on the basis of the report of the Odendaal Commission in 1963. The Commission pointed to the fact that the population of the Territory "consists of twelve different population groups which differ from one another both physically and spiritually in one or more important respects." It predicted "endless friction and clashes . . . if such divergent groups were to be represented in one central authority." It emphasized the great disparity in the size of the different groups, and asserted that

> if . . . a system of one man one vote were to be introduced for the Territory, with one central authority, the result would be that one group, the Ovambo, representing almost half the population, would completely dominate the other groups. The fear of domination by stronger groups has frequently been shown by the smaller non-White groups.

This, of course, is on the assumption that the voters would be moved by group loyalties rather than by loyalty to political parties cutting across group lines—an assumption that is quite plausible. The conclusion of the Commission was that "as far as practicable a homeland must be created for each population group . . . so that each group would be able to develop towards self-determination without any group dominating or being dominated by another."

> The Commission is desirous that the non-White groups of South West Africa should eventually become independent and that they should now be guided further in that direction. The development of the groups concerned has always been directed towards self-determination.[60]

Acting in conformity with the recommendation of the Commission, the South African government in March 1967 offered self-rule to "the Ovambo nation" (that is, to eight Ovambo tribes, said to constitute a nation), comprising 45 per cent of the total population of the territory.[61] And it expressed the intention of giving each "national" group in South-West Africa the same opportunity. In South Africa's view,

> it is clear that attempts at establishing integrated societies in conditions where substantial differences obtain amongst groups in one geographical area have not been successful at all. South Africa's approach cannot be used to uphold the assertion that her policy runs counter to civilized conceptions of human rights, dignities and freedoms. The fundamental aim of her policy is self-determination and the elimination of all domination of groups by one another. The very purpose is to build up each people into a self-governing organic entity, capable of cooperating with others in the political and economic spheres in such a manner as may voluntarily be agreed between them.[62]

Representatives of the white government claim that in both South and South-West Africa the non-whites welcome and support the policies of self-determination being applied to them.

In the light of what has already been said in the preceding section and in Chapter 3, it should not be surprising that South Africa's interpretation and application of the idea of self-determination are generally condemned. After all, if the various tribes of southern Africa constitute nations, then so might the tribes of Nigeria, Uganda, Tanzania, and so on. If self-determination were actually applied within the borders of one state, the pressures to apply it within the borders of others would be more difficult to resist. Moreover, within South Africa the whites themselves acknowledge that the policy will not in fact provide for the complete division of the population into territorially separated "nations"—the expectation being (as noted in Chapter 3) that some six million non-whites will be residing in the "white" area of the country in the year 2000, still outnumbering the whites. Non-whites in the "white" area will continue to be "subject to restrictions," as the Minister of Bantu Administration and Development says, "not because we regard him as an inferior being . . . [but because] we regard him as being present in another man's country."[63] Believers in human equality generally find the plan outrageous. If races are set apart from each other by the political boundaries of sovereign states, the fact is generally accepted. But if they are set apart within the state by deliberate governmental action, the fact is intolerable, above all if territorial separation is not achieved. No matter if the inequalities stemming from the division into sovereign states are greater than those stemming from domestic legislation.

In any event, as we have already noted, when the Security Council provided for the establishment of its expert committee to consider the South African problem, it referred to "all inhabitants of the territory as a whole, regardless of race, color or creed"—implicitly rejecting the claim that South Africa is comprised of a number of different race-nations. Almost all members of the United Nations reject above all the claim of the South African whites that they have a right to self-determination which justifies discrimination against non-whites living in the same geographical area with them. In addition, the policies that the whites propose for South-West Africa are explicitly denounced. In 1964 the General Assembly's Committee on Apartheid commented on the Odendaal Commission's plan for self-determination for the groups within South-West Africa.

> The Commission's plan is based on such an interpretation of "self-determination" as to make the term meaningless. "Homelands" with such small populations as are envisaged can never hope to become truly self-governing or independent. The objective would seem to be to divide the territory on tribal lines, create bantustans with small populations, and integrate the territory more closely with the Republic.[64]

After South Africa offered self-rule to the Ovambo "nation" in 1967, Ambassador Goldberg expressed the view of the United States, saying that "South Africa's proposals . . . to impose and promote the fragmentation of the Territory under the guise of self-determination . . . must be opposed because of their potential long-term harmful effect."[65] Canada indicated that it would "consider invalid any attempt by South Africa to take action which would have the effect of dividing the Territory into smaller parts. . . ."[66] And the Special Committee of Twenty-Four (on the granting of independence to colonial countries and peoples) adopted resolutions condemning the proposed application of self-determination to South-West Africa as illegal and contrary to the Charter of the United Nations and various resolutions of the General Assembly.[67]

## SPECIAL MINORITY RIGHTS WITHIN THE STATE?

Consistent with the view that groups within the state are not entitled to self-determination, most members of the United Nations also take the view that minorities, considered as collective entities, should not have special rights or status. In general, they prefer assimilation to differentiation, and whenever at all possible they are inclined to deny that their populations include minorities.

The explanation of the attitude is not far to seek. Among the various factors operating, the most important is undoubtedly the desire to promote and preserve the unity and the territorial integrity of the state and the belief that a minority constitutes an actual or potential threat. Especially after the rise of nationalism in Europe, it became quite possible if not likely that a minority would want to secede, whether to set itself up as an independent state or to join an adjacent kin state; and the kin state itself might champion the cause of its irredenta. Prior to World War I both the Austro-Hungarian and the Russian empires were plagued by troubles with dissident minorities, and before the war was over the first of these had broken up completely and the second (following the Bolshevik revolution) was forced to disgorge important territories. At the end of the war, a number of governments were obliged to give international guarantees concerning the treatment of minorities and to accept the supervision of the League of Nations over their implementation, but the governments involved, the minorities themselves, and the kin states were all more or less unhappy with the arrangements and unwilling to honor them. Especially with the rise of Nazism and Hitler's accession to power, Nazi elements within the German minorities gained in strength, and Hitler used them for his own purposes. "Actuated by nationalist and political motives, the bloc of states led by Germany undermined the League system by encouraging national minorities to be discontented with their position and immoderate in their demands. They went on to deal the system a fatal blow by promoting disloyalty. . . ."[68] The result was that after World War II the solution to the problem of minorities was sought, in the main, by methods other than the special guarantee of minority rights.

In truth, since World War II governments have generally been reluctant even to acknowledge that their population includes minorities. The reluctance shows up in efforts to define the term. Most of the Latin American countries, for example, have polyglot populations, including distinctive ethnic or cultural groups that might be called minorities. But the governments of Latin America have refused to do so. The Brazilian representative in the Third Committee of the General Assembly explained the outlook in 1961:

> For a minority to exist, a group of people must have been transferred "en bloc," without a chance to express their will freely, to a State with a population most of whom differed from them in race, language or religion. Thus groups which had been gradually and deliberately formed by immigrants within a country could not be considered minorities, or claim the international protection accorded to minorities. That was why Brazil and the other American States, which gave immigrants the same legal status as aliens and the same fundamental rights as their own nationals, did not recognize the existence of minorities on the American continent.[69]

The Chilean representative concurred, claiming that "the problem of minorities which arose in some European and Asian countries did not arise in the American States, particularly those of Latin America."

Comparable attitudes dominate the work of the UN Commission on Human Rights with respect to minorities. On a number of occasions in the early years of its activity, its Sub-Commission on the Prevention of Discrimination and Protection of Minorities suggested one or another definition of the term *minority*. The 1954 proposal was that "the term minority shall include only those non-dominant groups in the population which possess and wish to preserve ethnic, religious or linguistic traditions or characteristics markedly different from those of the rest of the population."[70] When the definition was submitted to the Commission on Human Rights, it withheld its approval, referring the matter back to the Sub-Commission for further study, as it had on previous occasions. Had the definition been adopted, a great many states (including many in Latin America) would have found it difficult to deny that their populations included minorities.

In addition to trying to avoid the admission that their populations include minorities, governments since World War II have, in the main, emphasized the idea of integration or assimilation, on the basis of pledges of equal and non-discriminatory treatment for individuals. In fact, when the Universal Declaration of Human Rights was being drafted, the view of the United States—in line with its own melting-pot tradition—was that provision for the rights of the individual made any reference to the rights of minorities superfluous.[71] And an inter-American conference in 1965, while reiterating support for the idea of individual human rights, reaffirmed "the goal of all the governments to develop a policy tending toward complete integration of all elements of their citizenry, without distinction of any nature based on racial origin."[72]

The Sub-Commission that formulated the definition of *minority* quoted above included a paragraph in its report suggesting the cross-pressures under which it worked.

> It is highly desirable that minorities should settle down happily as citizens of the country in which they live, and therefore in any measures that may be taken for the protection of their special traditions and characteristics . . . nothing should be done that is likely to stimulate their consciousness of difference from the rest of the population.[73]

Similarly the Covenant on Civil and Political Rights suggests ambivalence. Article 27 concerns minorities but its import is not clear. It reads as follows:

> In those states in which ethnic, religious or linguistic minorities exist, persons belonging to such minorities shall not be denied the right, in community with the other members of their group, to enjoy their own culture, to profess and practice their own religion, or to use their own language.

The article invites dispute over the question whether a minority exists in any given state; the circumstances of its adoption suggest an implicit recognition of the contention of the Latin American states that they have none.[74] Moreover, the reference to "persons . . . in community with the other members of their group" is open to more than one interpretation on the question whether any rights are assured to minorities as a group in addition to those assured to individual members of the group by other articles. For example, does the right "to use their own language" imply an obligation on the part of the state to provide education (elementary? secondary? higher?) in that language?

Though the emphasis since World War II has been on assimilation within a framework of respect for individual human rights, exceptions have occurred, among them the following.[75] In 1947 the General Assembly made recommendations for the future of Palestine that were not assimilationist. To be sure, the main emphasis was on equality and non-discrimination in the treatment of individuals, but group rights were also asserted, for example, in the provision that "the State shall ensure adequate primary and secondary education for the Arab and Jewish minority, respectively, in its own language and its cultural tradition." In 1950 the General Assembly recommended that Eritrea should become an "autonomous unit" within Ethiopia. In 1957 the International Labor Organization endorsed an Indigenous and Tribal Populations Convention which calls for the special treatment of those populations, though looking toward their progressive integration into the life of the country where they reside. In 1959 Greece and Turkey concluded an agreement on both individual and group rights in Cyprus; for example, the Greek and Turkish communities on Cyprus were to vote separately for members of the House of Representatives, Greeks electing 70 per cent of the members and Turks 30 per cent with a number of other such allocations being made as well. In 1960 UNESCO endorsed a Convention Against Discrimination in Education which speaks of the rights of both persons and groups and calls for a recognition of "the right of members of national minorities to carry on their own educational activities," without, however, obliging the state to give financial or other support to minorities for this purpose. Several agreements assure members of minority groups various rights having to do with language, for example, to receive instruction in school in their own language or to deal with public officials in their own language.

A notable test of attitudes in the United Nations toward the protection of minorities occurred in 1960, when Austria brought a complaint against Italy in connection with the treatment of the German-speaking inhabitants of South Tyrol. The complaint was based on a 1946 agreement between Austria and Italy which, among other provisions, specified that the populations of the Bolzano Province and of the neighboring bilingual townships of the Trento Province would be "granted the exercise of autonomous legislative and executive regional power."[76] Italy in fact then enacted an Autonomy Statute, but it included so many Italians in the region involved that the German-speaking element was a minority—a minority of one-third. Austria held that this violated at least the spirit of the agreement and asked for autonomy simply for the Province of Bolzano, where German-speaking people were a majority. But Austria got little support in the United Nations. Italy, of course, rejected Austria's demands. From its point of view, "the notion that every minority has the right to self-government is one which is foreign to the Charter and incompatible with the whole philosophy of the United Nations. In fact it was quite clear that rights granted to a minority should not be such as to form separate communities within a State which might impair its national unity or security."[77] Argentina also disagreed with Austria, and so did Lebanon. The representative of Argentina held that Austria was seeking "a decision of the General Assembly that would create inside the territory of a Member State an enclave in which the jurisdiction of that State would be seriously weakened," and he thought that this would constitute an "unfortunate precedent."[78] The representative of Lebanon said that "the UN could not possibly support claims by any ethnic, linguistic or religious minority for complete or partial autonomy within an independent, sovereign State." The principle that minorities should have some kind of international protection, he held, was obsolete, having served as "an excuse for interfering in the domestic affairs of States." Members of minorities were entitled to equal and non-discriminatory treatment as individuals, but minorities as collective entities had no right to special status.[79] The General Assembly gave Austria no help either on this complaint or on others. It terminated its consideration of the problem by adopting a resolution urging the disputing states to resume their negotiations and, if they failed, to resort to other means of peaceful settlement.

## ECONOMIC SELF-DETERMINATION

The first and third paragraphs of Article 1 of the Covenants are quoted at the beginning of this chapter. The second paragraph concerns "economic self-determination," and reads as follows:

> 2. All peoples may, for their own ends, freely dispose of their natural wealth and resources without prejudice to any obligations arising out of international economic cooperation, based upon the principle of mutual benefit, and international law. In no case may a people be deprived of its own means of subsistence.

Article 25 of the Covenant on Economic, Social, and Cultural Rights makes a supplementary statement:

> Nothing in the present Covenant shall be interpreted as impairing the inherent right of all peoples to enjoy and utilize fully and freely their natural wealth and resources.

These provisions were much fought over. An earlier version asserted that "the right of peoples to self-determination shall also include permanent sovereignty over their natural wealth and resources."[80] The general flavor and connotation of the original version carries over into a General Assembly resolution adopted at about the same time the Covenants on Human Rights were themselves approved. In the resolution, the General Assembly "reaffirms the inalienable right of all countries to exercise permanent sovereignty over their natural resources in the interest of their national development, in conformity with the spirit and principles of the Charter. . . ." It also:

> 5. Recognizes the right of all countries, and in particular of the developing countries, to secure and increase their share in the administration of enterprises which are fully or partly operated by foreign capital and to have a greater share in the advantages and profits derived therefrom on an equitable basis. . . .

Further, the General Assembly "considers that when natural resources of the developing countries are exploited by foreign investors, the latter should undertake proper and accelerated training of national personnel at all levels and in all fields connected with such exploitation."[81]

The above statements reflect the widespread belief of respresentatives from developing, capital-importing countries that they are morally entitled to more favorable terms in their arrangements with capital-exporting countries. The statements reflect the widespread belief that foreign owners and investors unfairly exploit the people of colonial and developing countries. It is beyond the scope of the present work to seek to determine to what extent such beliefs are justified. They no doubt are in part. At the same time, some of the representatives from developing countries, especially from Africa, are clearly guided by one or another variety of Marxism, and it is difficult to say what relative weight they give to doctrinal faith and to empirical observation. In any event, for good or bad reasons, more than two-thirds of the members of the General Assembly have obviously been willing to scold the richer, more advanced countries and to issue veiled warnings and threats. It goes without saying that the United States and other advanced countries have opposed such actions. Speaking of the alleged right of peoples to "permanent sovereignty over their natural wealth and resources," delegates of the United States have on various occasions pointed out that investors might be frightened away by language that seems to hint at the possibility of expropriation without compensation and at the possibility that the requirements of treaties, international law, and special contracts might not be honored.[82] Such warnings led to a modification of the wording of the relevant paragraph in the Covenants on human rights, but it is uncertain how much they may have modified the relevant underlying attitudes.

## CONCLUDING COMMENTS

The idea of internal self-determination has not so far been, and does not seem likely to become, a source of serious international difficulty. Governments resisting the movement for the international promotion and protection of human rights might, of course, claim that it challenges their rights of internal self-determination, but in fact they find it more advantageous to appeal to other symbols—to their rights of sovereignty and domestic jurisdiction.

The idea of external self-determination is far more unsettling. So far its major challenge has been to empires—to overseas colonialism—and in this realm, for a variety of reasons, it has triumphed. Some sources of trouble persist, notably Rhodesia and Portuguese colonialism, but outside southern Africa no major territory remains in colonial status.

The question is whether the application of the right of external self-determination should and can be limited to overseas colonies. The right is for "peoples," and it is arbitrary in the extreme to assume that "peoples" are to be defined automatically as the inhabitants of states and colonies within present boundaries. Many other groups—some entirely within an existing state, and some spread over the territory of two or more states—could also reasonably be called "peoples" entitled to self-determination. And in terms of the well-being of the individuals involved, it may be just as important for some of these groups to enjoy self-determination as it is for the inhabitants of sovereign states and colonies. Resentments against alien rule, and the sense of humiliation that goes with subjection, are perhaps strongest when the alien ruler is a white man from overseas. But resentments and humiliation also exist on many other bases—as the Ibos of Nigeria and many others can attest.

At the same time, to open the right of self-determination to all "peoples" who might reasonably claim it is to invite unending strife. Many states have already faced rebellions by dissident "peoples," and many more are sure to as well; moreover, what might in principle be a domestic insurrection is very likely to have international implications of some sort, and is almost bound to have such implications when the rebellious "people" are in a border region adjacent to their kin state. In any event, the United Nations would be in an extremely difficult position if it were to interpret the right of self-determination in such a way as to invite or justify attacks on the territorial integrity of its own members.

The problem would be simpler if self-determination had never been called a right and if the limits of its application had been more clearly specified from the first. But given the facts as they are, and given stability and peace as values, the limits specified in the United Nations—arbitrary as they are—have much to commend them. If self-determination is a right only for the inhabitants of colonies, the United Nations and its various members have a better chance of avoiding involvement in efforts to re-draw boundary lines over much of the world. And emphasis on individual human rights can potentially do much to minimize the injury within states to the various groups that would prefer to change their status.

# III

# International Obligations Concerning Human Rights

# 6

# International Obligations of the United States on Human Rights

In ratifying the Charter of the United Nations, the United States undertook to promote respect for human rights, but the meaning of this obligation is open to dispute. In subscribing to the Universal Declaration of Human Rights, the United States did not explicitly undertake any obligation except to regard it as a "standard of achievement," but some hold that more extensive obligations have developed. In joining the Organization of the American States and the International Labor Organization, and in ratifying various sorts of treaties, the United States has committed itself in one way or another in the field of human rights, but sometimes the commitment is more nearly moral than legal and sometimes it is quite vague. The object now is to examine the nature and extent of the obligations that have been assumed.

## THE OBLIGATIONS OF ARTICLES 55 AND 56

We have already quoted the principal articles of the Charter imposing obligations in the field of human rights—Articles 55 and 56—but they will be repeated here as a matter of convenience.

> Article 55. With a view to the creation of conditions of stability and well-being which are necessary for peaceful and friendly relations among nations based on respect for the principles of equal rights and self-determination of peoples, the United Nations shall promote:
> a. higher standards of living, full employment, and conditions of economic and social progress and development;

> b. solutions of international economic, social, health, and related problems; and international cultural and educational cooperation; and
>
> c. universal respect for, and observance of, human rights and fundamental freedoms for all without distinction as to race, sex, language, or religion.
>
> Article 56. All Members pledge themselves to take joint and separate action in cooperation with the Organization for the achievement of the purposes set forth in Article 55.

A number of other provisions of the Charter have to do with the authority of the United Nations to act in the field of human rights. In so far as they relate primarily to measures of implementation that the United Nations can take, they will be discussed in Chapters 8 and 9. Some of them, however, are relevant to the interpretation of Articles 55 and 56 and so need to be mentioned here. Article 10 authorizes the General Assembly to "discuss any questions or any matters within the scope of the present Charter." Article 11 authorizes it to discuss and make recommendations concerning "any questions relating to international peace and security," and to "call the attention of the Security Council to situations which are likely to endanger peace and security." Acting under these articles, the General Assembly has interpreted Articles 55 and 56; for example, as we will note more fully below, it has held that both racial discrimination and colonialism violate human rights and are threats to the peace. Article 13 authorizes the General Assembly to "initiate studies and make recommendations for the purpose of . . . assisting in the realization of human rights and fundamental freedoms for all without distinction as to race, sex, language, or religion." The Economic and Social Council (ECOSOC) has similar authority; Article 62 (2) authorizes it to "make recommendations for the purpose of promoting respect for, and observance of, human rights and fundamental freedoms for all" and to prepare draft conventions for submission to the General Assembly. Article 68 instructs ECOSOC to establish a commission on human rights to assist it in the performance of its functions. Under this combination of articles, the Commission on Human Rights, ESOSOC, and the General Assembly have adopted a series of resolutions, declarations, and conventions which are at least suggestive of meanings to be read into Articles 55 and 56. The most notable of these instruments are the Universal Declaration of Human Rights itself and the two Covenants on human rights.

For our purposes three principal questions arise about the meaning of Articles 55 and 56. A simplified version of the first concerns the meaning of *promote;* the second concerns the list of the rights and freedoms to be promoted, and the third relates to a fact already mentioned—that the phrase "without distinction as to race, sex, language, or religion" is by general consent interpreted to mean "without *adverse* distinction. . . ."

The first question could be quite complex. The words of Article 55 and 56 do not impose a clear-cut obligation on members to respect and observe human rights. Rather, the United Nations is to promote respect and observance, and members are to take joint and separate action in cooperation with the Organization to achieve the purposes set forth. This language leaves room for various questions (quibbles?), and some have in fact been raised.[1] But, in general, discussions in the United Nations proceed on the assumption that both the Organization and the individual members are under an obligation to promote respect for and observance of human rights. The Organization *promotes* in various ways; among other things, it seeks to define human rights and fundamental freedoms more clearly and fully than the Charter alone does, and it concerns itself with the problem of implementation. We will discuss these matters later. Here the question is what the obligation to *promote* entails for member states.

Obviously it calls for affirmative action; it rules out a do-nothing policy. But how vigorous and extensive must the affirmative action be, and where must it occur? Is it enough to give three cheers for human rights? Must all rights be promoted more or less equally? Does a government that is vigorous in combating racial discrimination excuse itself for inaction in other realms, or if it is vigorous in other realms does it excuse itself for inaction about racial discrimination? Suppose that a government does little or nothing about human rights at home, but loudly denounces their violation abroad. Is it meeting its obligation?

Another kind of question is whether the obligation is actually to assure respect for human rights or simply to take steps that go in the right direction. The question can be answered in general by the statement that an obligation to promote is not an obligation to accomplish specified results within a given time. Quite obviously, in most countries the implementation of economic, social, and cultural rights will require many years of effort. The goals fixed are indeed likely to recede as progress is made; that is, as it becomes possible for a government to meet higher standards, the international instruments are likely to be reinterpreted to require that the higher standards be met. Further, some countries are sure to require a long time to get certain civil and political rights implemented—for example, the right to equality of treatment without distinction because of race. The General Assembly itself has reflected this view in calling for "patterns of legislation and practice [that are] *directed towards* ensuring equality before the law of all persons regardless of race, creed, or color," and in declaring that "governmental policies . . . which are not *directed towards* these goals, but which are designed to perpetuate or increase discrimination, are inconsistent with the pledges of Members under Article 56 of the Charter."[2] The excoriations of South Africa and Rhodesia in the United Nations are to be attributed not simply to the fact of racial discrimination but even more to the fact that official policy is to accentuate the discrimination rather than to combat and reduce it. At the same time, the practice of a country with regard to a given right may already be so close to the international standard that the obligation to promote is indistinguishable from an obligation to observe, and it is difficult to see how certain rights (e.g. the right to a public trial) can be promoted without in fact being observed.

Is the obligation to promote human rights limited to the obligation to promote appropriate behavior on the part of agents of the central government itself? What obligation is assumed, if any, with respect to the behavior of agents of provincial, state, or local governments? Do the obligations of unitary governments differ from those of federal governments? In other words, do federal governments in effect escape some of the obligation because of the fact that the constitutional power to act is assigned not to them but to the states? Do obligations differ with respect to metropolitan and colonial territories? Does the obligation to promote human rights extend beyond the sphere of action of the government itself and call for efforts to influence or regulate the behavior of private persons? Does the obligation to promote human rights entail obligations with respect to the methods of doing it? Recall, for example, the provision of the Covenant on Civil and Political Rights which requires a restriction on freedom of speech and press as a way of combating racial and religious discrimination: "Any advocacy of national, racial, or religious hatred that constitutes incitement to discrimination, hostility or violence shall be prohibited by law." For the United States this would obviously involve problems relating to the first and fourteenth amendments.

The above paragraphs on the meaning of *promote* suggest more questions than answers. The obligation is vague. Semantic analysis can reduce its vagueness somewhat, but for the most part the clarity that is achieved will come through the international political (and perhaps the judicial) process.

As to the second question, the Charter does not identify the human rights and fundamental freedoms that are to be promoted. Jan Smuts of South Africa once contended that, in view of this, "member States did not have any specific obligations under the Charter, whatever other moral obligations might rest upon them."[3] But Smuts's view gets little support. The almost universal view is that "some rights are so basic that they need no definition."[4] The right to life illustrates the point. Surely anything at all comparable to Hitler's effort to exterminate the Jews would everywhere be regarded as a violation of the requirements of Articles 55 and 56, even if no other relevant international instruments existed. For that matter, officially enforced racial discrimination in South Africa is almost everywhere regarded as a violation of the requirements of these articles.

At the same time, the almost universal view is that human rights and fundamental freedoms need to be identified more precisely; and, as the preceding chapters indicate, the process has been going on ever since the United Nations came into existence. When the General Assembly adopted the Universal Declaration of Human Rights it explained itself in the preambular clauses by referring to the fact that members had pledged themselves to promote human rights and fundamental freedoms; and it pointed out that "a common understanding of these rights and freedoms is of the greatest importance for the full realization of this pledge." Many of the other resolutions of various United Nations agencies—most notably the declarations and conventions adopted by the General Assembly—are also obviously designed to promote a common understanding of the meaning of the obligations of Articles 55 and 56.

The General Assembly cannot impose its interpretation; it cannot by a two-thirds vote assign meanings to these articles that all members are obliged to accept.[5] This is quite explicit in the case of conventions, which become binding only on ratifying states. The United States, for example, voted for the Convention on the Elimination of all Forms of Racial Discrimination, and later signed it; but legal obligation awaits ratification by the President on the advice and consent of two-thirds of the Senate.

Nevertheless, the adoption of resolutions has some effect. When a delegate votes for a declaration or a convention, he indicates that his government endorses the rules and principles set forth. The endorsement may or may not apply fully to every single rule or principle involved; it may or may not be wholehearted; and (especially in the case of the United States) it may reflect the views of only the executive branch. But the qualifiers do not vitiate the proposition that votes in the General Assembly tend to commit the voting government, at least in a moral sense.

Whether governments tend to get committed even if they vote negatively or refrain is a different question; essentially the question is how customary law develops and whether a state can come to be bound by customary law developed against its will. The question has some point even for the United States and the other great powers, for they are not always able to block the adoption of resolutions that they oppose; indeed, given the distribution of voting strength in the General Assembly, the only practical goal for them in many cases is not to defeat a resolution but to reduce its objectionable features through re-drafting or through formal amendment. No doubt all of the great powers—and others as well—would deny that they are obliged to accept the rules and principles contained in resolutions that they do not support, but they are inevitably under pressure to abandon their positions and go along.

The third question concerning Articles 55 and 56 stems from the general agreement that "without distinction" should be interpreted to mean "without *adverse* distinction." The fact of this tacit agreement is mentioned in connection with the discussion of equality in Chapter 3. The agreement seems reasonable, but still it involves problems. What kinds of distinctions are adverse and what kinds are not? Who decides and by what standards? Assuming that a given distinction is not oppressive or unfair to a group as a whole, what is the legal situation if it has adverse effects on some individual members of the group? And what is the legal situation if, among the effects of a given distinction, some are adverse and some are not?

For the most part, answers to these questions remain to be worked out. Some of them went to the International Court of Justice in connection with the South-West Africa cases, with results that are of interest even if inconclusive. They are inconclusive mainly because the court avoided the substantive issues, rejecting the request for a judgment on the ground that the two states making the request (Ethiopia and Liberia) had failed to show that they had a legal right or interest in the matter. Further, a good deal of the argument turned on the terms of the original mandate, especially the requirement that South Africa "promote to the utmost the material and moral well-being and the social progress of the inhabitants of the Territory." Articles 55 and 56 of the Charter were not specifically and directly involved. Nevertheless, some of the argument and some of the opinions of individual justices are relevant to these and other articles and to other resolutions and agreements relating to human rights.

The central complaint against South Africa was that "in the light of applicable international standards or international legal norm, or both" it was failing to meet the obligation quoted above.[6] More particularly, Ethiopia and Liberia contended that a "norm of non-discrimination or non-separation" had evolved over the years, evidenced by international undertakings in the form of treaties, conventions, and declarations and by domestic law and practice. In their eyes the very definition of non-discrimination was "the absence of governmental policies and actions which allot status, rights, duties, privileges or burdens on the basis of membership in a group, class or race rather than on the basis of individual merit, capacity or potential."[7] They thus abandoned the view that distinctions are discriminatory only when adverse.

South Africa, of course, entered a denial. It held that none of the sources of law cited by Ethiopia and Liberia had given rise to a norm "which would entail that *any* differentiation on the basis of group membership, however beneficial such differentiation might be in intent or application, would be illegal."[8] On the contrary, it claimed that "the mandate system, by its very terms as well as its underlying philosophy . . . permitted and indeed required differentiation among various ethnic, linguistic or cultural groups, and, consequently, among their individual members, on the very basis of membership in such a group."[9] And it pointed to numerous international agreements as well as to domestic practices in a number of countries that approve distinctions based on membership in groups, the presumption being that the distinctions are not adverse. It intimated, as we have seen in discussing equality in Chapter 3, that adverse effects of its policies were confined to a small minority of individual members of the groups involved and were justified in the interest of the group as a whole.

The International Court of Justice in its opinion did not consider the above issues, but some of the individual justices did in separate opinions. Philip C. Jessup, in a dissent, expressed the view that, though apartheid might not have been contrary to the obligations of a Mandatory power in 1925, it is now.[10] Luis Padilla Nervo, in another dissent, held that "racial discrimination as a matter of official government policy is a violation of a norm or rule or standard of the international community."[11] In still another dissent the Japanese justice, Kotaro Tanaka, virtually ran the gamut of sources of international law in upholding the claims of Ethiopia and Liberia; in his eyes, natural law, the general principles of law, custom, and international conventions all made "distinction on a racial basis" illegal.[12] Moreover, he made the more general assertion that "from the provisions of the Charter referring to the human rights and fundamental freedoms it can be inferred that the legal obligation to respect human rights [not merely to promote respect for them] is imposed on member states."[13]

This indicates that considerable confusion exists concerning the precise meaning of the obligation to promote respect for human rights "without distinction. . . ." Within various countries, and with the approval of both the League of Nations and the United Nations, distinctions have in fact been made and are being made on some of the ostensibly forbidden bases. Where the distinctions are made, they are for the presumed benefit of the groups singled out for special treatment, but this is a matter of judgment, not of objective rule. Ethiopia and Liberia in effect wanted to give global application to the Supreme Court's finding that separate treatment is inherently unequal; but however justifiable this judgment may be in circumstances prevailing within the United States, it is not obvious that it is also justifiable where cultural differences of a grosser sort prevail. Moreover, assuming a hypothetical situation in which a modern state includes in its population a primitive indigenous tribe, it is odd to condemn it for practicing what it regards as favorable discrimination, but to praise it for a grant of independence that the tribe is really not prepared to exercise.

These references to the obligations of Article 55 and 56 are all to human rights, which are explicitly mentioned only in Article 55(c). The point made in Chapter 4 should be recalled, however, that Article 55(c) overlaps with 55(a) and 55(b), relating to obligations in the economic, social, and cultural fields. In any event, the clarification and implementation of 55(a) and 55(b) is as much the concern of the United Nations as the clarification and implementation of 55(c). Thus the promotion of full employment is no longer a purely domestic matter, but "an international obligation formally assumed under the Charter."[14]

## THE QUESTION OF DOMESTIC JURISDICTION

Articles 55 and 56 bind member states whether or not the United Nations can legally try to induce or compel them to live up to the obligations that they have assumed. Nevertheless, the question of the authority of the United Nations in this respect is important. The answer depends on the meaning given to Article 2(7) of the Charter, which reads as follows:

> Nothing contained in the present Charter shall authorize the United Nations to intervene in matters which are essentially within the domestic jurisdiction of any state or shall require the Members to submit such matters to settlement under the present Charter; but this principle shall not prejudice the application of enforcement measures under Chapter VII.

The questions raised by the above have already been debated so much that we will not attempt a thorough treatment of them here. We will, however, note them and the positions taken with respect to them. It will quickly be apparent that the crucial words are vague enough to give some basis for different interpretations, permitting states to make a selection according to the values and interests they want to promote. This being the case, the meanings assigned are likely to change through the years and never to become definitive. So far, appeals to the article in order to block action under Articles 55 and 56 have generally failed, but the explanation is more political than legal; and the precedents set may or may not hold in different political circumstances.

As a preliminary we should note the proposition that matters are within the domestic jurisdiction of a state when they are not regulated by international law, including treaties that the state has ratified. International law has not traditionally regulated the choice of forms of government, or the choice of constitutional systems; nor has it regulated the treatment of people within the state. Under general international law a state can have any kind of government, subscribe to any ideology, and treat people under its jurisdiction as it sees fit. These are traditionally matters of domestic jurisdiction.

Two exceptions to the above rule have long been advanced, both concerning the treatment of persons and both controversial. One is that humanitarian intervention may occur. Some of the more advanced and powerful states have engaged in such intervention (whether or not for exclusively humanitarian reasons) when another state—always a weaker state—was thought to be guilty of an "outrage upon humanity,"[15] for example, when it was encouraging or failing to prevent the massacring of people. The second exception concerns the treatment of aliens, the claim being that even if a state cannot be held internationally accountable for the treatment of its own citizens it is bound to meet a minimum international standard in its treatment of citizens of other states. The United States makes this claim, giving diplomatic protection to its citizens abroad; in some cases, especially in a few of the states of Central America and the Caribbean, the protection has taken the form of intervention.

Though the above exceptions have been claimed, the emphasis should be on the fact that action giving evidence of them is rare. The impact of the second exception has already been considerably modified by the acceptance on the part of the United States of the rule of non-intervention. Had Hitler begun exterminating Jews in peacetime—before international action against him was already occurring—it is not at all clear that other states would have had a right to interfere. Still less, under the old rules is it clear that the racial discrimination of South Africa gives other states any right to interfere.

The question is whether the provisions of the Charter concerning human rights brought significant change. South Africa says no. One of its arguments revolves around the first phrase of Article 2(7), and particularly around the word *nothing*. South Africa contends that the word should be taken literally—that neither the pledge concerning human rights nor anything else in the Charter authorizes intervention in essentially domestic matters. Another argument revolves around the word *intervention*. Those schooled in international law define the word as dictatorial interference: "a peremptory demand or an attempt at interference accompanied by enforcement or threat of enforcement in case of non-compliance."[16] But it is also possible to say that Article 2(7) refers not simply to dictatorial interference but to any interference, and of course South Africa makes this claim. Thus, so far as international action to implement human rights is concerned, South Africa claims in effect that the Charter does not change matters—that its realm of domestic jurisdiction is as wide as ever, and that nothing in the Charter authorizes interference in that realm.[17]

The contrary view, of course, is that the Charter wrought significant change. The fundamental proposition is that members of the United Nations accept international legal obligations in the field of human rights, and that in so doing they remove the subject from the realm of essentially domestic jurisdiction and make themselves internationally accountable for what they do. The obligation not to discriminate on the basis of race, sex, language, or religion is especially clear, and it is for racial discrimination that South Africa is arraigned. Moreover, the prevailing view, in contrast to the South African view, is that *intervention* should be given its technical meaning, thus leaving agencies of the United Nations free to take all kinds of actions relating to human rights so long as they stop short of dictatorial interference. This leads to the conclusion that so far as human rights are concerned Article 2(7) has no effect, for the Security Council is the only United Nations agency that can interfere dictatorially (i.e. take enforcement action), and in this respect Article 2(7) explicitly says that its authority remains unimpaired. The most that any other agency of the United Nations can do is to adopt a recommendation.

The case for the second of the above two views is stronger than the case for the first. Article 55 binds the United Nations to *promote* respect for and observance of human rights, just as Article 56 binds individual members; it requires affirmative action, and can readily be interpreted to authorize extensive affirmative action. The various other articles of the Charter cited above—most notably Articles 13 and 62(2)—supplement Article 55, clearly authorizing the making of recommendations; and anyone who wishes to do so can very plausibly contend that the authority to recommend implies the authority to inquire thoroughly into matters on which a recommendation might be made—for example, by receiving petitions and making investigations. Since the making of recommendations is explicitly authorized, the case is good for holding that recommendations are not intervention in the meaning of Article 2(7).

As indicated above, the precedents so far set are in accord with the second view; that is, they assume that Articles 55 and 56 mark a significant departure from traditional rules and that Article 2(7) does not safeguard those rules.

One of the tests, dating back to 1946, concerns Franco's fascist regime in Spain. Since Franco had been installed with the help of Mussolini and Hitler and had given them help during World War II, it is not surprising that members of the United Nations wished to bring about his downfall. In principle, what the General Assembly stood for was the establishment in Spain of

> a government which derives its authority from the consent of the governed, committed to respect freedom of speech, religion and assembly and to the prompt holding of an election in which the Spanish people, free from force and intimidation and regardless of party, may express their will.[18]

In calling for the establishment of such a government, the General Assembly did not explicitly invoke the human rights provisions of the Charter; but the significant point here is that it acted despite objections based on Article 2(7).

Other tests concern the Soviet Union and Hungary. In 1949 Chile complained that the Soviet Union was violating human rights in its treatment of Soviet women who had married nationals of other states: the Soviet government was refusing to allow these women to leave the country either with their husbands or to rejoin their husbands abroad. From the Soviet point of view, this was a matter of domestic jurisdiction and thus beyond the competence of the United Nations under Article 2(7). But the General Assembly rejected the contention and recommended to the Soviet Union that it change its policies.[19] In 1956 the Hungarian revolution and its savage repression by the Red Army again led to action by the General Assembly despite Soviet and Hungarian appeals to Article 2(7). The General Assembly adopted a series of resolutions in 1956 and later. It recalled "the obligations assumed by all Member States under Articles 55 and 56." It found that "the USSR, in violation of the Charter of the United Nations, has deprived . . . the Hungarian people of the exercise of their fundamental human rights, [and that] the present authorities in Hungary have violated the human rights and freedoms guaranteed by the Treaty of Peace with Hungary." It held that one of the fundamental rights of the Hungarian people, the right to hold free elections, should be implemented under the auspices of the United Nations.[20]

Almost all other tests of the import of Article 2(7) concern violations of human rights through racial discrimination and through colonialism or denials of self-determination. In these cases the defendant states—notably South Africa—regularly appeal to Article 2(7), and the General Assembly regularly rejects the appeal: racism and colonialism are not to be safeguarded by pleas relating to domestic jurisdiction.

As suggested at the outset, the above precedents are far from conclusive. They relate to very special circumstances—to emotions aroused by World War II, by communism and the cold war, and by racism and colonialism. They do not reflect any general and widespread determination in the United Nations to act on behalf of all sorts of human rights against all sorts of states, nor do they indicate that Article 2(7) will always be brushed aside. They involve acts of commission, but acts of omission are, if anything, even more significant in suggesting the import of Article 2(7) and, more broadly, of respect for domestic jurisdiction. No action analogous to that against Franco occurred against the Trujillo dictatorship in the Dominican Republic. Concern for the human rights of Hungarians under the heel of communism was not matched by concern for the human rights of people held in slavery or in bondage for debt. And, as we have already noted, action against racism is not matched by action against tribalism even when it becomes genocidal; and action on behalf of self-determination for colonies is not matched by support for self-determination for minorities and other groups within the state. In general, governments are sensitive about sovereignty. Articles 55 and 56 and other articles in the Charter involve obligations that modify the prerogatives of sovereignty, but these articles are so far being given only a limited application. The rights of domestic jurisdiction are so generally taken for granted that challenges to them in the form of overt pressures on specific states to respect human rights are rare.

In the light of the above, we should note the attitude of several of the great powers. France is perhaps most inclined to stress the rights of domestic jurisdiction and most consistent in refusing to support action that goes counter to those rights. It usually abstains even in connection with votes against South Africa's policies of apartheid. One statement of the French view, made in 1952, is as follows:

> The policy practiced by the government of any Member State toward its own nationals, within its own frontiers, is an intrinsic part of the sovereign rights reserved for the jurisdiction of each State and jealously safeguarded against even the best intentioned incursions by the organized collectivity of the other members of the international community. By committing one violation of those rights, no matter how important the particular case may be, the United Nations collectively commits a breach of the Charter and at the same time endangers the security of each Member.[21]

Britain is inclined in the same direction as France.[22] For many years it held that even the discussion of apartheid was outside the competence of the United Nations. It pointed to "great dangers" if an organization with peace as its main purpose is used for a "crusade of some Members against others, or conceivably of all against all."[23] It shifted its position in 1961, but with respect to apartheid only, explaining itself as follows:

> The question of apartheid was unique in that it involved the deliberate adoption, retention, and development of policies based entirely

> on racial discrimination. Moreover, those policies were directed amongst and against the permanent inhabitants of the territory concerned. The problem caused grave international repercussions, in Africa mainly, but also in other countries. . . . While the importance attached by the United Kingdom to Article 2, paragraph 7, of the Charter remained undiminished, it regarded apartheid as being now so exceptional as to be *sui generis*.

The British delegate went on to indicate that Britain was prepared to consider resolutions about apartheid on their merits.[24]

The Soviet Union takes an ambivalent position. On the one hand, it puts great stress on Article 2(7). As noted above, it appealed to this article in the case of the Russian wives. More generally, it holds that the implementation of international obligations is itself a domestic matter, and opposes international arrangements for implementation on the ground that this "would constitute an attempt at intervention in the domestic affairs of States and an encroachment on their sovereignty."[25] We will examine this view more fully in Chapter 8. On the other hand, Soviet delegates denounce racism and colonialism in strident terms, and demand action against them. In 1968 a Soviet delegate, referring to the obligations of Article 56 of the Charter, flatly declared that "the practices of racial discrimination and segregation in southern Africa were . . . a breach of treaty commitments freely contracted," and he declared that "the main task facing the Commission on Human Rights was to bring racial discrimination and segregation to an end."[26] Usually Soviet delegates base demands for international implementing action not directly on claims that human rights are being violated but rather on the claim that the violations threaten the peace; thus various articles of the Covenant other than Article 56 become involved, notably Article 39. The Soviet Union obviously wants the best of both worlds: to maintain a principle that gives safety to itself against international measures of implementation while denying the benefit of the same principle to South Africa, Southern Rhodesia, and countries possessing colonial territories; at a minimum risk to itself, it can thus cultivate the favor of virtually all peoples in the third world—the world of newly independent states with non-white populations.

The United States has been clear in asserting that Article 2(7) does not preclude discussion, but not quite as clear about other possibilities. In 1950, without saying why, it voted against the portion of a General Assembly resolution calling upon South Africa to refrain from implementing its

Group Areas Act; the vote may have reflected an interpretation of Article 2(7), or may have reflected appreciation for South Africa's support in Korea. In 1952 it faced a resolution that South Africa submitted in the General Assembly declaring that Article 2(7) forbade the adoption of proposals on the question of race conflict in South Africa. Britain and France supported the resolution, but the United States joined with the majority (including the Soviet Union) to defeat it, only to abstain from voting when the General Assembly then proceeded to establish a Commission on the Racial Situation in the Union of South Africa.[27] In 1958 it voted for a resolution chiding South Africa,[28] and since the Sharpeville incident in 1960 and the inauguration of Kennedy in 1961 it has voted for numerous resolutions condemning racism and colonialism, including the colonialism of Portugal, a North Atlantic Treaty ally. In 1968 Ambassador Goldberg was not deterred by Article 2(7) in accusing the Soviet Union of violating human rights in its treatment of the Soviet writers, Sinyavsky and Daniel, and those who sought to champion their cause. He pointed out that the two "have been accused, tried and sentenced as criminals for the sole offense of expressing themselves in writing in ways which did not please the authorities, and because these writings were sent abroad without official permission." To him, "a trial for the crime of writing a literary work [was] an outrageous attempt to give the form of legality to the suppression of a basic human right." Moreover, he complained that the trials connected with the Sinyavsky-Daniel affair were secret and thus contrary to the requirements of Article 11 of the Universal Declaration. Addressing the Human Rights Commission of the United Nations, he spoke of its "plain duty . . . to be concerned about transgressions against freedom of opinion and expression whenever and wherever they occur. . . . This commission has a responsibility to uphold the human rights of all peoples, regardless of their race or ideology or political system."[29] He did not, however, ask the Human Rights Commission to take specific action.

No real test has yet occurred of the attitude of the United States on the competence of the United Nations to exert pressures on a specific country in matters having nothing to do with fascism, communism, racism, or colonialism. In 1964 the Deputy Assistant Secretary of State for International Organization Affairs commented that the UN Commission on Human Rights

> regularly bypasses discussions of current problems in specific countries. In the vacuum thus created the General Assembly is tending to

> involve itself in politicized and emotional discussions of a few human rights problems without the benefit of a broad and analytical review of the entire subject.[30]

Whether the United States genuinely wants the United Nations to concern itself with all kinds of human rights problems in specific countries over the world is not really clear. Its own domestic legislation and practices put it in a relatively good position to stand as a champion of human rights elsewhere. But it is worth recalling that fears of the implementation measures that the United Nations might take were among those to which Senator Bricker appealed. He jumped from the idea that human rights are no longer essentially within the domestic jurisdiction of a state to the idea that these rights are subject to "enforcement . . . by an international authority."[31]

> No patriotic American will be able to support the United Nations if it continues to threaten national sovereignty by claiming jurisdiction over fundamental human rights. . . .
> The United Nations is obsessed by a dangerous ambition. That ambition is to define and enforce the rights and duties, both economic and political, of every human being in the world.[32]

In fact, of course, no member takes the view that enforcement action can occur through the United Nations except to counter a threat to the peace; and it is ambiguous and tendentious to say that the United Nations has "jurisdiction over fundamental human rights." Many of Senator Bricker's interpretations and charges were irresponsible. But his agitation in the name of the preservation of American sovereignty evoked a powerful response. We will discuss Senator Bricker more in the following chapter.

## THE UNIVERSAL DECLARATION OF HUMAN RIGHTS: IS IT BINDING?

The first section of this chapter was on the obligations of Articles 55 and 56 of the Charter, and we noted in the second section that those obligations stand whether or not Article 2(7) permits implementing measures directed at specific countries. Now the question is whether the Universal Declaration of Human Rights imposes obligations and, if so, what they are and on what basis they are imposed.

The Declaration does not itself suggest that it imposes a legal obligation. By its own terms it sets forth "a common standard of achievement."

Respect for the rights named is to be promoted "by teaching and education" and "by progressive measures, national and international." This is in keeping with the pledge of Article 56 of the Charter to promote human rights, but it obviously does not clear up the question of the meaning of *promote*.

At the time the Declaration was adopted, members of the United Nations disagreed on the question whether it had derivative legal effect, that is, whether it constituted an elaboration of the pledge that they had made in Article 56 by identifying the rights that they had bound themselves to promote. The preambular clause referred to above suggests this when it explains the adoption of the Declaration in part in terms of the need for "a common understanding" of the rights and freedoms to which the pledge of Article 56 relates. Among those who endorsed the thought was the Chinese delegate, though the fact that the first of his statements was in error does not commend the second: 'The Charter committed all Member States to the observance of human rights; the Declaration stated those rights explicitly."[33] Delegates from Chile, Lebanon, and Mexico took approximately the same view.[34] South Africa, which abstained from voting on the Declaration, explained its abstention in part in terms of a fear that the Chinese view might come to prevail.[35] New Zealand too expressed a fear that the Declaration "might be used for the purpose of definition of provisions of the Charter, a purpose for which the Commission on Human Rights had never intended it."[36] At a meeting of the Third Committee, the French delegate, Professor René Cassin, described the proposed declaration as an "authoritative interpretation of the Charter," but he did not repeat the claim in his address to the plenary meeting of the General Assembly.[37] Meantime the British delegate had registered a contrary view: "He did not agree with Professor Cassin that the declaration could be considered to have legal authority as an interpretation of the relevant provisions of the Charter. No General Assembly resolution could establish legal obligations."[38]

After reviewing the above, Louis B. Sohn draws the following conclusion:

> As the Declaration was adopted unanimously, without a dissenting vote, it can be considered as an authoritative interpretation of the Charter of the highest order. While the Declaration is not directly binding on the United Nations Members, it strengthens their obligations under the Charter by making them more precise. Members

> can no longer contend that they do not know what human rights they promised in the Charter to promote.[39]

The statement is not crystal clear, but it seems to side with the French delegate against the British. If so, the position is dubious. The General Assembly can obviously recommend a list of rights for promotion, but it is not authorized to determine precisely what obligations individual members assumed when they accepted Article 56.

Whatever the original status of the Declaration, some scholars say that it has taken on the character of customary law, or at least that it has ceased to be non-binding. A statement by the Office of Legal Affairs of the Secretariat concerning the significance of the adoption of declarations by organs of the United Nations suggests the process involved.

> A "declaration" may be considered to impart, on behalf of the organ adopting it, a strong expectation that Members of the international community will abide by it. Consequently, in so far as the expectation is gradually justified by State practice, a declaration may by custom become recognized as laying down rules binding upon States.[40]

The question then is whether practice has come to bear out the expectation.

A conclusive answer is impossible. No general agreement exists on the criteria for determining when practice has created customary law, any more than agreement exists on the question when footsteps across a lawn have created a path. Any answer must depend on judgment, and judgment is likely to be influenced by wish and hope. Those who suggest an affirmative judgment base their position on two kinds of evidence. In the first place, a great many states—above all, the states that have achieved independence since 1948—have in one way or another incorporated the principles of the Declaration in their constitutions, making them the law of the land. Moreover, without incorporating the Declaration in their constitutions, a number of other states, like the United States, substantially observe its requirements. In either a formal or a factual sense, then, the requirements of the Declaration are incorporated into domestic legal systems in a fairly widespread way; and this gives some basis for saying that customary law has been created. We might cite the provision in the Statute of the International Court of Justice which says that "the general principles of law recognized by civilized nations" are a source of international law.[41]

In the second place, a considerable number of international actions and instruments, most of them associated with the United Nations, reflect an assumption that the Declaration is to be regarded as binding. Within a few months after the Declaration was adopted the General Assembly took up the case of the Russian wives, mentioned above; and it cited two articles in the Declaration (Articles 13 and 16) among the bases for the conclusion that the policy of the Soviet Union was not in conformity with the Charter.[42] In 1950 the General Assembly adopted a resolution concerning non-self-governing territories, asking the administering powers to provide information on the extent to which they were implementing the Universal Declaration. The United States objected on the ground that this implied that the Universal Declaration was a treaty rather than a common standard;[43] and Britain objected on the ground that it was discriminatory to single the administering powers out and ask them for such reports. But the General Assembly went ahead and adopted the resolution nevertheless. Subsequently, it has regularly concerned itself with the implementation of the principles of the Declaration both in Trust Territories and in other non-self-governing territories. It obtains reports from administering powers, investigates on the spot, and receives petitions. We will deal with this more fully in Chapter 8.

In 1960 the General Assembly adopted a Declaration on the Granting of Independence to Colonial Countries and Peoples, to which we have referred before. It includes the following paragraph:

> All States shall observe faithfully and strictly the provisions of the Charter of the United Nations, the Universal Declaration of Human Rights and the present Declaration on the basis of equality, non-interference in the internal affairs of all States, and respect for the sovereign rights of all peoples and their territorial integrity.[44]

The vote on the resolution was 89 to 0, with 9 abstentions. The United States, Britain, and France all abstained. The next year the General Assembly established a Special Committee, which later became the Special Committee of Twenty-Four, to examine the application of the Declaration quoted just above and to make suggestions and recommendations on the progress and extent of its implementation.[45]

In 1963 the General Assembly adopted a Declaration on the Elimination of All Forms of Racial Discrimination, which concluded with an article like the one quoted above—specifying that "every State . . . shall fully and faithfully observe the provisions of . . . the Universal Declaration of Human Rights."[46] The vote was unanimous, but South Africa did not participate, and a number of states (including the United States, Britain, and France) put into the record the view that the Declaration did not impose legal obligations, implicitly agreeing with a statement by the delegate from New Zealand on the import of declarations.

> A declaration is a proclamation, a public affirmation of principles and aims. Its purpose is to set standards; its force comes from persuasion and the pressure of world opinion which it generates. A declaration should not create strict obligations, nor should it impose methods of implementation. These are the work of a convention.[47]

Ambassador Goldberg reiterated the view in 1967: "The declaration of human rights . . . is not a treaty obligation of any country. . . . It is at best a moral obligation as distinguished from a legal obligation."[48]

In 1968 the stronger interpretation showed up again. According to the Proclamation of Teheran, adopted unanimously at the official conference commemorating the twentieth anniversary of the Universal Declaration of Human Rights, the Universal Declaration "states a common understanding of the peoples of the world concerning the inalienable and inviolable rights of all members of the human family and constitutes an obligation for all members of the international community."[49]

On the basis of developments of the sort described above, though hesitant because of statements accompanying the 1963 declaration, Egon Schwelb concludes that the Universal Declaration "no longer fits into the dichotomy of 'binding treaty' against 'non-binding pronouncement,' but is rather an authoritative statement of the international community."[50] Sir Humphrey Waldock goes farther:

> This constant and widespread recognition of the principles of the Universal Declaration clothes it, in my opinion, in the character of customary law. Be that as it may, the Declaration has acquired a status inside and outside the United Nations which gives it high authority as the accepted formulation of the common standards of human rights.[51]

Like Schwelb, Waldock is obviously somewhat hesitant, and with good reason. Not only is there doubt whether enough states have incorporated the principles of the Declaration fully enough in their domestic legal systems and practice, but also there is doubt how much probative force ought to be attached to a declaration of the General Assembly that a previous declaration should be faithfully observed, especially when important powers abstain or attach reservations or record the view that no legal obligation is imposed. Moreover, it is no doubt significant that the last two declarations cited relate to colonialism and racial discrimination, subjects that arouse very special feeling and pressure; it is not at all certain that the states voting for these resolutions really wanted to push the Universal Declaration on toward the status of customary law. Even after the actions cited above, the General Assembly went on to adopt the Covenants on human rights, which it might or might not have done if it assumed that the Universal Declaration had already acquired the force of law. It seems very unlikely that states wishing to deny that the Universal Declaration has become law would be deterred by the kind of evidence cited above.

## INTER-AMERICAN OBLIGATIONS?

Participation in the OAS involves obligations with regard to human rights, but they are very vague. The major relevant treaty is the OAS Charter. In addition, numerous declarations and other kinds of pronouncements endorse principles, creating obligations that are moral rather than legal.

The preamble of the Charter of the OAS speaks of "the historic mission of America . . . to offer man a land of liberty, and a favorable environment for the development of his personality"; it speaks of the desire of the American peoples to live "in equality"; and it expresses the confidence of the American states that the

> true significance of American solidarity and good neighborliness can only mean the consolidation on this continent, within the framework of democratic institutions, of a system of individual liberty and social justice based on respect for the essential rights of man.

In Article 5 the American states reaffirm a number of principles. One of them is that "the solidarity of the American States and the high aims which are sought through it require the political organization of those states on the basis of the effective exercise of representative democracy," and another is that "the American States proclaim the fundamental rights of the individual without distinction as to race, nationality, creed, or sex." None of these statements seems to involve a specific pledge or promise. Article 13 reads as follows: "Each State has the right to develop its cultural, political and economic life freely and naturally. In this free development, the State shall respect the rights of the individual and the principles of universal morality." What the "rights of the individual" are —whether they are the same as human rights—is left uncertain; and so, for that matter, are the "principles of universal morality."

The American Declaration of the Rights and Duties of Man nowhere intimates that its purpose is to spell out obligations of the Charter; and it itself is non-binding. The United States voted against the Inter-American Charter of Social Guarantees adopted at Bogotá in 1948, and put a statement in the record, after the Charter was adopted, that it did not regard itself as bound.[52]

Numerous other pronouncements by inter-American conferences and agencies proclaim or extol this or that individual or human right. No one contends, however, that these pronouncements create legal obligations. If any obligation is created, it is moral.

We will note in Chapter 8 that in some respects the OAS, through its Commission on Human Rights, has gone farther than the United Nations in efforts to promote the observance of human rights, for example, by conducting investigations within the territory of certain member states. But inter-American documents are singularly lacking so far as any statement of specific and clear international legal obligations is concerned.

## OBLIGATIONS THROUGH THE ILO?

Membership in the International Labor Organization involves obligations with regard to human rights that are significant but general. The purpose of the organization, according to its constitution, is to promote objects named in the preamble and in the Declaration of Philadelphia of 1944, to which we have referred before. For the most part, the objects named relate to human rights, especially those of an economic and social sort. Among other things, the Declaration of Philadelphia affirms that:

> a. all human beings, irrespective of race, creed or sex, have the right to pursue both their material well-being and their spiritual development in conditions of freedom and dignity, of economic security and equal opportunity.
>
> b. the attainment of the conditions in which this shall be possible must constitute the central aim of national and international policy.

The United States makes this affirmation along with all other members, and it participates in the various activities of the ILO designed to promote the implementation of the principles named.

Other obligations have to do with conventions and recommendations that the General Conference of the ILO adopts. The obligation is to bring them "before the authority or authorities within whose competence the matter lies." In the case of a convention, this means that the President must refer it to the Senate, though he is not obliged to ask the Senate to advise and consent to ratification. In the case of a recommendation, it means that the President must refer it to the competent legislative or administrative agency, national, state, or local. Unratified conventions as well as recommendations, involve a further obligation: to make reports to the ILO concerning domestic law and practice relating to the matters dealt with. Reports concerning conventions are to include a statement of the difficulties that prevent or delay ratification. Delegates from other countries at ILO meetings are free to comment on the reports and to exert pressures for fuller implementation. We will comment more fully on the possibilities in the next chapter.

## ADDITIONAL OBLIGATIONS

Without attempting an exhaustive list of international obligations of the United States in the field of human rights, we ought to note a few others. The country is a party to various treaties having to do with slavery, the slave trade, and slavery-like practices, among them the Slavery Convention of 1926 and a Supplementary Convention of 1956. The Senate approved ratification of the latter only in 1967, its delay being explainable largely in terms of the surviving influence of Brickerism, militating against the acceptance of any international commitments in the field of human rights. A number of treaties of friendship, commerce, and navigation to which the country is a party include guarantees concerning the treatment to be accorded to nationals of one party who come within the jurisdiction of the other. The North Atlantic Treaty should be noted too. In the preamble the parties say that they are "determined to safeguard the freedom, the common heritage and civilization of their peoples, founded on the principles of democracy, individual liberty and the rule of law," and in Article 2 they pledge to "contribute toward the further development of peaceful and friendly international relations by strengthening their free institutions, by bringing about a better understanding of the principles upon which these institutions are founded, and by promoting conditions of stability and well-being." The fact that Portugal, with its dictatorship, was among the original signatories of the North Atlantic Treaty raises a question about the seriousness with which these provisions were taken.

Though the United States is party to a number of international obligations concerning human rights, it has avoided becoming a party to a number of others that have been proposed. In the next chapter we will examine the reasons for this policy and the question of its justifiability.

# 7

# Should Additional International Obligations Be Accepted?

In the early years of the United Nations it was clearly expected that the United States would be among the parties to covenants on human rights. President Truman at the closing session of the San Francisco Conference spoke of developing an international bill of rights that "will be as much a part of international life as our own Bill of Rights is part of our Constitution." As late as 1950 he expressed his faith that a covenant would be adopted, though he anticipated that language barriers and differences in legal systems would make it an arduous task to get general agreement.[1] Among the Republicans, John Foster Dulles took the same line. In the fall of 1948 he wanted the General Assembly to endorse the Universal Declaration of Human Rights, and he added:

> We must not stop there. We must go on with the drafting of a Covenant which will seek to translate human rights into law. It does not minimize our own Declaration of Independence to recognize that the Constitution and its Bill of Rights were required to establish the body of law necessary to achieve practical results. So with the Declaration before the Assembly.[2]

In 1950 Dulles was still speaking of the development of international standards in the field of human rights—standards that would be expressed "in terms of law which operates on individuals, not upon states, and which are enforceable by the courts and not by armies." "To abandon this goal," he said, "would involve substituting pious words for an effective result."[3]

Similarly with regard to the first of the specialized conventions before the General Assembly, the one on genocide, spokesmen for the United States anticipated ratification. In 1948 the United States delegate told the General Assembly:

> We should proceed with this convention before the memory of recent horrifying genocidal acts has faded from the minds and conscience of man. Positive action must be taken now. My Government is eager to see a genocide convention adopted. . . .[4]

The General Assembly soon approved the convention by a vote of 55 to 0, and in June, 1949, President Truman forwarded it to the Senate, urging it to advise and consent to ratification.

> In ratifying the Genocide Convention, we will let the world know that the United States does not condone mass atrocities any more now than in the past, and we will endorse the principle that such conduct is criminal under international law. This action by the United States will at least be a deterrent to the rulers of certain countries who consider genocide a justifiable means to promote their political objectives. I also regard speedy ratification of the Genocide Convention as essential to the effective maintenance of our leadership of the free and civilized nations of the world in the present struggle against the forces of aggression and barbarism.[5]

The Deputy Under Secretary of State, Dean Rusk, supporting President Truman's recommendation, pointed to the "inescapable fact that other nations of the world expect the United States to assert moral leadership in international affairs." It was a familiar role, he said, for the United States "to take the lead in raising moral standards of international society. And prevailing international conditions make it imperative that the United States continue to play this role."[6]

But both with regard to the proposed international bill of rights and with regard to the Genocide Convention, the unexpected happened. Movement toward the acceptance of additional international obligations concerning human rights precipitated a miasmal reaction, led in Congress by Senator Bricker, with effects that are still powerful. In the light of the Bricker reaction, Secretary of State John Foster Dulles announced in 1953 that the United States would not sign or ratify any covenant on human rights, and that it would not sign the Convention on the Political Rights of Women which the General Assembly had adopted; and in effect he indicated that the Administration would not press for Senate approval of the Genocide Convention. The policy applied to other conventions adopted by the General Assembly, the ILO, and UNESCO during Eisenhower's presidency.

President Kennedy, with obvious hesitation and diffidence, reverted more nearly to the original policy, holding that the various proposed international instruments should be considered on their merits.[7] In 1963 he asked the Senate to approve the Convention on the Political Rights of Women, the Convention on the Abolition of Forced Labor, and the Supplementary Convention on the Abolition of Slavery, the Slave Trade, and Institutions and Practices Similar to Slavery. After considerable delay, the Senate finally approved the Supplementary Slavery Convention toward the end of 1967, and formal accession of the United States followed. In the same year Ambassador Goldberg declared that the Johnson administration was "determined to press forward vigorously for ratification of all the United Nations conventions that have been signed but not yet ratified by this country."[8] But vigorous determination did not in fact manifest itself. In a belated Executive Order Establishing Observance of the International Year of Human Rights (1968), President Johnson confined himself to a reference to Senate approval of the Supplementary Slavery Convention and to the expression of "earnest hope" that the Senate would "complete the tasks before it by ratifying the remaining Human Rights Conventions."

### BRICKERISM

A committee of the American Bar Association—curiously named the Committee on Peace and Law Through the United Nations—preceded Senator Bricker in agitating against the Genocide Convention and against the idea of an international bill of rights. The Committee and the Senator were mainly responsible for the reversal of administration policy described above; and the Committee is still active (though in 1968 its name was changed to the Committee on World Order Under Law and its jurisdiction and functions were redefined). In 1967 it opposed all three of the conventions that Kennedy had recommended, but the House of Delegates of the American Bar Association overruled it with regard to the Supplementary Slavery Convention; and the Senate then endorsed this convention alone.[9]

### *Domestic Jurisdiction and the Proper Subject Matter of Treaties*

The central issue in "Brickerism" and in the eyes of the ABA Committee is that of domestic jurisdiction, or of the "proper" subject matter of treaties. To put it in other words, the central issue is the desirable relationship between man and the state, and the nature of a desirable world order. Again and again Senator Bricker and members of the ABA Committee quoted a statement by an official in the Secretariat:

> What the United Nations is trying to do is revolutionary in character. Human rights are largely a matter of relationships between the state and individuals, and therefore a matter which has been traditionally regarded as being within the domestic jurisdiction of states. What is now being proposed is, in effect, the creation of some kind of supra-national supervision of this relationship between the state and its citizens.[10]

They quoted the statement, of course, only to denounce and to decry the change that it describes.

Two somewhat different but interrelated assumptions are basic to the stand of the ABA Committee. One is the usual assumption that the country has a choice about the extent of its domestic jurisdiction, and that it could transfer ("surrender") some matters to the international realm. The Committee regards such a surrender as undesirable.

> It is the view of the Committee that international relations have not yet reached the stage at which the United States should surrender its exclusive jurisdiction over the regulation of its own internal order and the relations between its own national and local governments and their citizens. It is submitted that the cause of human rights neither justifies nor requires participation in treaties which would prejudice the domestic jurisdiction of the United States and the federal/state structure.[11]

Contrasting with this assumption is another, held simultaneously, that denies the country a right of deliberate choice. The second assumption focuses on "the line of demarcation between matters of 'international concern' and those falling exclusively within 'the domestic jurisdiction.'" In principle, the Committee grants that the line can be changed. "Matters which have traditionally been regarded as solely within the 'domestic jurisdiction' of a state may, in the course of time and by virtue of extensive international concern with them, become matters of 'international concern.'" Nevertheless, the Committee regards the line as highly resistant to change, and rejects the usual rule for bringing change about and for determining whether it has occurred: "It is sophistry to insist that matters cease to be domestic whenever they are made the subject of international agreement."[12] Why this is sophistry is not explained, and no substitute rule is offered. Apparently the view is that the line of demarcation cannot be shifted by any single deliberate act; it is beyond direct control. "The course of time" and "extensive international concern" will somehow produce change, but not the decision of governments. The Committee's stand reflects a judgment that developments associated with the United Nations have not brought the change about in the field of human rights—not Article 56 of the Charter pledging cooperation with the United Nations to promote them, nor almost a quarter century of international activity in which the United States has played a prominent role. And the intimation is that the Committee's conception of the location of the line is an objective finding of fact rather than a reflection of personal values and preferences.

Serious consequences flow from the location of the line and the rejection of the rule that it can be altered at will through international agreement. Holding that "many" human rights "have no direct relationship to the external affairs of the United States," and pointing out that these "concern the relationship of the citizen to the government of his country," the Committee asserts that they may not properly "form the subject . . . of international compacts."[13] If an international compact is nevertheless accepted, it marks not the transfer of a matter to the other side of the line of demarcation, but a violation of the line—an improper encroachment on the realm of domestic jurisdiction.

> Once the door has been opened to international regulation of such an area of relations between a State and its own citizens, the existing limitations on the treaty power to matters of "international concern," and the exclusion from matters essentially within the domestic jurisdiction, would become a mirage and not a limitation at all. Those supporting this report cannot accept such a revolutionary change in our legal structure.[14]

At the same time the Committee says that it "unqualifiedly supports the position of the United States" in promoting human rights "in every country" through the United Nations and that it "favors recommendations by the United Nations on all human rights and fundamental freedoms."[15] It is all right to promote and to recommend, then, even on matters that fall within what the Committee regards as the domestic jurisdiction of states, but not to accept a treaty obligation.

Though the House of Delegates of the American Bar Association overruled the Committee with regard to the Supplementary Slavery Convention, it did not clearly reject the principles that the Committee espoused. To be sure, the convention largely concerns matters that, according to Committee principles, are domestic; for example, it concerns debt bondage, serfdom, the purchase of brides. But the convention supplements a treaty of 1926 to which the United States was already a party and, in any event, matters connected with the slave trade and slavery long ago came within the realm of international concern. The House of Delegates apparently concurred with its Committee that another of the conventions before the Senate—the Convention on the Political Rights of Women—"invades the domestic jurisdiction of the United States."[16]

### *Other Themes of the ABA Committee and Senator Bricker*

In the early 1950's the Committee included other themes in its agitation against accepting international obligations in the field of human rights, themes that Senator Bricker took up and elaborated, and themes that might well be taken up again if the acceptance of additional international obligations in the field is pressed. One of them was that far from promoting human rights in the United States or even leaving them unimpaired, ratification of the proposed international Covenant or Covenants would place them in jeopardy. Frank E. Holman, for example, cited an article in the draft Covenant permitting derogation from obligations during a state of emergency and went on to assert that this "authorized" the President, once he declared a state of emergency, "to close all newspapers in the United States."[17] Senator Bricker spoke of the draft Covenant under the title, "Blueprint for Tyranny."[18] In another speech he said that "the United Nations . . . is setting up a form of government that is directly imperiling the basic fundamental freedoms of the citizens of the United States."[19]

> I do not want any of the international groups, and especially the group headed by Mrs. Eleanor Roosevelt, which has drafted the Covenant of Human Rights, to betray the fundamental, inalienable, and God-given rights of American citizens enjoyed under the Constitution. That is really what I am driving at.[20]

The arguments involved grossly exaggerated fears and were ill-considered and tendentious if not completely unfounded, doing no credit to the probity and trustworthiness of those who advanced them. But they had powerful political effect.

Another major theme of the ABA Committee and of Senator Bricker was a reaction to the dominant view in the United Nations that human rights include those of an economic, social, and cultural character. We have already noted in Chapter 4 the denial that these are "rights or freedoms in any true sense." "In the final analysis," said Senator Bricker, "human rights are synonymous with the rights and freedoms enjoyed by the American people."[21] To insist on a recognition of economic, social, and cultural *rights* was to insist on socialism. To provide for such rights in an international covenant was "Socialism by Treaty."[22] Frank E. Holman spoke of the "grandiose grant of power" that ECOSOC allegedly enjoyed, and charged it with using that power "to reform and remake the world." "One of the first documents produced under this program of world-wide reform was the so-called Declaration of Human Rights. . . . This declaration, among other things, is a complete blueprint for socializing the world."[23] George A. Finch, also a member of the Committee, warned against the use of the UN Charter as "a Trojan horse by those who would continue the social and economic revolution in this country through extraconstitutional means."[24] Senator Bricker was impressed, too, by a resolution of the U.S. Chamber of Commerce claiming that the ILO was being used "as a propaganda forum for statism and socialism" and that "by and large the staff of the ILO is non-objective and dangerously devoted to the accomplishment of statist and Socialist ideologies."[25]

Though spokesmen for the Executive branch have never taken the view that to accept the idea of economic, social, and cultural rights was to accept socialism, they have displayed a notable lack of enthusiasm about spelling those rights out in treaties. In 1951, after an earlier failure, they managed to get agreement on the point that instead of one Covenant on Human Rights there should be two, which could be ratified independently of each other; the United States might then choose to accept only the Covenant on Civil and Political Rights.[26] And when the General Assembly finally adopted the two Covenants in 1966, the American delegate spoke critically of the one on Economic, Social, and Cultural Rights. That Covenant, she said, "speaks of 'rights' that in fact are objectives which no government, no matter what its human and financial resources, could implement immediately. . . ." And she objected to a passage in Article 2 requiring each party "to take steps, individually and through international assistance and cooperation, especially economic and technical, to the maximum of its available resources, with a view to achieving progressively the full realization of the rights recognized in the present Covenant. . . ."[27] Her fears were suggestive of those advanced many years earlier by Frank E. Holman concerning Article 22 of the Universal Declaration: "Its loose and general language can easily mean that through international cooperation by Uncle Sam and in accordance with our resources we are to provide, or in large part to provide, social security for all the rest of the world."[28]

Another theme concerned the constitutional division of powers between the states and the federal government. The problem was, and remains, both real and difficult. In *Missouri v. Holland* the Supreme Court endorsed the principle that through a treaty the federal government might acquire a power that it did not otherwise have. This suggests the possibility that treaties and conventions on human rights might enhance federal powers at the expense of the states. The possibility is troublesome to other federal states as well as to the United States. In the ILO the principle followed is that federal governments are required to adopt implementing legislation only within their already established jurisdictional limits; where action is called for outside those limits, the obligation of the federal government is to refer the matter to state governments or other proper authorities, recommending that they take appropriate action. Early drafts of the human rights covenants included a similar provision, but it was inadequate to satisfy the Committee on Peace and Law Through the United Nations or Senator Bricker. Eberhard P. Deutsch, a member of the Committee, saw it as the "underlying long-range objective" of treaties on human rights "to destroy local government while expanding the sphere of national power and setting a course toward world totalitarianism."[29]

Following the change in United States policy forced by the ABA Committee and Senator Bricker, the United States no longer fought for the inclusion of an ILO-type federal-state clause in the Covenants on Human Rights, and the clause was dropped.[30] Both Covenants now specify that their provisions "shall extend to all parts of federal States without any limitations or exceptions." Similarly, the United States failed to fight for the inclusion of a federal-state clause in the Convention on the Elimination of All Forms of Racial Discrimination, explaining that the effort was likely to fail and that United States influence could be "more productively directed to securing satisfactory substantive provisions." The ABA Committee finds this attitude "shocking," and comments that "the fact that 'there is little support in the United Nations General Assembly for the inclusion of federal-state clauses in human rights conventions' is not pertinent to whether or not we wish to change our form of government."[31]

Still another theme of the Bricker movement was that international treaties on human rights might be construed to be self-executing, that is, to become law of the land without legislative action by Congress and without giving it a role in interpreting and providing for the implementation of the obligations assumed.

The above themes related not only to the proposed international bill of rights but also to the first of the specialized conventions approved by the General Assembly—the Genocide Convention. It was and is vulnerable in distinctive ways; even the "Section on International and Comparative Law" of the American Bar Association, which favored ratification, thought that seven reservations were desirable. The Convention specifies that "causing serious . . . mental harm" to members of a national, ethnic, racial, or religious group constitutes genocide if done with the intent to destroy the group. It declares that "direct and public incitement to commit genocide" shall be punishable. The high probability is that neither provision would ever cause a problem, but still questions relating to freedom of speech and press might arise. These provisions, as well as several others (e.g. the very ban on "killing members of the group") also raise potential questions about federal-state relationships. The convention does not include governmental complicity as a definitional feature of genocide, raising the question what the prohibition of genocide would accomplish that is not already accomplished by the prohibition of homicide.

Objections to the Genocide Convention and the proposed international bill of rights were not confined to Senator Bricker and the ABA Committee, nor were misinterpretations and misconceptions, and resort to distortion, exaggeration, and innuendo. For example, William H. Fitzpatrick got a Pulitzer Prize for distinguished editorial writing on human rights, the extent of his knowledge and the flavor of his views being suggested by the following. Speaking of the Universal Declaration of Human Rights, he remarked:

> If this is adopted as a treaty by the Senate, this country may no longer be as we have known it. We will have instead a world-wide

social and economic system with Uncle Sam paying the bills. We will have an International Court of Human Rights to which every one of us may be held responsible. Our immigration laws will become ineffective. Laws of many States will be thrown out. The customs of the people will be disregarded. It attacks the institution of marriage by social recognition of illegitimacy just as Nazi Germany did and Communist Russia does. It invades the rights of people to choose their own intimates and fellow workers and it would strike a serious blow at religious beliefs and tenets.

It is a far-reaching, revolutionary document which could easily drive this country to the poorhouse and its people to totalitarianism.[32]

### *Contrasting Attitudes in Europe*

Reactions of the kind cited above to the international movement for the promotion of human rights stand in sharp contrast to reactions in Europe. The governments there, far from opposing the movement and the use of treaties in principle, decided not to wait for the United Nations but to proceed independently. The danger of communism seemed great, and the memory of Nazism was fresh. "It was when the European countries were acutely aware of the challenge of communism that they felt the need to reaffirm the principles of their own political faith; it was the danger of dictatorship that made them conscious of the value of democracy."[33] And they wanted to prevent the recrudescence of Fascism. There must be no more Führers, no more crematoria! "It is necessary to intervene before it is too late. A conscience must exist somewhere which will sound the alarm to the minds of a nation menaced by this progressive corruption, to warn them of the peril and to show them that they are progressing down a long road which leads far, sometimes even to Buchenwald or Dachau."[34] In consequence the Statute of the Council of Europe obliges each member to "accept the principles of the rule of law and of the enjoyment by all persons within its jurisdiction of human rights and fundamental freedoms," and the European Convention on Human Rights and its various protocols make the obligation more specific. Sixteen of the eighteen members of the Council of Europe—all except France and Switzerland—have ratified the Convention.

### *The Bricker Proposals and Dulles's Retreat*

The resolution that Senator Bricker first proposed in 1951 related directly to the question of international action on behalf of human rights:

> Resolved, That it is the sense of the Senate that—
> 1. The Draft International Covenant on Human Rights . . . would, if ratified as a treaty, prejudice those rights of the American people which are now protected by the bill of rights of the Constitution of the United States;
> 2. The President of the United States should advise the United Nations that the proposed International Covenant on Human Rights is not acceptable to the United States; and
> 3. The President of the United States should instruct United States representatives at the United Nations to withdraw from further negotiations with respect to the Covenant on Human Rights, and all other covenants, treaties, and conventions which seek to prescribe restrictions on individual liberty which, if passed by the Congress as domestic legislation, would be unconstitutional.[35]

Later in 1951 Senator Bricker broadened his efforts, proposing a constitutional amendment that went through several revisions in the ensuing years. The 1955 version reads as follows:

> 1. A provision of a treaty or other international agreement which conflicts with this Constitution, or which is not made in pursuance thereof, shall not be the supreme law of the land nor be of any force or effect.
> 2. A treaty or other international agreement shall become effective as internal law in the United States only through legislation valid in the absence of international agreement.[36]

The proposed amendment shifted the focus of debate away from human rights as such to the question of constitutional arrangements for conducting foreign relations. And alarm at the potential consequences of the amendment in the broader area led Secretary of State Dulles to a strategic retreat in the field of human rights. Peace treaties with the defeated states of Europe had included articles binding them to respect human rights and fundamental freedoms, but Dulles refused to include a comparable provision in the peace treaty with Japan, explaining himself explicitly in terms of objections that had arisen in the United States to any attempt to make human rights a matter of enforceable treaty obligation.[37] Then in 1953 he extended the retreat to the question whether the United States should itself accept international obligations in the field. He testified to Senator Bricker's committee that "the trend toward trying to use the treatymaking power to effect internal social changes" had been reversed. "This administration is committed to the exercise of the treatymaking power only within traditional limits." With regard to human rights, the administration would encourage their promotion everywhere, but it would favor "methods of persuasion, education, and example rather than formal undertakings. . . ."

> Therefore, while we shall not withhold our counsel from those who seek to draft a treaty or covenant on human rights, we do not ourselves look upon a treaty as the means which we would now select as the proper and most effective way to spread throughout the world the goals of human liberty to which this Nation has been dedicated since its inception. We therefore do not intend to become a party to any such covenant or present it as a treaty for consideration by the Senate.

Mr. Dulles went on to say that the Eisenhower Administration did not intend to sign the Convention on the Political Rights of Women, "because we do not believe that this goal of equal political status for men and women can be achieved by treaty coercion or that it constitutes a proper field for the exercise of the treatymaking power." And he declared that the same principles would guide the administration in other fields in which treaties had been suggested.[38]

The stand to which Dulles retreated was not new. Faced with a movement for an inter-American treaty on equal rights before World War II, the United States had taken the position that "Equal Rights is not an appropriate subject for a treaty."[39]

Dulles's retreat deprived the Bricker movement of some of its appeal, but it did not satisfy either the Committee or the Senator. Hostility toward the United Nations with respect to human rights, and distrust of the Department of State, were extreme. Senator Joseph McCarthy's agitation supplemented Bricker's. Said Senator Bricker, "I would suspect the State Department of almost anything it might be charged with in connection with the ulterior purposes of the United Nations and its representatives to undermine the liberties of the people of America."[40] The fear was that a future administration would revert to the policy of championing international conventions on human rights, so efforts continued to get the Bricker amendment approved. Frank E. Holman reports a conversation with the Legal Adviser in the Department of State: "He told us, 'You American Bar people have done a great job. . . . Why don't you go home;

you have defeated the Genocide Convention; you have defeated the Covenant on Human Rights.' " To which Holman's response was, "We are not asking for this amendment as against the present administration. We are asking it against all administrations. . . ."[41]

> Only an adequate Constitutional Amendment can protect the American people against the Communistic and Socialistic inclusions and omissions of the Covenant on Human Rights if and when at some future time it is submitted to the Senate for ratification and under the pressures of the time is unfortunately ratified.[42]

Holman went on to describe the Bricker amendment as "a symbol or a line of demarcation dividing those who believe that the American concept of a constitutionally limited government (a Republic) should *not* be sacrificed to international plans and purposes, and those who believe that such a sacrifice should be made in the interest of so-called international cooperation." Whether the amendment was adopted or not, he was gratified that the fight for it had "served to expose and unmask the insidious propaganda program, begun several years ago, of quietly inoculating the American people with the virus of 'one-worldism.' "[43] In the end, of course, the movement for the amendment faded out, but in 1967, when the Senate was considering the three conventions recommended to it by President Kennedy, the ABA Committee predicted (threatened?) that their ratification would lead to its revival:

> When the so-called "Bricker Amendment" to limit the domestic effect of treaties in the United States was being considered, the American Bar Association was assured that it could trust the Executive Department not to sign and submit treaties affecting the internal affairs of the United States.
>
> If such treaties as are now proposed for accession or ratification should be approved, it will again become necessary to seek constitutional limitations on the treatymaking power.[44]

## TREATY OBLIGATIONS AND BEHAVIOR

### *Attitudes on Protecting Rights Through Constitutional and Treaty Law*

The extent to which the domestic practices of states are likely to be affected by the acceptance of treaty obligations is debatable. An analogous question exists within countries—how much difference it makes if there is a written constitution that includes a bill of rights—and informed judgments differ.

With respect to modern France, according to Sherman Kent, "The generalization which stands out is that . . . there has been very little correlation between the guarantee of rights (or the absence of such a guarantee) and the enjoyment of rights."[45]

With respect to Latin America, appraisals of very different sorts are made. Austin F. Macdonald comments that, in the eyes of Latin Americans, a constitution is "a record of what should be done under ideal conditions. When those ideal conditions have been achieved, the constitution will be respected in its entirety. But, until that happy day arrives, more practical solutions must be found for pressing problems."[46] Though not necessarily disagreeing with this view, Jacques Lambert adopts a different emphasis.

> The contrast between the lengthy statement of guarantees and the resistance to their application in immature societies has led too many observers to conclude that the men who framed the constitutions merely paid lip service to lofty principles and, once they had put them into words, gave little thought to their application. The conclusion is unfair; it is not completely untrue, however, because there are enough differences among the twenty Latin American countries to justify any thesis by numerous examples.[47]

Lambert goes on himself to cite Latin American countries in which the behavior of governments justifies negative appraisals. Moreover, he stresses the dualism of most Latin American societies, that is, the urban-rural division, and indicates that constitutional guarantees of rights are relevant mainly, if not exclusively, to the urban areas. "A segment of society—in some countries the largest segment—is outside the scope of the government's protection or exactions." Nevertheless he says that "on the whole, Latin America is a land of personal freedoms, and the exercise of those freedoms is more apt to be curtailed through the helplessness of governments than by their despotism." In his view, too, constitutional provisions on economic and social rights "have not remained empty words; everywhere legislation has tried to keep up with the promises of constitutions. . . . It would be a serious mistake to regard . . . declarations of social rights as never-enforced declarations of intention."[48]

Especially in dealing with colonies, Britain has faced the question of the value of bills of rights in written constitutions. The Simon Commission in 1930 decided against a bill of rights for safeguarding minorities in India.

> We are aware that such provisions have been inserted in many constitutions, notably in those of the European States formed after the War. Experience, however, has not shown them to be of any great practical value. Abstract declarations are useless, unless there exists the will and means to make them effective.[49]

Sir Ivor Jennings, writing on *The Approach to Self-Government,* shows similar skepticism. He holds it to be "generally agreed that the essential political and personal freedoms are even better protected in the United Kingdom than they are in the United States," even though the United Kingdom has historically lacked a written Bill of Rights. For new countries approaching self-government, he opposes the provision of constitutional guarantees of civil and political rights: " . . . there can be a great deal of potential harm in any formulation of constitutional guarantees. No draftsman can produce a formula which will be satisfactory even in the short run. . . . The constitutional guarantees in the Constitution of the United States have often been used by vested interests to obstruct legislation which was clearly desired by the people." Observing that "a most careful formulation of constitutional guarantees" in fact came to be included in the Constitution of independent India, he comments that "almost before the ink was dry difficulties were discovered. . . . The unusual step had to be taken of validating by constitutional amendment no less than thirteen legislative acts. According to Sir Ivor, "the less one puts into a Constitution the better." With specific reference to the use of a Bill of Rights to prevent discrimination in respect of race, religion and caste, he holds that "such provisions are rarely successful. . . . Laws cannot be effective if they go far beyond public opinion. . . . One cannot overthrow a social system by drafting a Constitution."[50] Benn and Peters likewise make the judgment that "the American device of a Bill of Rights" is a "doubtful way" of safeguarding the rights of citizens, for the rights have to be framed so broadly as to give "virtually absolute discretion" to the Supreme Court in interpreting them.[51]

Regardless of the above attitudes, however, Britain became a party to the European Convention on Human Rights in 1951. It remains without a written constitution, but has accepted a written bill of rights as a matter of international obligation. Moreover, after 1951 Britain began extending the provisions of the European Convention to its dependent territories by making declarations under Article 63,[52] and as it granted independence to such territories it began to incorporate into their constitutions guarantees of human rights based on the provisions of the European Convention. At least in part it did this to allay the fears of minority groups.[53] A commission studying the problem of a constitution for Nigeria endorsed the practice. Guarantees of fundamental rights, it said,

> are difficult to enforce and sometimes difficult to interpret. Nevertheless we think they should be inserted. Their presence defines beliefs widespread among democratic countries and provides a standard to which appeal may be made by those whose rights are infringed. A Government determined to abandon democratic courses will find ways of violating them but they are of great value in preventing a steady deterioration in standards of freedom and the unobtrusive encroachment of a Government on individual rights.[54]

Rhodesia illegally declared its independence in 1965 to avoid the constitutional and international obligations concerning human rights that otherwise would presumably have been imposed upon it.

However effective bills of rights may be, a great many countries include them in their constitutions; indeed with written constitutions this is customary.[55] Moreover, a great many also hold it desirable to develop a network of international obligations. This is evidenced by the fact that members of the United Nations went ahead with the formulation of the Covenants on human rights and of various specialized conventions despite the Dulles retreat of 1953. In 1965 (a year before the adoption of the Covenants) the General Assembly urged particularly the ratification of nine of the specialized conventions—some of them developed by the ILO or UNESCO. The subjects of the nine are given below, together with the year they were adopted and the number of states that had ratified by the end of 1967.[56]

1. The Abolition of Slavery, the Slave Trade, and Institutions and Practices Similar to Slavery (1956-72)
2. The Abolition of Forced Labor (1957-79)
3. Discrimination in Respect of Employment and Occupation (1958-63)
4. Equal Remuneration for Men and Women Workers for Work of Equal Value (1951-60)

5. Freedom of Association and Protection of the Right to Organize (1948-76)
6. Discrimination in Education (1960-41)
7. The Prevention and Punishment of the Crime of Genocide (1948-71)
8. The Political Rights of Women (1952-55)
9. The Elimination of All Forms of Racial Discrimination (1965-18)

Thirty-one states had ratified the ninth of these conventions by the spring of 1969—enough to bring it into effect.

Within the Organization of the American States, too, voices are raised for the promotion of human rights through treaties. In 1948 the Bogotá Conference instructed the Inter-American Juridical Committee to prepare a draft statute for an "Inter-American Court to guarantee the rights of man,"[57] only to have the Committee decline the assignment on the ground that the time had not arrived for such a court.[58] In 1959 the Fifth Meeting of Consultation of Ministers of Foreign Affairs adopted a resolution declaring that "the climate in this hemisphere is favorable to the conclusion of a convention" on human rights, and instructed its Council of Jurists to prepare one.[59] The Council accepted the assignment, but its Juridical Committee revealed some ambivalence on the matter, on the one hand taking the stand that the development of a convention was not practicable,[60] and on the other hand submitting a study favoring a convention on the ground that "mere declarations and resolutions" would not be observed. According to the study,

> democracy in America is beset by an absolute contradiction between the written law and reality. All the constitutions establish broad guarantees and rights, but these guarantees and rights are not always respected in practice. From which it follows, with the clarity of noon, that, today, the protection provided by domestic law is not enough.

"And from which it also follows," said the study, whether or not with irony, "that we must think in terms of a system of international protection."[61] The upshot is that a system of international protection is under active consideration. In the fall of 1968 the Council of the OAS referred a preliminary draft convention on human rights to the members, inviting them to make observations and propose amendments within three months. It is then to convene a specialized conference to consider the matter.[62] According to an OAS report to the UN in 1968, "the most important goal of the OAS [in the field of human rights] is the approval of a regional convention."[63] Given the fact that the Latin American states voted in the General Assembly to adopt the Covenants put before it in 1966, approval of a regional convention might obviously occur. Prospects for ratification are quite uncertain.

*Reasons for Favorable Attitudes*

No comprehensive study has yet been made of the reasons why governments think it desirable to formulate and ratify conventions on human rights, but a variety of considerations are cited.

One of the considerations clearly is a belief that the rights in question are moral values that ought to be safeguarded and promoted. As noted above, it is not an accident that the movement for international action on behalf of human rights gained great impetus during and immediately after World War II. Victory seemed to call for a reaffirmation of the human values for which the war was in part fought. The peace treaties imposed on the defeated states bound them to respect human rights and fundamental freedoms. The Charter bound members of the UN similarly. No question at all exists but that the Genocide Convention was formulated as a gage that states would give to each other not to permit in their territory crimes such as those perpetrated by the Nazis against the Jews, simply because such crimes are wrong. Similarly, as we have noted, the fear of totalitarianism, whether Nazi or communist, influenced the European states in providing for human rights in the Statute of the Council of Europe and in accepting the European Convention on Human Rights. A sense that the requirements of morality ought in large measure to be made requirements of law pervades discussions of human rights in the United Nations.

The above attitude rests on an assumption, of course, that the requirements of morality are more likely to be observed if they are also the requirements of law. It reflects the old conviction that law may reinforce virtue. And the assumption and conviction are no doubt sound. In the first place, conceptions of the requirements of morality are likely to be clarified in the process of formulating the law—or the international convention. In the second place, the relatively simple statements in the law or convention are likely to provide a better basis than would otherwise exist for educational and propaganda efforts on behalf of the principles involved. In the third place, so far as the use of international conventions is concerned, a government accepting them may strengthen its hand against domestic opponents of policies that it wants to carry out; and governmental leaders, knowing that they may sometime lose power, may make it more difficult for a succeeding government to change policies entrenched through an international convention, and may assure themselves in advance of a better basis for pressures against future governments than they otherwise might have. To put this point more generally, governments accepting an international commitment strengthen the hand of domestic elements that especially want to see it observed; of course, a future government of a recalcitrant or dictatorial sort may be able to deter or suppress those who might otherwise exert pressure, but international obligations are likely in the long run to make a government more vulnerable to domestic pressures than it would otherwise be. ILO conventions, for example, give leverage to trade unions wanting to see the conventions observed. Finally, in the fourth place, international obligations entail the possibility of various kinds of pressures from other governments and from international agencies; that is, they open the way to international measures of implementation, which constitute the subject of the following chapter.

Other considerations also suggest the desirability of conventions on human rights. The constitution of the ILO, in its preamble, points out that "the failure of any nation to adopt humane conditions of labor is an obstacle in the way of other nations which desire to improve the conditions in their own countries." The desire to maintain or improve labor standards at home, then, is a reason for attempting to get them maintained or improved abroad; and one of the ways of doing this is through conventions. In addition, countries whose nationals engage to any considerable extent in international travel or in international commercial activities of any sort have an interest in the fairness and reasonableness of law and practice in the foreign countries involved.[64] Much more generally, the international significance of domestic developments in countries over the world tends to increase along with the increase in international relationships of all sorts. Countries seeking domestic welfare, social justice, and stable progress for themselves are likely to find their efforts made easier if other countries are seeking the same goals. A world environment conducive to the promotion of these domestic goals is precious, and a world environment that threatens them is by definition dangerous. Domestic developments relating to human rights in Germany had much to do with the origins of World War II. Domestic developments relating to human rights in the Soviet Union and in the countries that it reduced to satellite status had much to do with the origins and development of the cold war. Domestic developments relating to human rights in South Africa and Rhodesia have already created international strains and tensions; according to the General Assembly they are threats to the peace. Quincy Wright endorses this theme:

> Barbarities that shock the conscience of mankind and persecutions of minorities, especially if they have the nationality of the population of another state, have been an important cause of war. Suppression of freedom of speech and press and terrorization by secret police, characteristic of totalitarian states, tend to prevent contacts of the population so oppressed with other peoples and to create a fanatical and uninformed national opinion, unaware of the attitudes of other nations or of the conditions of world opinion and, therefore, dangerous to peace.[65]

Finally, it should be noted that affirmations of support for human rights have come to be necessary to good standing among the virtuous. This is suggested by a unanimous vote in an African Regional Conference of the ILO "that ratification and strengthened application of ILO conventions concerning human rights should be regarded by all African countries as a question of 'honor and prestige' "[66] A government that refuses in principle to consider the acceptance of conventions raises questions about the seriousness of its support for what is almost everywhere said to be the right.

## REACTIONS AGAINST BRICKERISM

### *American Attitudes on Protecting Rights Through Treaties*

Not everyone agreed with Dulles that his retreat was desirable, and voices urging the promotion of human rights through treaties began shortly to be raised again. Senator Lehman deplored Dulles's refusal to press for the ratification of the Genocide Convention. He thought that, apart from domestic politics, there could be "no substantial argument" against ratification.[67] Later he described it as "shameful" that we had not ratified.[68] In 1957, in the House of Representatives, Henry S. Reuss pointed to "the melancholy fact" that the United States "stands almost alone in opposing in principle treaties relating to human rights." And he said: "It is time that we give up being afraid. . . . It is time for us to resume a position of leadership in the United Nations struggle for human rights." He wanted to use international conventions "to promote justice for the individual," and he thought that "a decent respect for human rights . . . is a precondition of world peace." The Universal Declaration was not enough. "If these human rights are to have meaning, they must be embedded into the organic law of member nations. This can be done most effectively by treaty or convention."[69] Senator Humphrey in 1958 submitted a resolution requesting the President "to resume the participation by the United States in the United Nations and in other international bodies in the effort to draft and sign international instruments to promote and protect human rights and fundamental freedoms throughout the world." It pleased him that the State Department had invoked the Universal Declaration in denouncing the execution of Imré Nagy and others in Hungary.[70] In 1959 the Assistant Secretary of State for International Organization Affairs saw fit to note evidence that in Tibet "the Chinese Communists have committed acts violating the norms established by the Genocide Convention of 1948,"[71] and in the following years a number of members of Congress spoke up for ratification of that Convention.

Meantime a committee under the chairmanship of Joseph E. Johnson, appointed by the Departments of State, Commerce, and Labor, made a report on the stance of the United States with respect to the International Labor Organization. American participation in the ILO had been under attack, especially by employer and business groups, e.g. the National Association of Manufacturers. In general, they shared the views of the ABA Committee on Peace and Law Through the United Nations and of Senator Bricker. The Chairman of the Board of the NAM, who served as the employers' delegate to an ILO conference in 1957, even objected to the proposed convention on the abolition of forced labor.

> The employers of the United States support the principle that it is inappropriate to embody in an international draft treaty provisions governing the relationship of an individual to his own government. We believe that international treaties are proper only when they deal with the relationship of a national or his government to foreign citizens or their governments.[72]

Another employer delegate objected also to ILO recommendations. "Once a recommendation along a certain line has been passed, then the majority Socialist group will sharpen it into a convention which those who have previously consented to the recommendation find it difficult to oppose."[73] Other employer delegates took the view that the standards recommended by the ILO "are often neither economically feasible nor practicable," and that conventions tend to create the illusion that legislation can raise living standards.[74]

In the light of the above attitudes the Johnson committee included the following among its recommendations:

> a. That the United States continue to work for decreased emphasis on the use of conventions and recommendations; but
> b. That when, nevertheless, conventions or recommendations are under consideration by the General Conference, it should be U.S. policy to support or oppose them on their substantive merits, and not to oppose a proposal with which the United States is in agreement on principle simply because the measure is in convention form or is thought not to be properly a subject of legislation under the American system.[75]

The report spoke of "the embarrassing, in fact almost impossible, situation" in which the United States then found itself with respect to the convention on forced labor. The country had played a leading role in bringing the issue of forced labor before the world, with Soviet practices as the main object of attack. It helped stimulate an ILO inquiry, which gave publicity to massive evidence. But when the inquiry led to the proposal of a convention on the subject, the matter took on another aspect. U.S. labor delegates vigorously supported the idea of a convention.[76] Employer delegates opposed. Government delegates squirmed.

> As a result, instead of the United States leading the fight for a convention against forced labor, an issue over which we fought a bloody war, we hedged ourselves around with reservations and amendments and gave the appearance in the propaganda outlets of the world of opposing this convention. Moreover, our intractable stand against conventions, in this case as in others, reduces our ability to negotiate a document more satisfactory to us.[77]

As already indicated, President Kennedy switched to the principle endorsed by the Johnson committee of considering conventions on their merits, but his stand cannot be described as strong. Perhaps he was influenced by Southern fears.[78] The Committee on Foreign Relations took no action in 1963 when Kennedy recommended approval of three conventions, including the one on forced labor. According to Senator Dodd in 1965, "Our entire moral position, and our claim to leadership in the fight for freedom and justice and human decency, is prejudiced by our failure to ratify" these conventions and the one on genocide.[79] In 1965 the Committee on Human Rights of the National Citizens' Commission on International Cooperation urged that all of these conventions be ratified and that others adopted by the General Assembly, UNESCO, and the ILO be referred to the Senate for approval.[80] Continued inaction by the Committee on Foreign Relations led Senator Proxmire in January 1967 to begin making a speech a day in the Senate for ratification of the pending treaties. He found it "a cruel paradox as well as a national disgrace that the United States, which has proved conclusively to the world the practical effectiveness of our own Bill of Rights, must hang our national head in shame at our irresponsible unwillingness to lead the fight for the establishment of basic human rights for all men."[81] Finally, in March 1967, the Committee on Foreign Relations arranged for hearings on the three conventions that Kennedy had recommended.

### *Other Themes Supporting Favorable Attitudes*

Themes suggested above and others are advanced in support of the proposition that the United States should accept additional international obligations relating to human rights. It is not that American domestic law and practice fall short and that treaties should be used as a basis for bringing domestic change about. Instead, the themes relate to human rights abroad and to the basis for American participation in efforts to promote them.

One of the themes, as stated by Richard N. Gardner, is that ratification by the United States of the three conventions that President Kennedy recommended "will encourage other nations to adhere to them and implement their provisions in their own territories."[82] Ambassador Goldberg makes a similar point:

> There are strong reasons to believe that, in countries where a long tradition of human rights is lacking, these international conventions provide a meaningful standard and a target for future development. . . . Many nations tend to look to the community of nations for help in developing their own modern standards, in human rights as in many other fields.[83]

In other words, treaties might be used to encourage the development of underdeveloped countries along desired lines. Not that nations accepting international obligations would necessarily interpret them in the same way or implement them fully or immediately. Ambassador Goldberg points out that one hundred years after the adoption of the Fourteenth Amendment

> we are still working to assure the "equal protection of the laws" to all citizens regardless of their race. In the same way, I believe, the international conventions will bear fruit in due time. The making of an international commitment is in itself a foundation stone on which the nations can build.[84]

Conventions, and for that matter the Covenants, are actual or potential supplements to the various declarations of the General Assembly in encouraging the development of uniform minimum standards in the treatment of human beings throughout the world.

Another theme, as stated by Richard N. Gardner, is that "ratification will put the United States in a better legal and moral position to protest infringement of these human rights in countries that have ratified the conventions but failed to implement them."[85] Actually, as we will see in the next chapter, one of the questions concerning the problem of implementing human rights conventions is the extent to which reliance should be placed on the right of diplomatic protest. The point is commonly made that extraneous considerations are likely to influence the relevant decisions —that decisions whether or not to protest (and, if so, in what terms) are likely to be influenced or controlled not so much by concern for human rights as such as by concern for political alignments and political struggles centering around other goals and issues. But the fact is that the United States is already protesting violations of human rights abroad. It is protesting apartheid in South Africa, discrimination in Rhodesia, and the denial of self-determination in Portuguese territories. On an episodic and sporadic basis it protests undemocratic seizures of power, and failures to hold elections, e.g. in Latin America and in Greece. As noted in the preceding chapter, it has appealed publicly to the USSR with regard to violations of human rights in prosecuting authors for their literary work. The fact that such protests are made indicates that they do not depend on ratification of relevant special conventions, but ratification would surely strengthen American efforts. Especially with the domestic developments of recent years relating to civil rights and racial discrimination, the country could withstand international scrutiny very well; and, given emphasis on the value of human rights rather than on the sensitivities that go with sovereignty, a willingness on the part of the United States to accept the implications of international accountability might be very significant.

Another theme concerning the three conventions recommended by Kennedy, again as stated by Richard N. Gardner, is that "ratification will increase United States influence in the continuing U.N. process of drafting legal norms in the field of human rights. . . ."[86] The record since the Dulles retreat of 1953 suggests at least that the reverse of this proposition is true: that the United States reduced its influence over the drafting of covenants and conventions by announcing that it would not ratify them regardless of their terms. Various provisions then came to be included or omitted in several instruments which will surely involve problems for the United States if ratification is ever seriously contemplated. Most notable is the omission from various instruments of a clause like the one employed by the ILO concerning the obligations of federal states. As the covenants on human rights now stand, for example, ratification by the United States would involve the acceptance of obligations in legislative fields so far reserved to the states; and ratification would thus presumably extend federal powers at the expense of the states. Similarly, as we have noted, both the Covenant on Civil and Political Rights and the Convention on the Elimination of All Forms of Racial Discrimination include requirements going counter to traditional American conceptions of freedom of speech and press. Of course, it is impossible to prove that a different stand with regard to the question of ratifying covenants and conventions would have given the United States sufficient influence to get these instruments drafted differently; and, for that matter, a case can be made for the terms that the General Assembly approved. Still, if the retreat that Dulles made in 1953 had any effect it was surely to reduce the influence that the United States might otherwise have exerted. In a sense, of course, the Dulles policies were terminated by the decision of the Kennedy Administration to consider human rights treaties on their merits, but the meager and slow response of the Senate raises a question about the extent of the change.

The final theme that Richard N. Gardner advances is that "ratification will dissipate the embarrassing contradiction between our failure to ratify these conventions and our traditional support of the basic human rights with which they are concerned."[87] Ambassador Goldberg makes a similar point. He speaks of our traditional commitment to human rights and then takes the view that "we are not entirely faithful to this commitment when we show concern for human rights at home and yet appear indifferent to the same rights abroad." The result of the Dulles retreat, he says, "has been to confuse our friends, give ammunition to our enemies, and embarrass our country in the councils of the world."[88] He urges "a decent respect for the opinions of mankind. . . . Human rights is the great concern of the member states of the United Nations, and they have changed dramatically since Secretary Dulles filed his statement."[89] Morris B. Abram, when he represented the United States on the Human Rights Commission, likewise spoke of the "serious embarrassment to the conduct of our policy at the United Nations stemming from our failure to ratify these conventions."[90]

We might note incidentally that running through a number of the quotations given above is the idea that the natural and proper role for the United States is one of leadership, and that it is humiliating not to be the leader. Value attaches to leadership as such. President Truman declared in 1950 that "on us, as a nation, rests the responsibility of taking a position of leadership in the struggle for human rights."[91] With specific reference to the view that the United States should acknowledge human rights of an economic and social sort, Edgar Turlington once endorsed the principle, "There go my followers. I must lead them."

> It sometimes seems to me [he told Senator Bricker's committee] that our Government, in its desire to maintain its leadership in the field of economic and social relations, is obliged to do what it thinks is desired by those who must follow it.[92]

Congressman Dow came close to the same principle in urging appropriate action during Human Rights Year:

> Here we have a chance to formulate the keystone that our foreign policy needs; namely, a means whereby we can advance to the front of the column of those millions of people on this globe who are moving forward into a new era. . . . We above all nations ought to lead others.[93]

Ambassador Goldberg in 1967 declared that "it is only fitting that a country which has taken such great strides should play a leading role in the attempt to see human rights respected in all sectors of the globe."[94] And in the view of Morris B. Abram, "To be included—we who lay claim to the position of leadership of the free world—among states which have failed to participate in the principal means available to the world for developing international standards in the field of human rights, I submit, is a national embarrassment and indignity."[95]

The contention is frequently made that the promotion of human rights is a way of promoting peace. Quincy Wright is quoted above to this effect. In listing the requisites of peace, President Truman once gave second place to "common respect for basic human rights," and then went on to name a third requisite that also falls within the realm of human rights, "the free and full exchange of knowledge, ideas, and information among the peoples of the earth, and maximum freedom in international travel and communication."[96] He held that "the attainment of basic civil and political rights for men and women everywhere—without regard to race, language, or religion—is essential to the peace we are seeking."[97] Secretary of State Marshall expressed similar views in 1948.

> Systematic and deliberate denials of basic human rights lie at the root of most of our troubles and threaten the work of the United Nations. It is not only fundamentally wrong that millions of men and women live in daily terror of secret police, subject to seizure, imprisonment, or forced labor without just cause and without fair trial, but these wrongs have repercussions in the community of nations. Governments which systematically disregard the rights of their own people are not likely to respect the rights of other nations and other people and are likely to seek their objectives by coercion and force in the international field.[98]

As we will note more fully in a later chapter, more than two-thirds of the members of the General Assembly are pressing the view that racial discrimination is a threat to the peace, and in the case of Rhodesia the Security Council formally accepted that view, the United States concurring. Scholarly evidence is not such as to permit the addition of a Q.E.D. after clear-cut statements about the relationship between human rights and peace. Moreover, even if the judgments cited are correct, they do not necessarily call for the promotion of human rights through treaties; other means are available. But both the importance of the contention and its plausibility strengthen the challenge to the view that conventions are to be ruled out automatically.

## ALTERNATIVES TO CONVENTIONS

Though this chapter has been devoted to the question of accepting formal international obligations, other means of promoting human rights are available and are being used. The ILO adopts more recommendations than conventions (128 conventions and 131 recommendations through 1967). The General Assembly adopts declarations that, for the most part, are similar in import to ILO recommendations. Moreover, methods of implementation are relevant. They influence decisions concerning the acceptability of conventions, and they may promote observance of principles and obligations already accepted. It is to this general subject that the following two chapters are addressed.

# IV

# The Problem of Implementation

# 8

# The Problem of Implementation: Persuasion

The problem of implementation is the problem of seeing to it that human rights are in fact respected. In principle, the problem might be left to the good faith of individual states, to be solved by the legislative and other measures that they can take within the limits of their domestic jurisdiction; and, in truth, domestic measures are obviously necessary and crucial. But almost all states (the Soviet Union being the principal exception) take the view that international agencies must be involved, authorized to act in specified ways. The question concerns the agencies and the methods of action that are or might be employed.

We will attack this question first by identifying and briefly describing the existing international agencies that are involved in efforts to implement human rights.

Then, in a group of sections, we will ask about the kinds of activities in which these agencies engage. We will ask about educational activities and reporting systems. We will ask about permitting one government to complain about another's violations of human rights, and about staging international investigations; a major part of the chapter will be devoted to this subject, the sections focusing on one international agency after another. And we will ask about the right of petition.

Finally, we will describe and appraise proposals to establish new agencies of implementation: a High Commissioner for Human Rights, and international courts of human rights in addition to the European Court of Human Rights.

The question of the use of coercive methods of implementation is reserved for Chapter 9.

As a preliminary and general matter, we might note that the problem of implementation varies considerably depending on the kind of right and the kind of circumstances that are in question. The right of an accused person to be presumed innocent until proved guilty obviously differs in kind from his right to a high standard of physical and mental health; more generally, civil and political rights differ in kind from economic, social, and cultural rights, and the right to self-determination differs from all the others. Similarly, the problem of implementation varies greatly depending on the attitude of the government immediately responsible; it is one thing to seek implementation by helping a cooperative government and another thing to seek it by trying to persuade or coerce the uncooperative. Measures of implementation that may be highly suitable and effective in one kind of circumstance may be irrelevant or useless in another.

## EXISTING INTERNATIONAL AGENCIES

This is not the place to attempt a comprehensive description of existing international agencies that seek the implementation of human rights, but a brief listing is essential.

The United Nations is, of course, the principal organization involved. Within it the Security Council has "primary responsibility for the maintenance of international peace and security." In this connection it may "investigate any dispute, or any situation which might lead to international friction or give rise to a dispute." If it finds that peace is somehow endangered, e.g., by racial discrimination, it may take any of a number of possible actions under Chapter VI of the Charter, on "Pacific Settlement of Disputes." For example, it may condemn a state, or make recommendations either to an accused state or to others. If the Security Council finds a "threat to the peace," it may order the mandatory application of sanctions under Chapter VII. As we will note more fully in the next chapter, the Security Council has found that the situation in Rhodesia constitutes a threat to the peace because of the efforts of the whites, constituting about 4 per cent of the population, to keep the blacks in a position of permanent political inferiority. The Security Council confronts demands that it take comparable action against South Africa for its racism, and against Portugal for its denial of self-determination to colonial territories.

The General Assembly is much more fully engaged in promoting respect for human rights. As we noted at the beginning of Chapter 6, it may "discuss any questions or any matters within the scope of the present Charter." It may discuss and make recommendations concerning "any questions relating to international peace and security." It may "initiate studies and make recommendations for the purpose of . . . assisting in the realization of human rights and fundamental freedoms for all without distinction as to race, sex, language, or religion." These provisions do not authorize the General Assembly to order enforcement action against a recalcitrant state or to create new legal obligations; but short of such measures, the General Assembly is free to adopt any resolutions on human rights that two-thirds of the members will support.

The Economic and Social Council (ECOSOC) has comparable powers. According to Article 62, "it may make recommendations for the purpose of promoting respect for, and observance of human rights and fundamental freedoms," and it may prepare draft conventions pertaining to these rights and freedoms. Further, ECOSOC "may make arrangements with the Members of the United Nations and with the specialized agencies to obtain reports on the steps taken to give effect to its own recommendations and to recommendations falling within its competence made by the General Assembly," and it "may communicate its observations on these reports to the General Assembly." Moreover, Article 68 of the Charter requires ECOSOC to "set up commissions in economic and social fields and for the promotion of human rights." Again, as in the case of the General Assembly, what ECOSOC can do (short of ordering enforcement action or creating new legal obligations) depends on the will of the members.

For our purposes the principal commission set up by ECOSOC is the Commission on Human Rights. It consists of the representatives of thirty-two states elected by ECOSOC for three-year terms; eight of the member states come from Africa, six from Asia, six from Latin America, four from Eastern Europe, and eight from Western Europe and other areas.[1] Subordinate to ECOSOC, the Commission must operate not only within ECOSOC's own limits but also within any others that ECOSOC chooses to impose; among them is a requirement that sessions, which occur once a year, shall last no longer than six weeks. But the terms of reference of the Commission are very broad, permitting it, within the limits mentioned, to do what the members choose. As we will note more fully below, they decided in 1947 not to take "any action in regard to any complaints concerning human rights"; in other words, they decided not to consider specific cases of alleged violations of human rights, but to confine themselves to general studies and recommendations. The activities of the Commission are described below, together with signs that the 1947 rule is being modified.

Various other UN agencies are also active in rather specific spheres. In addition to the Commission on Human Rights, ECOSOC in 1946 established a Commission on the Status of Women. The Commission on Human Rights itself established in 1947 a Sub-Commission on Prevention of Discrimination and Protection of Minorities. The General Assembly established the Office of the High Commissioner for Refugees, its activities beginning in 1951. At various times, too, the General Assembly and other agencies have established special committees or commissions concerned with human rights. The two now most active are the Committee of Twenty-Four (the Special Committee on the Situation with Regard to the Implementation of the Declaration on the Granting of Independence to Colonial Countries and Peoples), established in 1960, and the Special Committee on the Policies of Apartheid of the Government of the Republic of South Africa, established in 1962. The Charter itself provides for the existence of the Trusteeship Council, which, among other things, is "to encourage respect for human rights and fundamental freedoms . . ." in the trust territories with which it is concerned.

It goes without saying that several parts of the UN Secretariat are deeply involved in the problem of implementation as well as in other problems in the field of human rights.

Various specialized agencies also concern themselves with human rights. Most noteworthy among them for our purposes is the International Labor Organization. Its principal organs, apart from the International Labor Office, are a General Conference, to which all members send four voting delegates—two representing the government and the other two representing workers and employers, respectively—and a Governing Body of 48 persons representing governments, workers, and employers in a ratio of 24-12-12. In international organizations, the presence of non-governmental voting delegates is distinctive to the ILO, and has demonstrably made a difference in the efforts of the ILO to promote the implementation of human rights. Under the Governing Body is a Committee of Experts on the Application of Conventions and Recommendations, a Committee on Freedom of Association, and a Fact-Finding and Conciliation Commission on Freedom of Association; in addition, special committees or commissions are appointed from time to time. We will note the functions of these various agencies below.

Regional arrangements for the implementation of human rights exist both in Europe and among the American republics. The European Convention on Human Rights, developed under the aegis of the Council of Europe with its Consultative Assembly and Committee of Ministers, provides for both a European Commission and a European Court of Human Rights; they are to "ensure the observance of the engagements undertaken by the High Contracting Parties." Members of the Commission serve in their individual capacities, though they are elected by the Committee of Ministers. The same is true, of course, of the members of the Court (who, however, are elected by the Consultative Assembly). Each body has the same number of members as the Council of Europe itself (18), and no two members can come from the same state.

The American republics, more inclined toward declarations of general principle than toward international legal commitments in the field of human rights, have been relatively bolder in developing methods of implementation. In 1960 the Council of the OAS elected an Inter-American Commission on Human Rights, consisting of seven persons who "represent all the member countries of the OAS and act in its name." Nominally, at least, its terms of reference at first limited it to the kinds of activities pursued by the United Nations Commission on Human Rights; that is, they did not include a right to act on complaints of specific violations of human rights.[2] But the Commission strained at its leash. It resolved that its right to make recommendations to governments in general included a right to make general recommendations to an individual government.[3] It interpreted its terms of reference to give it, after all, the authority to act on specific complaints.[4] It recommended that its functions be formally expanded—and the Second Special Inter-American Conference acquiesced in 1965, authorizing it "to examine communications submitted to it and any other available information, to address to the government of any American state a request for information deemed pertinent by the Commission, and to make recommendations, when it deems this appropriate, with the objective of bringing about more effective observance of fundamental human rights."[5] We will note more fully below the surprising activities of this Commission.

## EDUCATIONAL METHODS OF IMPLEMENTATION

In the effort to see to it that human rights are in fact respected, educational methods are used, as might be expected, and involve no great problem of a political sort. Their effectiveness is difficult to measure.

The United States gave special emphasis to educational methods after the reversal of policy forced by Senator Bricker in 1953. Compelled virtually to withdraw from the main stream of action in the UN Commission on Human Rights, the United States proposed what it called an "action program," including studies of specific aspects of human rights, the holding of "seminars" (conferences), the extension of advisory services to governments requesting them, and the offer of training fellowships. The "action program" also called for periodic reports from member governments on progress achieved—a subject to be discussed below.

In practice, little demand developed for the proffered advisory services, and few training fellowships were offered.[6] Numerous "seminars" have, however, been held under the joint sponsorship of the United Nations and the government of a host country, for example, "seminars" on criminal procedure, on habeas corpus, on the status of women in family law, on freedom of information, on the rights of the child, on the rights of the police, on apartheid, on the realization of economic and social rights, on human rights in developing countries. Similarly, numerous studies have been made, whether on behalf of the United Nations or one of the specialized agencies, for example, a study of slavery, a study of discrimination in the matter of political rights, a study of discrimination in education. But the studies themselves are superficial. The rule is that they must reflect only the information that governments supply and that they must be "general" and "objective." In other words, nothing is to be included that a government finds offensive. For that matter, the sensitivities of governments are at least as important as the inherent significance of the subject in determining whether the study is to be made at all. Moses Moskowitz points out that the studies so far made were not a part of a coherent program with clear ends. And he comments that "it made little sense to engage in studies of discrimination when governments denied human rights indiscriminately."[7]

The Inter-American Commission on Human Rights has issued a number of studies of a vastly different sort from those of the UN Commission, giving detailed accounts and appraisals of the situation with regard to human rights in specific countries. They will be dealt with below.

### REPORTING SYSTEMS

Reports and reporting systems vary. Reports can range from the exhaustive and specific to the brief and general, and from the frank and candid to the carefully contrived. The agency receiving a report can file and forget it, or can go over it with various degrees of care, perhaps asking for additional information and possibly making critical comments. In a fully developed supervisory system, a report may simply be the first step in an exhaustive investigation in which, in effect, a government goes on trial.

The reporting system developed in the UN as a part of the "action program" that the United States proposed in 1953 is of the superficial sort. There was little enthusiasm for it, an earlier reporting system having been allowed to lapse. The Soviet delegate thought that reports on what he considered domestic matters might lead to a violation of Article 2 (7), that is, to intervention in matters within the domestic jurisdiction of states. The Chilean delegate objected especially to the possibility that the Commission on Human Rights might comment on the reports received. He believed that the Commission "should avoid direct criticism of States. No one wanted the Commission to become a kind of tribunal. Tensions and conflicts caused by the play of political forces must be avoided at all costs in the field of human rights."[8] Since the reporting system was to be based on a recommendation and would not be obligatory, it was clear that some states would simply fail to act. Their silence might condemn them in some sense but the penalty would be light. At the other extreme, any state that reported fully and frankly might expose itself to criticism and to invidious comparison.

Despite objections and doubts, however, the Commission on Human Rights adopted the American proposal. The United States itself denied any thought that through the reports states would be held internationally accountable.[9] And the Commission adopted the principle that any comments, conclusions, or recommendations that it made would be "objective" and "general." Individual governments would not be criticized by the Commission itself, whatever these governments might choose to say about each other in the UN or elsewhere.[10]

The reporting system remains in operation, with problematical results. Great sensitivity about sovereignty and about avoiding official accountability is evident. In 1962 ECOSOC invited non-governmental organizations in consultative status to submit comments and observations relating to the observance of human rights. It specified that they must be "objective" in character. When some of them came to be considered, however, spokesmen for Iraq, Saudi Arabia, and the United Arab Republic denounced them as biased and slanderous, and a reporter's summary was "withdrawn."[11] The official view of the Commission on Human Rights is that the reporting system "is not only a source of information, but also a valuable incentive to Governments' efforts to protect human rights and fundamental freedoms and the implementation of the Universal Declaration of Human Rights."[12] A contrary view, attributed to one delegation on the Commission, is that the system "served no useful purpose. The appeals for reports were being ignored by the vast majority of Member States; and such reports as were being received created a misleading picture of almost exclusively positive developments. . . ."[13]

A much greater degree of international accountability is insisted upon and accepted in connection with trust and non-self-governing territories. Reports by the administering powers, including materials pertaining to human rights, are regular features of the systems. But the Trusteeship Council and the Committee of Twenty-Four also obtain information in other ways—e.g. through petitions and hearings and sometimes through actual visits to the territories involved. It is thus more suitable to consider the matter under the heading "Complaints and Investigations," below.

The ILO has a reporting system that differs vastly from that of the UN Commission on Human Rights. The constitution of the organization requires members to report on all conventions and recommendations that the ILO adopts—biennial reports now being the rule. If a member has ratified a given convention, it is to report the measures which it has taken to meet obligations assumed. Even if it has not ratified, it must still submit a report—a report on the position of its law and practice in regard to the matters dealt with and on the difficulties which prevent or delay ratification. Reports concerning recommendations are to be similar to those concerning unratified conventions; they are to "show the extent to which effect has been given, or is proposed to be given, to the provisions of the recommendation and such modifications of these provisions as it has been found or may be found necessary to make in adopting or applying them." A government's report goes not only to the ILO but also, within the country, to representative organizations of workers and employers; and these organizations, as well as other private organizations, are invited to submit observations which the government is bound to forward to the ILO along with any comments it cares to make. Within the ILO the reports and any observations made on them go to a Committee of Experts on the Application of Conventions and Recommendations, consisting of persons selected for their technical competence; they do not represent governments. The Committee may request additional information from governments, or seek it from any other source; on-the-spot investigations for the purpose of checking on implementation are barred, though missions that the ILO sends out for other purposes may incidentally collect relevant information.[14]

For whatever reason, the proportion of members submitting reports is far higher in the ILO than in the UN. Over the years, some 83 per cent of the expected reports have been received by the time of the meeting of the Committee of Experts, and others have come in later.[15] In fact, the problem in the ILO is not so much to induce governments to report as to get them to report on time; and then, within the ILO, the problem is to handle the flood of material in an effective way.

Consideration of the reports by the Committee of Experts leads to the adoption of observations for the benefit of the General Conference, including observations that criticize governments by name. As noted above, half the members of the General Conference represent governments and the other half represent workers and employers respectively. Focusing on this arena, E. A. Landy, in a very impressive appraisal of the experience of the ILO with international supervision, speaks of "the reluctance of governments to participate actively in supervising other governments." But the governments do not block action. Rather, they simply "leave the main burden of mutual supervision to the workers and employers." As Landy puts it, "the whole system depends on the active interest of the non-governmental groups."[16] In the thirty-year period on which Landy focuses, ending in 1964, the Committee of Experts and the corresponding committee of the General Conference examined the question of implementation in connection with 3422 ratifications. In 72 per cent of the cases measures of implementation were found to be satisfactory. In the remaining cases, "operative observations" were made, calling for governmental action. Of the operative observations, according to Landy, 32 per cent led to "full action, either directly or by stages," 29 per cent led to "partial action," 2 per cent led the government involved to denounce the relevant convention, and 37 per cent had had no apparent effect at the time he completed his tabulation.[17] Official reports speak of the "large measure of cooperation from governments. . . . Significant progress is noted each year. In 1964 and 1965 alone, more than 102 cases of progress . . . relating to 71 countries . . . were noted with satisfaction by the Committee of Experts."[18] C. Wilfred Jenks considers the ILO arrangements for supervision "highly effective,"[19] and Ernst B. Haas describes the ILO record as one "of which any international agency can be intensely proud."[20] It is noteworthy, too, that, despite a few denunciations, the supervisory system has apparently not deterred states from ratifying ILO conventions.

> Over a period when the technical and mutual examination procedures have noticeably gained in strictness, the rate of ratification has accelerated rather than slowed down. It is obvious, then, that governments have not refrained from assuming additional obligations because they thereby subjected themselves to international scrutiny and perhaps to criticism.[21]

The European Social Charter provides for a reporting system patterned more or less after the ILO system. The principal difference, at least in terms of the formal arrangements, relates to the part of the process that comes after the work of the Committee of Experts. In place of the Conference Committee of the ILO, in which workers' and employers' delegates play a major role, there is a committee on which only governments are represented; delegates of workers and employers participate, but only in a consultative capacity. Similarly, the ILO model has influenced the reporting systems set up in connection with the European Code of Social Security and in connection with UNESCO's Convention Against Discrimination in Education.

The human rights covenants call for reports. The Covenant on Civil and Political Rights specifies that ratifying states are to elect a Human Rights Committee of eighteen members. One of the functions of the Committee is the consideration of the reports that the parties are periodically to submit. The Committee is then to make its own report, including "such general comments as it may consider appropriate." The Covenant on Economic, Social, and Cultural Rights also calls for reports, which are to be considered not by a Human Rights Committee but rather by ECOSOC, which may transmit them to the Commission on Human Rights "for study and general recommendation or, as appropriate, for information. . . ." In both instances the language is much more suggestive of practices under the "action program" than of practices in the ILO.

Similarly the International Convention on the Elimination of All Forms of Racial Discrimination, adopted by the General Assembly in 1965, calls for reports. They are to go to a Committee on the Elimination of Racial Discrimination, elected by states' parties to the convention. On the basis of a government's own reports—and not on the basis of information received from any other source—the Committee is to be authorized to make "suggestions and general recommendations" to that government.[22]

In 1966 the Inter-American Commission on Human Rights decided to make annual reports from members of the OAS a regular feature of its work. Members are to report on the measures that they have adopted to adjust their laws to the principles of the American Declaration of the Rights and Duties of Man and the Universal Declaration of Human Rights.[23]

## GOVERMENTAL COMPLAINTS AND INTERNATIONAL INVESTIGATIONS

Under existing and proposed arrangements, a complaint may be the first step in the process of international supervision—an accusation by a government that another government is not living up to its obligations. The question is whether the international agency to which (or in which) the complaint is made has the authority to act on it.

### *Complaints and Investigations: The Principal UN Organs*

Obviously the General Assembly, the Security Council, and ECOSOC are authorized to take action when complaints are made. Numerous resolutions concerning racial discrimination and colonialism in southern Africa illustrate the fact. So does the investigation that ECOSOC and the ILO launched in the early 1950's concerning the use of forced labor in the world—an investigation designed particularly to expose and give publicity to forced labor practices in the Soviet Union. Also illustrating General Assembly activity is the work of the Special Committee on the Problem of Hungary, established after the suppression of the Hungarian uprising in 1956; the report of this committee led to a finding by the General Assembly "that the USSR . . . has deprived the Hungarian people of the exercise of their fundamental human rights," and that "the present authorities in Hungary have violated the human rights and freedoms guaranteed by the Treaty of Peace with Hungary."[24] Noteworthy, too, is the mission that the General Assembly sent to Vietnam, on the invitation of the Diem government, to investigate complaints concerning the treatment of Buddhists; among other things, the General Assembly authorized the mission to receive petitions and hold hearings. The overthrow of Diem led to a decision in the General Assembly against taking any action on the report that the mission made.[25]

The jurisdiction of the International Court of Justice extends in principle to legal disputes between states over alleged violations of international obligations, including those in the field of human rights. Issues in this field came up in the South-West Africa cases, but were left unresolved when the court dismissed the cases on procedural grounds.

*Complaints and Investigations: The UN Commission on Human Rights*

The right of the UN Commission on Human Rights to entertain complaints against governments, or itself to initiate action critical of a specific government, is not so clear-cut. In 1946 the Commission looked toward the assumption of such a right. It took the view that the purposes of the UN "could only be fulfilled if provisions were made for the implementation of the observance of human rights," and it suggested that pending the establishment of an agency of implementation it might itself point to cases where the violation of human rights constituted a threat to the peace.[26] Not many months later, however, the Commission reversed itself; it "recognized" that it had "no power to take any action in regard to any complaints concerning human rights,"[27] and ECOSOC later approved. The decision related both to possible complaints by one government against another and to complaints emanating from private persons and organizations. The decision was a matter of choice, not of legal necessity, for the Charter and the terms of reference of the Commission could readily have been interpreted to permit it to consider and act on complaints.[28]

Steps have occurred in recent years away from the stand of 1947, the impetus coming mainly from African states preoccupied with the problems of racial discrimination and colonialism in southern Africa.[29] Disappointed that a number of countries, including the United States, declined membership in the Special Committee on Apartheid, they seek to enlist the Commission on Human Rights in the struggle. In so doing they enlarge the involvement not only of the United Nations as an organization but also of individual members, such as the United States. But other states, again including the United States, do not like to abandon the 1947 stand solely for the purpose of dealing with problems in southern Africa. Whether out of genuine concern for human rights elsewhere or in order to cool the campaign against South Africa by pointing to the potential ramifications of international action on human rights, they cite problems in other parts of the world as well.

Various resolutions relate to the above. In 1966 the General Assembly invited ECOSOC and the Commission on Human Rights "to give urgent consideration to ways and means of improving the capacity of the United Nations to put a stop to violations of human rights wherever they might occur."[30] ECOSOC had in fact already asked the Commission to prepare recommendations on this problem, "including policies of racial discrimination and segregation and of apartheid in all countries,"[31] and the Commission in turn had invoked the aid of the Sub-Commission on Prevention of Discrimination and Protection of Minorities. Later the Commission also invited the Sub-Commission to bring to its attention "any situation which it has reasonable cause to believe reveals a consistent pattern of violations of human rights and fundamental freedoms, in any country, including policies of racial discrimination, segregation and apartheid, with particular reference to colonial and other dependent territories,"[32] and it established an Ad Hoc Working Group of Experts to investigate charges of torture and ill-treatment of prisoners in South Africa, authorizing it to "receive communications and hear witnesses and use such modalities of procedure as it may deem appropriate."[33]

The resolutions are not clear-cut on the question whether the Commission on Human Rights is prepared actually to concern itself with violations "wherever they might occur" and "in all countries." The question was put to the test when complaints were made concerning not only South Africa and Rhodesia but also Burundi, Israel, Greece, and Haiti.

No problem arose about the principle that the Commission might direct criticisms against South Africa and Rhodesia by name, and it has begun to do so in terms similiar to those used by ECOSOC and the General Assembly.[34]

It was another matter, however, to condemn governments outside southern Africa. Burundi came up for consideration because of the action of the ILO. In considering allegations that trade union rights were being violated there (e.g. by the execution of trade union leaders without trial), the

Governing Body of the ILO concluded that a question should be raised of violations of other categories of rights, and proposed that the matter be put on the agenda of the UN Commission on Human Rights.[35] The issue was not whether to condemn or criticize Burundi but whether to allow for the possibility by putting the item on the agenda. An observer from Burundi objected, indicating, however, that his government was willing to hold thorough discussions with the ILO on the matter. Given this assurance, the ILO representative "did not press for the inclusion of the proposed item" on the agenda, and it was not included.[36]

As for Israel, the question concerned the fate of those who fled from territory that it occupied as a result of the June 1967 war. In effect, the decision went against Israel, though it was not named. The Commission affirmed that the refugees had a right to return and that "the Government concerned" should take the necessary measures to facilitate the return. In 1968 the General Assembly itself established a special committee of three member states to "investigate Israeli practices affecting the human rights of the population of the occupied territories."[37]

Greece and Haiti went scot free. In a formal sense, the issue was whether "gross violations" and "consistent patterns of violations" existed in these countries. But the issue was also whether the Commission on Human Rights should concern itself with the implementation of its principles everywhere or only in southern Africa and, perhaps, Israel. The Sub-Commission on Prevention of Discrimination and Protection of Minorities, composed of experts who do not represent governments, had found "particularly glaring examples of situations which reveal consistent patterns of violations of human rights" in both Greece and Haiti, and sought authority to investigate these situations further.[38] When the matter came to the Commission on Human Rights a split developed. The United States, which wanted the Commission to "consider violations of human rights and fundamental freedoms in all countries," sought a compromise, conceding implicitly that sufficient information had not been presented to justify a recommendation but requesting the two governments to make additional information available. These governments objected. Haiti characterized the reports about it as unjustified and slanderous, and anyway it held that action by the Commission would violate Article 2(7) of the Charter. Greece held that temporary derogations from its obligations concerning human rights were justified by its emergency situation (a military group having staged a coup d'état in 1967), and that human rights were gradually being restored. Spokesmen for Nigeria and Tanzania took the part of Greece and Haiti. If the Commission were to act on the situation in Greece and Haiti, said the delegate from Nigeria, "there was nothing to prevent it from taking a similar action with regard to any other member State." If communications concerning Greece and Haiti "were felt to be an adequate basis for discussing the situation in Greece, the two or three hundred communications relating to eastern European countries should in all fairness be treated in the same way." Anyway, according to the Nigerian delegate, no evidence existed of "gross" violations in Haiti, and the military government in Greece had not been in existence long enough (ten months) to establish a "consistent pattern" of violations.[39] Similarly, the Tanzanian delegate and others made it clear that they wanted to differentiate sharply between the kinds of violations "exemplified" in southern Africa and the kinds that occurred elsewhere.[40] The Soviet delegate shared the Tanzanian view, asserting that "the Commission had never been asked, and could not be asked, to consider violations of human rights and fundamental freedoms 'in all countries,' without any qualification."[41] An impasse thus occurred, and no action could be taken. South Africa could be condemned, but Greece and Haiti could not even be asked to supply additional information.

Potentially contradictory developments ensued, giving further evidence of struggle over the question whether, in connection with the problem of promoting the implementation of human rights, the UN will confine itself substantially to violations that occur in southern Africa. On the one hand, the Commission on Human Rights asked for an increase in the size of the Sub-Commission on Prevention of Discrimination and Protection of Minorities in the name of "equitable geographical representation," which means increased Afro-Asian representation; and this in turn will accentuate tendencies to focus on southern Africa and to ignore violations in other parts of the world.[42] On the other hand, when the Sub-Commission met in October 1968, it set up a working group to sift, prior to its next meeting, communications received by the UN relating to violations of human rights, with a view to calling the attention of the Sub-Commission to communications disclosing consistent patterns of gross violations. Moreover, the Sub-Commission requested the Commission on Human Rights and ECOSOC to authorize and give enduring basis for what it proposed to do.[43] The future role of the Commission and Sub-Commission with regard to implementation is thus uncertain.

*Complaints and Investigations: The International Labor Organization*

The ILO has gone much farther than the UN toward making international supervision a matter of routine, but its record is varied. Not much in fact is done on the basis of specific complaints that a convention has been violated, but a good deal is done (quite apart from the question of a violation of any convention) in the field of freedom for trade unions.

According to the ILO constitution, in case the violation of a convention is at issue, associations of employers or workers may make a representation and when this happens the Governing Body of the ILO may invite the accused government to comment and may give publicity to the materials involved. Only nine such representations have ever been made.

The constitution also permits a government to complain about the alleged violation of a convention on the part of another government, and in the fifty-year history of the ILO this has happened twice. In 1961 Ghana complained that Portugal was not observing the Abolition of Forced Labor Convention in several of its African colonies, and shortly thereafter Portugal made a comparable complaint against Liberia. In both cases, the Governing Body appointed a Commission of Inquiry, and both of the accused governments cooperated, e.g. by allowing the Commissions of Inquiry to conduct investigations in their territory. The Commission that went into the Portuguese colonies noted in its report that Portugal had adopted some reforms following Ghana's complaint, and it asked for additional reforms. The Commission that went to Liberia found bases for relatively extensive recommendations, to which Liberia meekly acquiesced.[44]

These episodes are worth noting. They illustrate the possibility of international supervision of an acceptable sort. But the rarity of action under the constitutional articles in question is also worth noting. It reinforces a point made above: that, far from looking for ways to embarrass each other through international supervisory agencies, governments shy away from developing and using them. At the same time, the desire to embarrass another government—or at least to serve ulterior political purposes—no doubt played a significant role in inducing Ghana and Portugal to lodge their complaints.

The ILO is much more active in the restricted area of freedom of association. In 1950 the Governing Body set up a Committee on Freedom of Association, authorizing it to take up complaints on this subject presented either by governments or by workers' or employers' organizations. Included are complaints by these organizations against their own government. Moreover, the complaints are entertained whether or not the accused government has ratified any of the conventions on the subject. According to the ILO's count, the Committee had examined over 500 complaints by 1967. Ernst Haas's analysis shows that, down to 1963, 20 per cent of the cases led to a recommendation to the accused government to change its law or practice.[45] Two of the cases went on from the Committee on Freedom of Association to a joint UN-ILO Fact-Finding and Conciliation Commission on Freedom of Association, though one of the two (concerning Greece) was withdrawn by agreement between the parties involved.[46] The other case concerned Japan, which consented to what became an extensive investigation, occurring in part in Japan; and the upshot was an extensive report, calling for various changes in Japanese law and practice.[47] The significant point is that Japan accepted the propriety of international supervision, and added to its formal international obligations in the field by ratifying the ILO's Freedom of Association and the Right to Organize Convention 1948.

### *Complaints and Investigations: The Inter-American Commission on Human Rights*

The Inter-American Commission on Human Rights has perhaps the most striking record in connection with action on complaints and the making of investigations. As noted in part above, its terms of reference give it wide latitude. It is free to examine communications from any source, to prepare studies and reports, to request governments to supply information, and to make recommendations. With the consent of the government concerned, it is free to hold its meetings in any of the American republics and to make the meetings an occasion for on-the-spot observation as well as for the holding of hearings and the receipt of petitions. A change in its terms of reference made in 1965 calls for the submission—either to the Inter-American Conference or to a Meeting of Consultation of Ministers of Foreign Affairs—of an annual report describing progress achieved, identifying areas in which further steps are needed, and making any other observations it considers appropriate.

In comparison with the UN Commission on Human Rights, the Inter-American Commission has been bold in using its powers. In fact, from the first it fought for an extension of those powers, and began acting pretty much as if the desired extension had in fact been made; and when it was made, it amounted to an authorization to the Commission to continue the practices it was already following.[48] Its most spectacular activities have pertained to the Dominican Republic. With the consent of the government, the Commission visited or held meetings in the Dominican Republic in 1961 and 1963, and it maintained a "continuous presence" there for a number of months in 1955-56. (The Inter-American Peace Committee had similarly visited the country in 1959, but was denied permission to make a second visit in 1960 on the ground that this would mean a "serious intervention" in its domestic jurisdiction.)[49] Occurring after the overthrow of Trujillo, the 1961 and 1963 visits included interviews with high officials, hearings at which spokesmen for local groups could voice their complaints, and travel within the Dominican Republic. They led to notes to the government calling its attention to violations of human rights, and to the issuance of open reports. Members of the Commission also visited the Dominican Republic as individuals in 1962 to attend a Symposium on Representative Democracy scheduled so as to span the day on which national elections were held.[50] In the crisis of 1965 two governments contended for power in the Dominican Republic, and the United States intervened. Both of the governments requested the presence and activity of the Commission, making formal pledges to respect the principles set forth in the American Declaration of the Rights and Duties of Man and promising to facilitate the work of the Commission. It dealt officially with both governments, regardless of the question which one was entitled to represent the state.[51] By September 1965, when the Provisional Government assumed power, the Commission "had handled more than 1500 complaints of persons imprisoned for political reasons and more than 200 specific charges affecting, directly or indirectly, the right to life. On the eve of the inauguration of that Government, the Commission succeeded in obtaining the release of all the political prisoners remaining in Dominican jails."[52] The establishment of the Provisional Government was based, among other things, on another formal pledge to respect human rights (including a pledge to hold free elections) and on an undertaking "to cooperate with the Commission to enable it to observe compliance" with the pledge.[53] As Durward V. Sandifer rightly says, the role of the Commission during the Dominican crisis was far more extensive than its creators had anticipated. Members and agents of the Commission ranged over the country, checking insofar as they could into reports of violations of human rights. The mission was not simply to observe but "to help bring an end to the excesses and violations." Rarely if ever has an international agency exercised so close a supervisory role in day-to-day developments in the field of human rights.

The Dominican case is unique, and thus does not go far toward testing either the capacities of the Commission or the willingness of the American republics to accept its efforts to promote and protect human rights in their territories. Still, activities occur in connection with other countries. The Commission has been probing persistently into the situation with respect to human rights in Haiti and Cuba, undeterred by the refusal of the governments of those countries to permit meetings of the Commission to occur on their territory. It has obtained information as it could (e.g. by holding hearings in Miami concerning Cuba), has used requests for information (e.g. about the fate of individuals who had disappeared in Haiti) as a means of emphasizing its concern, and has published detailed studies and reports.[54] It requested but was denied permission to meet in Nicaragua during the period of an electoral campaign. At one time or another since 1962, Bolivia, Costa Rica, and Honduras have all requested services connected with elections—either technical assistance of some sort or the sending of observers to witness elections. Both Ecuador and Honduras have invited visits by the Commission. In connection with allegations that human rights have been violated, the Commission has requested information from a number of governments, e.g. from Bolivia, Colombia, Ecuador, Guatemala, Paraguay, and the United States,[55] and it has been reasonably successful in obtaining responses. Given the very special sensitivity of the Latin American countries on the question of intervention, and given the magnitude of the changes that would be required for the full implementation of human rights, rapid progress is not to be expected.

### *Complaints and Investigations: The European Commission of Human Rights*

The European Convention on Human Rights permits both inter-governmental complaints about violations and, in certain circumstances, complaints or petitions by private persons or organizations. Four governmental complaints have been made since the European Commission of Human Rights was established in 1954. Greece made two of them in 1957 against Britain, Austria made one in 1960 against Italy, and a group of members of the Council of Europe made one against Greece in 1967.

Greece acted on behalf of Greeks on Cyprus, where Britain had declared, under Article 15 of the Convention, that an emergency situation existed justifying derogations from its obligations. Greece denied this claim, and the European Commission confirmed a principle already established by the European Court of Human Rights that such claims were subject to international review. Britain accepted the jurisdiction of the Commission, pleading its case and permitting on-the-spot investigations in Cyprus. While the Commission was still considering the matter, Britain and Greece came to agreement on the future status of Cyprus, and by common consent the Commission decided to take no further action.[56]

Austria acted on behalf of German-speaking inhabitants of South Tyrol, alleging that Italy had not given them a fair trial in a murder case. Italy, like Britain, acquiesced in and assisted the inquiry that the Commission of Human Rights inaugurated. The inquiry led the Commission to exonerate Italy, and the Council of Ministers endorsed the ruling.[57]

In the above cases, the complaining state was acting on behalf of ethnic elements in which it had a special interest. The complaint of 1967 against Greece is therefore distinctive in that it reflects a disinterested effort to secure respect for the European Convention. The problem of Greece has been mentioned above, in connection with the discussion of the UN Commission on Human Rights. A military group seized power and openly suspended various human rights, claiming (as Britain had with regard to Cyprus) that its action was justifiable under Article 15 of the convention. This others denied. In less than a month after the coup d'état the European Parliament—an agency of the six states of the Common Market—adopted a resolution referring to the fact that Greece had taken a step toward joining the Common Market by becoming an associated state. The Parliament indicated that it was profoundly disturbed by the suspension of democratic and parliamentary life in Greece and declared that the agreement relating to Greece's association with the Common Market could be applied only if democracy, political liberty, and trade union freedom were restored; and it emphasized the importance of respect on the part of Greece for its obligations under the European Convention on Human Rights.[58] Soon thereafter the Consultative Assembly of the Council of Europe also expressed its grave concern "at the many serious reputed violations of human rights and fundamental freedoms" and recommended that parties to the European Convention on Human Rights should file a complaint with the European Commission.[59] Denmark, Norway, Sweden, and the Netherlands did so, asserting that the military government in Greece was violating various obligations in the field of human rights and denying that the circumstances justified a derogation from those obligations, as Greece claimed; and the European Commission in February 1968 found the complaint admissible.[60] Meantime the Consultative Assembly resumed its own consideration of the problem, condemning the violation of normal constitutional procedures in Greece and deciding "to recommend to the Committee of Ministers, at the latest in the spring of 1969, the suspension or expulsion of Greece from the Council of Europe if by then an acceptable parliamentary democracy has not been restored."[61]

### *Complaints and Investigations: The Committee on the Elimination of Racial Discrimination*

The International Convention on the Elimination of All Forms of Racial Discrimination provides for the establishment of an implementing Committee authorized to receive complaints from one party about alleged violations of another. Given such a complaint, a series of steps may then occur. The Committee is to transmit the complaint to the accused state for explanation and comment. Failing a satisfactory response, and given the exhaustion of all relevant domestic remedies, the matter may then go to an *ad hoc* Conciliation Commission, which will strive for a friendly settlement between the complaining state and the accused. The Conciliation Commission is to make a report which, in the absence of friendly settlement, may contain findings of fact and recommendations. The parties then have three months within which to state whether they accept the recommendations, it being left uncertain what the consequences of a rejection would be.[62]

The above review indicates that intergovernmental complaints have been scattered and sporadic and thus suggests that, however useful they may on occasion be, they are not reliable as means of bringing about the implementation of human rights. ILO activities on behalf of freedom for trade unions have become more or less routine, involving no great crisis; but governments rarely initiate or lead in action against other governments. In connection with racism in South Africa, and colonialism anywhere, governmental complaints are common. But for promoting the realization of human rights in other areas, the lodging of governmental complaints and the staging of international investigations are from from routine. Despite the accusations against Greece in 1967, the overwhelming emphasis is still on sovereignty and the rights of domestic jurisdiction.

## PETITIONS

On the same day that the General Assembly adopted the Universal Declaration of Human Rights it also adopted a resolution concerning the right of petition: "Considering that the right of petition is an essential human right, as is recognized in the constitutions of a great number of countries," the General Assembly "decides not to take any action on this matter at the present session." Ambivalence on the problem persists. On the one hand, the view is quite widely accepted that, to be fully effective, a system for assuring human rights must include a right of aggrieved individuals to petition to an international agency for redress against their own government. On the other hand, governments are extremely reluctant to accept this kind of international supervision.

The so-called "right of petition" has varied meanings. In its most elementary form (and in the context of the problem of international action concerning human rights), it refers simply to a right to communicate—a right to give information; the agency receiving the information may or may not give it consideration, and may or may not take any other action. It must, however, be authorized to consider communications from private parties, else no right of petition would exist. In a more meaningful form, the "right of petition" is a right to seize an international agency of a matter—that is, a right to obtain consideration and to expect that action of some kind will occur. Petitions must, of course, meet certain qualifications. For example, they must not be trivial, and they must relate to a right that the international agency is authorized to protect. It is a common view that petitions are not suitable as a means of promoting the implementation of economic and social rights. The international agency that hears petitions may be political, quasi-judicial, or judicial. It may exist solely to handle petitions, or it may have other functions as well. To obtain justice for an aggrieved petitioner, it may have to rely entirely on publicity, moral authority, and the arts of persuasion, or it may be able to render a judgment that is binding on the accused government. It may or may not be a part of the requirement that domestic remedies shall be exhausted prior to the appeal to an international agency. In its strongest form, the right of petition does not depend on a prior exhaustion of local remedies, and it involves appeal to an international agency (presumably a court) that is obliged to consider the matter and is authorized to make a binding decision.

Precedents exist for an international right of petition prior to World War II.[63] In connection with the implementation of the minorities treaties imposed on some of the European states after World War I, the Council of the League of Nations accepted petitions as sources of information—and then might or might not take action concerning them. A convention concluded between Germany and Poland in 1922 concerning Upper Silesia gave the right of petition a much stronger form; it gave individuals a right to expect that an especially created Mixed Commission would act on their petitions, and it permitted them to petition the Council of the League of Nations either directly or via the Mixed Commission, the Council also being obliged to act. And the mandates' system of the League of Nations included a right of petition—inhabitants of the mandated territories being free to direct petitions to the League (and thus to the Permanent Mandates Commission) via the government of the mandatory power.

As the quotation at the beginning of this section suggests, debate about the right of petition began in the United Nations when the Universal Declaration was being formulated, and the debate has gone on intermittently ever since. At an early point the Commission on Human Rights set up a Working Group on Implementation, and it is said to have found no difficulty in reaching agreement in 1947 on the principle that "the right to petition in respect of the violation of human rights shall be open not only to States, but also to associations, individuals, and groups."[64] The French delegate took the view that "in questions concerning human rights it is morally impossible to declare petitions *a priori* inadmissible unless they are sponsored by a State,"[65] and he proposed the creation of an International Bureau of Human Rights, authorized (among other things) to consider petitions submitted by individuals either directly or through a non-governmental organization. In 1949, when the Commission on Human Rights was at an early stage in drafting a Covenant, the members divided about equally on the question of including a right of individual petition to an international agency.[66] Both the United States and the Soviet Union were in the negative. From the Soviet point of view, to provide for the right of individual petition would be to violate sovereignty. The attitude of the United States was more temporizing: it was that "for the time being" complaints should be handled only when "sufficiently important to be brought to the Commission by States."[67] Even before the activities of Senator Bricker began, the United States thought it essential that the provisions of the proposed Covenant "should not interfere unduly with the domestic jurisdiction of member states. . . . To allow an individual to appeal from a decision of his country's court of last resort is a serious step; yet this might be the consequence of recognizing the right of individual petition."[68] Britain too had serious doubts. One of its fears was that a UN agency authorized to consider petitions would be swamped by them. Another was that a right of petition might be abused for cold war purposes. The implication was that the Soviet Union might be able both to deter petitions by its own citizens and to incite them by citizens of other countries—perhaps by members of communist parties there; the results of this, Britain feared, would be invidious and troublesome. In truth, a system providing for private petitions would work unequally with respect to individual countries, depending (among other things) on the extent of fear of some kind of retribution.[69]

The principal considerations favoring the acceptance of a right to petition are both negative and positive. On the negative side are those indicating that implementation should not be left entirely to governments. The fear is that the decision of a government whether or not to go to the defense of human rights in another country would be based largely on political considerations of an ulterior sort. To do it would almost inevitably be regarded as an unfriendly act, and it would thus accentuate international strains and tensions, and it might well lead to retaliation in kind. Governments would thus be unlikely to act as the disinterested champions of human rights abroad, but would be more likely to treat accusations concerning violations of human rights as weapons in struggles over other matters, to be used or not as considerations of national interest suggested. On the positive side, of course, is the view that aggrieved individuals should have every reasonable opportunity to seek justice for themselves, that they are the most likely champions of their own rights, and that action by aggrieved individuals is the best way of de-politicizing the defense of human rights—the best way of seeing to it that problems can be considered on their merits, with political implications minimized.

The upshot of years of struggle over the right of petition is a compromise, at least so far as the Covenants on human rights are concerned. It was, of course, never expected that a right of petition would exist in connection with economic and social rights. The issue has concerned civil and political rights. The compromise is that the right is not provided for in the Covenant itself, but is provided for in an Optional Protocol. Separate acts of ratification are necessary for the two instruments, meaning that states are free, if they wish, to ratify the Covenant without ratifying the Protocol. A state that ratifies the Optional Protocol thereby permits the Human Rights Committee provided for in the Covenant to "receive and consider communications from individuals subject to its jurisdiction" who claim that their rights under the Covenant have been violated, provided that the petitioner has exhausted domestic remedies. The Committee is not authorized to receive communications (meaning petitions) from non-governmental international organizations; thus, these organizations are not to be permitted to act on behalf of the aggrieved, championing their rights. The aggrieved must act directly and openly, without a reliable safeguard against retribution. On receiving a communication, the Human Rights Committee is to forward a copy to the state involved, which within six months is to provide written explanations or statements, along with a description of any remedy it may already have adopted. The Optional Protocol does not give the Committee authority to make binding decisions; it can only "forward its views to the State Party concerned and to the individual." Thus only a weak form of the right of petition is provided for. Even so, should the Protocol ever come into force, it might have notable effect. Moses Moskowitz is especially optimistic, though he does not say how many states are likely to ratify either the Covenant or its Protocol. It is the Optional Protocol and its right of petition, he says, that

> more than anything else will breathe life into the Covenants and help them evolve into instruments for the creation of a new international public order. The Optional Protocol is the first important step toward the emancipation of the individual from the restraints of nationality and his entry into the international community in his own right as a human person, as an object and subject of international concern.[70]

The International Convention on the Elimination of All Forms of Racial Discrimination contains an optional arrangement for petitions similar to that in the Optional Protocol.

Despite the reluctance and caution of most of its members concerning a general right of petition, the United Nations acknowledges and acts on the right in limited spheres, i.e. in connection with trust territories, other non-self-governing territories, and South Africa. The Charter itself authorizes the General Assembly and, under its authority, the Trusteeship Council to "accept petitions and examine them in consultation with the administering authority." The article is interpreted to permit the receipt of petitions through the Secretary-General and through visiting missions sent into the Trust Territories as well as through the administering government, and it is interpreted to permit oral argument by petitioners. Similar practices hold for other non-self-governing territories, the UN agency most directly involved being the Special Committee of Twenty-Four. This Committee has a Sub-Committee on Petitions which received 1283 communications during the years 1962-66, of which it decided to circulate 1208 as petitions.[71] The Special Committee on Apartheid likewise accepts petitions within its sphere of interest. Like the Trusteeship Council, both of the special committees permit petitioners to present their case either orally or in writing or both.[72]

Neither the Trusteeship Council nor the special committees can make binding decisions relating to petitions submitted. If they are to obtain justice for petitioners, they must therefore rely on publicity, moral authority, and persuasion. The Special Committee on Apartheid, however, is so virulently hostile to the government of South Africa that cooperative responses from it are very unlikely. So far as the Special Committee is concerned, petitions are bases for agitational and propaganda efforts on behalf of equality, not bases for seeking redress for individuals.

The European Convention on Human Rights includes an optional article on the right of petition, analogous to the Optional Protocol of the Covenant on Civil and Political Rights. States willing to accept the article may make a special declaration to that effect—and eleven of the parties have now done so, Britain adding itself to the list in 1966. Petitions may be filed by "any person, non-governmental organization or group of individuals claiming to be victim of a violation by one of the High Contracting Parties of the rights set forth in this Convention." They go to the European Commission of Human Rights, which decides whether they meet the various conditions of admissibility, for example, whether the relevant domestic remedies have been exhausted, whether the petition is directed against a state that has accepted the right of petition, whether it concerns a right protected by the convention, whether the petitioner has a prima facie case justifying further inquiry. Of approximately 3300 petitions filed by September 1967, only 47 were considered admissible.[73] Once the Commission accepts a petition it is obliged to examine it together with the parties and to "place itself at the disposal" of the parties with a view to securing a friendly settlement. Failing such a settlement, the Commission reports to the Committee of Ministers, stating the relevant facts and giving a judgment on the question whether a violation of human rights has occurred. Either the Commission or the state concerned may refer the case to the European Court of Human Rights, but if this does not happen, the Committee of Ministers is to make a judgment by a two-thirds vote, and the judgment is binding. By late summer, 1967, the Commission had ruled against the accused governments in four cases or groups of cases. It or its Sub-Commission had effected a friendly settlement in two cases. In a number of other cases, the petitioner withdrew his petition and a number of cases were still pending. None of the cases aroused serious international tensions. The Secretary of the Commission testifies to the effectiveness of unofficial cooperation with the various governments, and to the responsiveness of governments to the fact or prospect of criticism.[74] In some instances the activities of the Commission or of other agencies of the European Convention led governments to change their legislation or take other actions reflecting respect for their international obligations in the field of human rights.

The Inter-American Commission on Human Rights has from the first interpreted its Statute to permit the examination of communications from individuals, and the Second Special Inter-American Conference approved and regularized the practice in 1965.[75] To obtain redress for individuals, the Commission depends on inquiry, moral suasion, and publicity. A draft convention is under consideration which provides more fully and explicitly for petitions, after the pattern of the European Convention. It permits any person, group of persons, or legally constituted association to lodge a petition with the Commission. If the petition is admissible, the Commission is to request relevant information from the accused government, and it may conduct an investigation "for the effective conduct of which the States concerned shall furnish all necessary facilities." It is to seek a friendly settlement. Failing in this effort, it is to make a private report to the parties, including such proposals and recommendations as it sees fit. As a last resort, it may decide that a state has violated its obligations and prescribe remedial measures; and if the accused state remains recalcitrant the Commission may publish its report.[76]

### A HIGH COMMISSIONER FOR HUMAN RIGHTS?

In 1967 the ECOSOC recommended to the General Assembly that it establish a United Nations High Commissioner's Office for Human Rights.[77]

The idea has been debated through the whole post-war period. The Soviet Union opposes it adamantly, charging that if a High Commissioner had significant authority he would violate the sovereignty of states and interfere unduly with their domestic affairs; the Soviet Union finds it particularly objectionable to entrust the powers of the office to one man (who, given the distribution of votes in the General Assembly, almost surely would not be a communist). Most other states have taken a more flexible attitude, the question being precisely what authority the High Commissioner and his Office might have.

According to a plan submitted by Uruguay at the fifth and sixth sessions of the General Assembly, the High Commissioner was to have an imposing array of powers, to be used in promoting the implementation of a Covenant. He was to collect and examine information with regard to all matters relevant to the observance and enforcement of the rights set forth in the Covenant, without limit on the sources from which the information might come. He was to receive reports from parties to the Covenant and was to be authorized to initiate consultations with governments. He was to be permitted to receive and examine complaints by individuals, groups of individuals, national and international non-governmental organizations, and international organizations, and to conduct investigations concerning complaints received, including hearings within the territory of the state concerned. The government of that state was to "afford all facilities necessary for the efficient conduct of the inquiry," and the High Commissioner was to have the power of subpoena. In effect, he was to be able to issue injunctions—"to call upon the State Party concerned to comply with such provisional measures as he may deem necessary and desirable in order to prevent an aggravation of the situation." He was to seek a negotiated settlement with that state, and if this proved impossible could make an accusation, which would have the effect of seizing the Security Council of the matter. Responsibility would then pass to the Security Council, but the High Commissioner was to be entitled to be present at meetings of the Security Council and to make oral and written presentations to it.[78] It is not surprising, given all the other signs of governmental concern about sovereignty, that the Uruguayan proposal was not adopted.

The plan endorsed by ECOSOC in 1967 is much more modest, though it is quite possible that interpretations and informal practice may give it a broader significance than a strict construction of the words suggests. According to the plan the High Commissioner is to advise various agencies of the UN and individual member governments, doing this formally only on their request. He is to have access to communications concerning human rights addressed to the United Nations—including communications that amount to complaints or petitions—and to be free to bring them to the attention of the government concerned; but formally the government concerned is under no obligation to respond. He is to report on developments in the field of human rights, "including his observations on the implementation of the relevant declarations and instruments . . . and his evaluation of significant progress and problems," and his reports are to be separate items on the agenda of the General Assembly, the ECOSOC, and the Commission on Human Rights; it will be his choice whether to make the reports general and bland or specific and challenging. He is to be advised and assisted by a panel of expert consultants, appointed by the Secretary-General, the principal legal systems and geographical regions being represented.[79]

The requirement that the various UN agencies named are to put the High Commissioner's report on their agendas is significant; this assures attention to whatever he chooses to say. Various other aspects of the plan give the High Commissioner informal access to international agencies and member governments, which might lead to nothing or which might permit him and his office to play a crucial role. Obviously he will not be conducting hearings in Mississippi, obtaining witnesses under subpoena, as Uruguay's High Commissioner might presumably have done, but he will be in a position to exercise more or less gentle suasion and to mobilize mild pressures. The United States is among the states supporting the ECOSOC plan.

## JUDICIAL IMPLEMENTATION

The UN Commission on Human Rights gave sporadic attention to the question of establishing an international court of human rights up to 1955, but then dropped the question from its work program.

Differences of judgment appeared from the first. In 1947 a Working Group on Implementation supported the idea that a convention on human rights should include provision for a court, but the representative of the United States (among others) opposed. She felt "that such a proposal . . . could not be put into effect in the foreseeable future. She further had grave doubts regarding the desirability of making it more difficult for States to ratify the convention by inserting in it far-reaching provisions regarding an international tribunal."[80] Presumably the assumption was that the United States—or at least the Senate—would not be favorably disposed toward an international court of human rights. In 1949 Australia advanced a statute for a court in connection with discussions of a covenant on human rights. It specified that "any party" to the covenant could refer to the court a dispute arising out of its interpretation and application, and that "parties in cases before the Court" might be states, individuals, groups of individuals, or associations, whether national or international. This left it somewhat unclear whether private parties could seize the court of a case, but it was a far-reaching proposal nevertheless.[81] Little support for the proposal developed. The truth is that, in general, states are reluctant to commit themselves in advance to the judicial settlement of any disputes, and this is true above all of the new states that have come into existence since World War II. If anything, the reluctance is greater in the field of human rights than in other fields, for the law that a court would apply is especially vague—still in process of development. To give a court compulsory jurisdiction in connection with economic and social rights would obviously be unworkable; and, in the eyes of many countries to give it jurisdiction in connection with civil and political rights would be to give it legislative powers (i.e. a right to assign clear meaning to vague principles) that the governments want to retain for themselves.[82]

Like the United Nations, the OAS has given consideration to the establishment of an international court on human rights. A resolution at the Bogotá conference (1948) calling for the preparation of a statute for such a court proved to be abortive, but a similar resolution of the Fifth Meeting of Consultation of Ministers of Foreign Affairs (Santiago, 1959) has produced results. The preliminary draft inter-American convention adopted by the Council of the OAS in 1968 includes provision for the creation of an Inter-American Court of Human Rights. Only the states parties to the convention, or the Commission itself, are to have the right to submit cases to the Court, and any state against which a complaint is lodged can refuse to submit to the judgment of the Court. Parties may, however, accept an optional clause agreeing in advance to the compulsory jurisdiction of the court.[83]

Formally at least, the parties to the European Convention on Human Rights have gone much the farthest with judicial settlement, though they do not make much actual use of the Court that their Convention established. Cases reach the Court only after having been submitted to the European Commission of Human Rights, and then only through the action of the Commission or a state party to the Convention; individuals do not have direct access to the Court. The Convention includes an optional clause, permitting parties to agree in advance to accept the jurisdiction of the Court, and at the end of 1967 eleven of the sixteen parties to the Convention had done so. A total of seven cases have been submitted to the Court, while twenty cases have gone from the Commission to the Committee of Ministers. However important the judgment of a court may be in individual cases, other methods of implementation have, in general, proved more acceptable and therefore more useful.

In some circumstances, of course, the judicial implementation of obligations concerning human rights could be accomplished through the International Court of Justice. Its jurisdiction extends to all legal disputes submitted to it. A number of treaties give the International Court of Justice compulsory jurisdiction over disputes concerning the meaning of their terms, and among such treaties are some concerning human rights. For example, the International Convention on the Elimination of All Forms of Racial Discrimination, adopted by the General Assembly in 1965, provides that any dispute between its parties with respect to its interpretation or application which is not otherwise settled shall, at the request of any of the parties to the dispute, be referred to the Court. The Covenant on Civil and Political Rights, adopted by the General Assembly a year later—after the Court displeased many UN members by its decision on South-West Africa—contains no reference to the International Court of Justice or to judicial settlement.[84]

Ambassador Goldberg describes it as "ideal" if an international judiciary existed that could grant writs of habeas corpus, but the achievement of such an ideal is obviously remote.[85]

Finally, we might note the fact that after World War II the peace treaties with Bulgaria, Hungary, and Rumania envisaged the use of arbitration in case of dispute over the fulfillment of the treaty terms. The arbitral tribunal was to consist of three persons, each party appointing one of them and the Secretary-General appointing the third. All of the treaties included an article binding the defeated states to take all the measures necessary to secure to all persons under their jurisdiction the enjoyment of human rights and fundamental freedoms. In the eyes of the United States, all three states violated this obligation; and when they denied the accusation the United States declared that a dispute existed which, according to the terms of the treaty, should be referred to arbitration. The three governments, however, refused to appoint arbitrators. The General Assembly condemned them for their "wilful refusal . . . to fulfil their obligations," but arbitration did not occur.

## CONCLUDING COMMENTS

The two preceding chapters showed that the international legal obligations of states in the field of human rights are, for the most part, still general and vague. The expression of good intentions about the achievement of minimum standards is more common and prominent than the making of legal commitments. It is not surprising that a corresponding kind of situation should exist with regard to measures of implementation. In truth, it is to be expected that states would be even more hesitant about subordinating themselves to international supervision and enforcement than about accepting obligations to be fulfilled simply on their own initiative and responsibility.

The subordination that has occurred or is being attempted is very uneven. It is uneven in terms of the existence and powers of regional organizations. The sixteen states that have ratified the European Convention on Human Rights—and, even more, the eleven that have accepted the optional provisions of the convention concerning individual petition and compulsory adjudication—have gone much the farthest both in commitments to respect rights and in terms of international arrangements for implementation. The catastrophe that Hitler brought upon them and the threat of another catastrophe at the hands of Stalin and the communists were among the powerful forces leading them to establish safeguards that other states have resisted. The American republics have gone relatively far too—though farther in international measures designed to encourage national respect for human rights than in the formal acceptance of legal obligations; the leadership in this has not belonged to the United States. The Organization of African Unity has shown little interest in human rights in general, and the same is true of such other regional organizations as exist.

One of the questions pertaining to the UN's activities—a question that has come up and will come up again in connection with the proposed High Commissioner's Office for Human Rights—is whether to put more stress on regional arrangements. The record in Western Europe argues especially for this, the implicit suggestion being that countries with similar traditions and values should be encouraged to push forward as rapidly as they can, adjusting action for human rights to regional situations and possibilities. At the same time, it would be somewhat anachronistic for a global organization promoting human rights to follow policies that might promote regional differentiations and contrasts.[86]

The development of international implementing measures is also uneven in another respect. A very considerable proportion of the activity of the United Nations in the field relates to racial discrimination, and in connection with racial discrimination a high proportion of the activity concerns apartheid and its counterpart in Rhodesia. This will come out more fully in the next chapter. White Americans, and for that matter white Europeans, are perhaps not very acceptable as judges of the relative importance of racial equality among the human rights, or of the relative importance of the practices in southern Africa in the field of discrimination. But at least a question should be raised about the consequences of policies that seem to identify human rights almost entirely with racial equality, and that seem to identify racial equality almost entirely with the elimination of apartheid. On the one hand, it may be natural and proper to concentrate on an especially egregious kind of violation of human rights as a first step toward action against other kinds of violations. But on the other hand it may discourage support for human rights if those demanding action against apartheid give the impression that this is the only problem in the field in which they have serious interest.

Somewhat similar sorts of statements apply to the emphasis on self-determination as a human right and on measures to bring an end to colonialism. The argument has some merit that special measures of implementation are justified in this realm because they involve the promotion rather than the violation of the sovereignty of colonial peoples. But it would be a poor service to the cause of human rights if it results in the establishment of more sovereignties like those of Nkrumah and Duvalier. To paraphrase Moses Moskowitz, it is not defensible to concentrate on bringing an end to discrimination and colonialism without also showing concern for the violations of human rights that are wholesale and indiscriminate. A statement by Morris B. Abram to the UN Commission on Human Rights is in point. The United States, he said, "believed in an even-handed approach to human rights problems everywhere in the world. . . . The Commission's work should be far-reaching and balanced. . . . He freely admitted that there were violations in his country, and he would welcome it if the Commission or any other body examined them, provided that the same was done in respect of violations occurring elsewhere. . . . Serious wrongs were not confined to Southern Africa."[87] Possibly the Inter-American Commission on Human Rights is the agency that might put these principles to the test. Its serious probing has so far mainly concerned Cuba, the Dominican Republic, and Haiti. An even-handed approach would encompass additional countries, including the United States.[88]

Abram's statement reflects a major problem in the activities of both the United Nations and the Organization of the American States. They have at their disposal a considerable array of measures of implementation. These measures are open to improvement, to be sure, but the main question is whether the various states involved are in fact willing to have them applied in an even-handed way.

# 9

# The Problem of Implementation: Coercion

Neither the Charter of the United Nations nor the comparable document of any other international agency provides explicitly for the enforcement of obligations concerning human rights, i.e. for coercive pressures or sanctions. For the most part, states find this situation agreeable. If they hesitate about developing international arrangements and methods for implementation that rely on moral authority and persuasion, as the preceding chapter shows, it follows that they would hesitate all the more about approving coercive methods.

Nevertheless, demands for enforcement action arise. In 1946 there was a demand for action against the Franco regime in Spain, established with the help of Hitler and Mussolini. Intermittently through the years voices have been raised in Latin America in favor of some kind of enforcement of certain human rights. Above all in terms of current urgency and potential importance are the demands relating to southern Africa—to South Africa, to South-West Africa, to Southern Rhodesia, and to Portugal as the ruler over Angola and Mozambique.

The demands for enforcement raise questions of both legality and practicality. Legally the General Assembly is of course free to recommend sanctions, and (as we shall see) it has repeatedly done so. But many members of the UN fail to implement these recommendations, or at least fail to do it fully. This leads advocates of sanctions to demand that the Security Council make them mandatory—which it could do, but not for the explicit purpose of enforcing respect for human rights. To make sanctions mandatory, the Security Council must first find—under Article 39, Chapter VII, of the Charter—that there exists a "threat to the peace, breach of the peace, or act of aggression." If it makes such a finding, it may then decide what measures members of the UN shall take "to maintain or restore international peace and security." The question thus is whether violations of human rights can be said to be threats to the peace. At the San Francisco Conference the possibility was envisaged.[1] But it is intrinsically likely that any such threat will be ambiguous, not subject to easy determination as a clear matter of fact. Preference is then bound to influence findings, and, at the extreme, the finding of a threat will depend not so much on objective circumstances as on the desire or willingness of states to apply sanctions. Moreover, if peace is threatened by violations of human rights, the question remains who is responsible—the harsh government that probably wants to be left alone or the outraged government that prepares to intervene.

Questions of practicality are at least as difficult. What kinds of sanctions will produce what kinds of results with what degree of probability? Precisely what results are in fact desired? Are sanctions-short-of-force likely to be adequate? Must sanctions-short-of-force be backed by a willingness to use force if necessary? If the application of sanctions becomes costly in any country, what will be the domestic effect on the political fortunes of the government responsible? After Vietnam, political leaders in the United States are likely to be especially anxious about gaining and retaining popular support for costly foreign ventures, but at the same time they are also likely to be concerned about the country's moral posture and moral leadership.

The above questions are most acute with respect to southern Africa, and most of this chapter will be addressed to them in that context. But we will give some attention first to the problem of Franco and to questions concerning enforcement that have arisen in Latin America.

## FRANCO'S FASCIST REGIME IN SPAIN

In the spring of 1946 Poland asked the Security Council to declare that "the existence and activities of the Franco regime in Spain [had] led to international friction and endangered international peace and security"; and it asked for mandatory sanctions of a very mild sort—the severance of diplomatic relations with that regime.[2] Though Poland based its case on the fascist character and record of the Franco regime rather than on an explicit appeal to enforce respect for human rights, the problem raised is reasonably analogous to the problem relating to southern Africa.

Members of the Security Council divided on the issue. The Soviet Union sided with Poland. Normally, it said, the internal situation in a state was a domestic matter in which the United Nations should not interfere, but when that situation constitutes a threat to international peace and security, "definite measures" are necessary; and a fascist regime was by its very nature a threat. Mexico and France took a similar view. According to the French spokesman, "Dictatorial regimes inevitably lead to war. . . . There is great danger in allowing a regime which, by its nature is directed towards war and cannot continue to exist without the glory of war, to develop in any country and not to take any counter-measures."[3] The Netherlands and Britain opposed the Polish resolution. The Netherlands pointed out that the Polish delegate had not said "one word which pointed with any degree of certainty or even probability to fundamental offensive action on the part of the Spanish armed forces," and he feared that action based on the kind of evidence presented would establish a "precedent for all sorts of ill-founded intervention." A Sub-Committee to which the Security Council referred the matter sought middle ground. It concluded that the situation in Spain, "though not an existing threat within the meaning of Article 39, is a situation the continuation of which is in fact likely to endanger the maintenance of international peace and security."[4] The finding did not satisfy Poland. It held that in order to be recognized as a threat to the peace, a situation did not need to involve an "immediate danger." "Potential, as well as imminent, dangers can be construed as a threat to the peace in the sense of Article 39. . . . Unless threats to the peace are taken care of by the Security Council at an early stage while they still are potential and easy to remove, the United Nations may find themselves in face of situations beyond their power to control."[5] The upshot was that the Security Council rejected the Polish resolution.

The General Assembly then took the matter up, adopting a resolution referring not to human rights or to a threat to the peace but rather to the fascist nature and wartime record of the Franco government. It recommended that the government be debarred from membership in the specialized agencies and from participation in their activities, that members of the UN should recall their Ambassadors and their Ministers plenipotentiary from Madrid, and that

> if, within a reasonable time, there is not established a government which derives its authority from the consent of the governed, committed to respect freedom of speech, religion and assembly and to the prompt holding of an election in which the Spanish people, free from force and intimidation and regardless of party, may express their will, the Security Council consider the adequate measures to be taken in order to remedy the situation.[6]

Obviously, many states voted for this resolution that did not meet its requirements themselves. In addition to the measures that the General Assembly recommended, Spain was barred from NATO and from the various organizations established by the states of Western Europe.

Several years after the adoption of the resolution Secretary of State Acheson expressed the opinion that it had not only failed of its intended purpose, but had actually strengthened the Franco regime. He said that the United States was continuing its efforts "to persuade the Spanish Government that its own interest in participating in the international community, and particularly in the Western European community, requires steps toward democratic government, which offers the best hope for the growth of basic human rights and fundamental freedoms in Spain." Acheson thought it "difficult to envisage Spain as a full member of the Western community without substantial advances in such directions as increased civil liberties and as religious freedom and the freedom to exercise the elementary rights of organized labor." At the same time, he reaffirmed a view taken earlier that the General Assembly action of 1946 had been a mistake, and he wanted it revoked.[7] Not many months later revocation occurred, and in 1955 Spain, still controlled by the Franco regime, was admitted to the United Nations.

## THE QUESTION OF UPHOLDING REPRESENTATIVE DEMOCRACY IN LATIN AMERICA

The question of the use of some kind of coercive pressure in support of human rights has come up repeatedly in inter-American relations.

In 1945 the Foreign Minister of Uruguay, Mr. Larreta, asked for consideration of one aspect of the question. Vague in all his crucial statements, he said that the concept of the interdependence of democracy and peace had become absolute truth. He spoke of the "common determination to make effective, to any necessary extent, the defense of the democratic ideal and of the individual." "The repeated violation of such rules," he said, "is not only disastrous itself, but sooner or later produces grave international repercussions." The principle of non-intervention was "inspired by noble and just claims," but states had no right "to invoke one principle in order to be able to violate all other principles with immunity." Finally he intimated that "multilateral collective action, exercised with complete unselfishness" might occur for the "reestablishment of essential rights" in any country suffering under a dictator.[8]

The United States quickly announced its "unqualified adherence" to Larreta's principles. According to Secretary Byrnes, ". . . men everywhere may properly demand that human rights and dignity be respected as an essential condition for the maintenance of peace and security throughout the world." He said that if the American republics are to preserve the peace, they "cannot permit oppressive regimes to exist in their midst."

> Violation of the elementary rights of man by a government of force and the non-fulfillment of obligations by such a government is a matter of common concern to all the republics. As such, it justifies collective multilateral action after full consultation among the republics in accordance with established procedures.[9]

Though some of the other American republics also responded favorably to Mr. Larreta's suggestion, a decisive majority turned it down.[10]

Similar suggestions come up in connection with the question of the recognition of *de facto* governments. At the close of World War II and for some time thereafter Guatemala pressed a proposal for the denial of recognition to "anti-democratic" governments on the ground that such governments, through their violation of the rights of man, constituted a menace to international peace, but the Inter-American Juridical Committee, to which the proposal was referred, concluded that it would be impossible to determine what was or what was not an "anti-democratic" regime without violating the principle of non-intervention.[11] At the Bogotá conference in 1948, the government of Uruguay, in line with the Larreta proposal mentioned above, suggested that in the event of grave violations of human rights by an American government, other governments should consult on the question of recognizing it or, if it was already recognized, of severing diplomatic relations with it.[12] Neither Guatemala's proposal nor Uruguay's was ever adopted.

One of the preambular clauses of the Inter-American Treaty of Reciprocal Assistance (1947) asserts that "peace is founded on justice and moral order and consequently on the international recognition and protection of human rights and freedoms." In line with this "manifest truth" the Foreign Ministers of the American republics in 1959 adopted a statement that "the existence of anti-democratic regimes constitutes a violation of the principles on which the OAS is founded, and a danger to united and peaceful relationships in the Hemisphere." On this basis the Foreign Ministers called for a study of the possibility of taking enforcement action on behalf of human rights and representative democracy—though they must have known in advance that the international obligations of the American republics did not provide clear basis for such action. The committee to which the question was referred gave them no encouragement. It agreed that "a political organization established on a democratic basis" is among "the high ideals with which the Charter [of the OAS] is imbued," but it asserted that action in conformity with those ideals was left entirely to the good faith of the member states. It saw "no place for collective action in defense of or for the restoration of democracy under that heading alone." It held that no machinery could "be put into motion in defense of democracy, or to maintain or restore it, except in cases in which such defense would also be, and for other reasons, a defense against aggression." To try to enforce democracy would be to intervene, to threaten the independence of states. It would be suggestive of a new Holy Alliance. The Committee spoke of the possibility of action in case a country fell under the control of international communism, but held that "domestic corruption of democracy . . . escapes completely from the control of the Organization."[13]

The Foreign Ministers in 1959 also asked the Inter-American Peace Committee to examine "the relationship between violations of human rights or the nonexercise of representative democracy, on the one hand, and the political tensions that affect the peace of the hemisphere, on the other." The report that the Committee later made confirmed the view that a relationship exists, illustrated by the fact that opposition leaders tend to flee from dictatorial countries and take refuge abroad, there engaging in activities that create or accentuate tensions.[14] An investigation of the situation in the Dominican Republic under Trujillo led the Committee to conclude that Trujillo had aggravated tensions in the Caribbean by his "flagrant and widespread violations of human rights,"[15] and a similar conclusion flowed from an investigation of Castro's Cuba.[16] But these conclusions did not lead to overt action. Had the OAS acted against either Trujillo or against Castro because they were dictators who violated human rights, it would have raised troublesome questions about other Latin American regimes that were dictatorial. The Foreign Ministers came to the conclusion that Castro's government had "voluntarily placed itself outside the inter-American system" but their explanation did not rest on the fact of dictatorship or on the violation of human rights; rather, it rested on the proposition that "adherence by any member of the OAS to Marxism-Leninism is incompatible with the inter-American system."[17] This permitted action against Cuba alone.

Finally in 1967 the Second Special Inter-American Conference adopted a resolution in line with Uruguay's proposal of 1948. The resolution called for an exchange of views when the question of recognizing a *de facto* government came up, and it said that in exchanging their views governments should consider the following circumstances:

> a. Whether the *de facto* government proposes to take the necessary measures for the holding of elections within a reasonable period, giving its people the opportunity to freely participate in the consequent electoral process; and
> b. Whether the *de facto* government agrees . . . to respect the human rights expressed in the American Declaration of the Rights and Duties of Man. . . .[18]

This suggests the possibility of mild pressure, whether or not it deserves to be called coercive.

In sum, with respect to both Spain and Latin America, moves have occurred in the direction of declarations that violations of human rights or of the principle of representative democracy are the concern of the international community and may endanger peace. But the idea that the violation of human rights may threaten peace and thus justify enforcement action has not been accepted.

### THREATS TO THE PEACE IN SOUTHERN AFRICA?

Issues concerning the relationship between human rights and peace are especially sharp with regard to southern Africa. The United States is among the small minority of UN members that refuse to say that a threat to the peace exists because of violations of human rights in South Africa, South-West Africa, and the colonies ("overseas provinces") of

Portugal. The overwhelming majority have repeatedly cast votes on the other side. However, the United States is with the majority in saying that the situation in Rhodesia constitutes a threat to the peace and in applying the sanctions made mandatory by a Security Council vote.

What is the nature of the alleged threat? Not really that any of the accused governments might launch an armed attack across its borders against a neighboring state. To be sure, in a patently strained attempt to fit the alleged threat with traditional conceptions, some decry the measures of military preparedness that South Africa has been taking, and point to the vulnerability of some of South Africa's neighbors (especially Lesotho, an enclave). Further, they cite the fact that the Security Council has condemned Portugal for allowing mercenaries to use Angola in connection with activities in the Congo. But evidence of a threat of aggression is transparently flimsy. In truth, South Africa, Portugal, and Rhodesia, beleagured as they are, have every reason to be extremely careful not to threaten aggression, lest they give a decisive argument to those in the UN who seek their undoing.

The threats to the peace said to exist in southern Africa are of a different sort. South Africa is rascist, as we have repeatedly noted in preceding chapters; discrimination against the non-white population is the official policy and is carried to very great lengths. Portugal's chief offense is that it denies self-determination to the peoples of its colonies. The offense of the whites in Rhodesia, comprising about 4 per cent of the total population, is that they declared independence illegally for the specific purpose of assuring the preservation of white supremacy; they would not go along with British demands for constitutional arrangements looking toward majority rule. South-West Africa, mandated to South Africa after World War I and never placed under trusteeship, involves special problems. South Africa is enforcing apartheid there, is denying self-determination in the sense accepted in the UN, and is insisting on preserving its rule despite a declaration by the General Assembly that its legal right to be there has terminated. If South Africa is a threat to the peace because of policies pursued within its own boundaries, it is surely also a threat because of its policies in South-West Africa.

The proposition that threats to the peace exist in southern Africa rests on actual and prospective reactions of others to the racism and colonialism of the dominant white regimes. Most easily ascertained are the reactions of governmental delegates in the United Nations, and among them, not surprisingly, delegates from the black African republics are especially outspoken. From their point of view the black peoples of Africa have in the past been denied human dignity—have been compelled to live in humiliation and degradation. It is not enough for these spokesmen that white colonialism and racism have ended in their own countries; it must end elsewhere too. They are strident and adamant in this demand, and extremely sensitive to white attitudes and actions that go in a different direction. It is a matter of gaining pride and self-respect, if not for themselves then for the people with whom they identify. For example, the delegate from Tanzania told the General Assembly in 1967 that the

> African revolution for the recovery of freedom and dignity is not complete so long as any part of Africa remains under alien domination, so long as any African is humiliated because of his color. . . . There need be no doubt that the oppressed people will fight, whatever the cost, because no human being worth the name can permanently allow himself to be regarded as a sub-human-racial type and subjected to degradation and humiliation.[19]

A few months later the Tanzanian delegate mixed metaphors with great abandon in comparing the problem of a non-proliferation treaty with the problems of southern Africa. He thought there was no urgency about the treaty.

> But there is a burning, immediate and compelling urgency about the problems of southern Africa. This is a sweltering volcano, a powder keg. Time has run out for that area. In southern Africa we are living on borrowed time. When this volcano erupts, when the fuse has burnt its course, we shall all—the whole world—be caught up in the lava of hate, bloodshed, and the nastiest racial war that human experience has ever encountered.[20]

Others give similar warnings. U Thant has spoken of the "prospect that racial conflict, if we cannot curb and finally eliminate it, will grow into a destructive monster, compared to which the religious and ideological conflicts of the past will seem like a small family quarrel."[21] The British delegate to the General Assembly went on record along the same general line.

> We see the forces of African nationalism north of the River Zambesi and the forces of white supremacy south of the river facing each other in a confrontation. That confrontation creates, so I have long believed, one of the greatest dangers of the world—the danger of

> race conflict, a conflict which could inflame the whole of Africa and involve the whole world.[22]

Similarly Moses Moskowitz, who has long represented one of the nongovernmental organizations at the UN and who devotes himself to the cause of human rights, takes a very serious view of the problems of southern Africa.

> The revolt of the Afro-Asian world against the myth of White superiority and its resentment of any and all forms of racial segregation have exploded with a torrential force which will not be contained until it has spent itself. The dignity and self-respect of the African States dictate that they shall not rest until they have achieved majority rule in South Africa.[23]

Though a great many share the above views, both the timing and the magnitude of the dangers are very difficult to assess. No one credits the black African states with sufficient military power to have a chance of success through armed attack in southern Africa, and the pressure that they can exert through economic sanctions is slight. Lacking the necessary naval and air power, they could not reinforce economic measures by blockading the coasts of southern Africa even if the United States, Britain, and France took a benevolent attitude.

It is less certain to what extent the African states and others may be able to stir up or support guerrilla activities and sabotage. Some of them have been engaged in efforts along these lines at least since 1963, when the Summit Conference at Addis Ababa established a Special Fund "to supply the necessary practical and financial aid to the various African national liberation movements."[24] Senator Brooke says that in the fall of 1967 the thirty-eight members of the Organization of African Unity voted to give $2 million of their $3 million budget to various groups promoting liberation in southern Africa.[25] News reports indicate that "black Rhodesians are being trained as guerrillas in Algeria, North Korea, the Soviet Union, China, and Cuba. They get further tactical instruction in camps in Tanzania. In Zambia they are drawn up into fighting units. . . ."[26] South African authorities claim that by the spring of 1967 "more than 2,000 young Africans had been taken out of South Africa for training as 'terrorists.'" In the late summer of 1967 the security forces of South Africa and Southern Rhodesia are said to have combined in "serious warfare" against adherents of the African National Congress of South Africa, who were attempting to return to their homeland through Southern Rhodesia; 31 were reported killed, and 20 captured. Similar operations occurred in the spring of 1968 and presumably will continue to be necessary.[27] Both South Africa and Southern Rhodesia have executed a number of persons whom they call terrorists and who in UN documents are commonly called freedom fighters or political prisoners. According to the Tanzanian delegate,

> Algeria has shown the way. The people of Viet Nam have shown the way. The so-called Mau Mau people of Kenya have shown the way. . . . We do not flinch from force when all the avenues of pacific settlement have been exhausted. We submit that we have now reached that stage in southern Africa. . . . We shall fight until Africa has sacrificed its life for freedom or until total freedom is won at last on our continent.[28]

In a report issued in 1968, the General Assembly's Special Committee on Apartheid "takes note of the decision of the liberation movement of the oppressed people of South Africa that . . . armed struggle is now the only feasible and effective means to secure the human rights and fundamental freedoms of all the people of South Africa, and understands the circumstances that have led to this decision."[29] The General Assembly itself has adopted more than one resolution recognizing the "legitimacy" of the struggles for national liberation in Africa and urging all states to provide "moral and material assistance." A number of states, most of them from Africa, propose a draft resolution which first asserts that all forms of colonialism are "a violation of international law" and which then goes on to declare that "peoples who are deprived of their legitimate right of self-determination and complete freedom are entitled to exercise their inherent right of self-defense, by virtue of which they may receive assistance from other States."[30] This does not necessarily mean an endorsement of violence, but at least it raises the question.

The statement is made above that evidence is lacking of an intention on the part of South Africa, Southern Rhodesia, or Portugal to launch an attack across frontiers. It should be noted, however, that from their point of view they already face great provocation, and the situation might worsen. Under general international law they could build a reasonably good case in support of armed action against a neighboring state that permits the use of its territory as a base of hostile operations. The Special

Committee on Apartheid has some fear of this, for it has asked the General Assembly to "warn the South African Government that any action taken by that Government against other States for their support of the legitimate struggle of the people against apartheid would not be tolerated by the international community."[31]

In light of this, almost all UN members agree that dangers to the peace exist in southern Africa. The first question is whether any of the dangers should be called a *threat*—the crucial word of Article 39. As noted above, if the Security Council finds that a *threat* exists, it may order the mandatory application of sanctions, whereas in the absence of a threat it may not. What states naturally do, therefore, is to decide whether or not they want Security Council action on the basis of Article 39, and then choose their words accordingly. If a threat is found, various other questions follow—among them the question against whom any action that is taken should be directed. Obviously the Tanzanian delegate did not think of his own state as the source of a threat calling for action by the Security Council. In effect his position with respect to the white regimes in southern Africa is this: that since I find your policies intolerable and therefore intend to use force to end them, you are a threat to the peace. He can make a case for his view, just as South Africa can make a case for a contrary view; but the issue is one that needs to be argued.

## RECOMMENDATIONS AND APPEALS OF THE GENERAL ASSEMBLY

An overwhelming majority in the General Assembly find threats to the peace in southern Africa and call for sanctions. To begin by giving a summary, the General Assembly has since 1960 adopted formal resolutions describing all of the following as threats to the peace: "the situation in South Africa," "the policies and actions" of South Africa, "the practice of apartheid," "the explosive situation" in Southern Rhodesia and southern Africa, "the colonial war" carried on by Portugal in Angola, "the continued refusal of Portugal to recognize the legitimate aspirations of the Angolan people to self-determination and independence," "the attitude of Portugal towards the African population of its colonies and of neighboring states," "the increasing cooperation between the authorities of Southern Rhodesia, South Africa, and Portugal," "the continuation of colonial rule," and "all forms of racial discrimination." To add to the indictment, the General Assembly has also described the policy of apartheid and all forms of racial discrimination as a "crime against humanity." ECOSOC and various committees of the General Assembly take similar stands. The UN Commission on Human Rights, as noted in the preceding chapter, has shifted in this specific context to the taking of action on complaints and has started adopting resolutions of the sort suggested above. For example, in March 1968, it condemned "all ideologies, including nazism and apartheid, which are based on racial intolerance and terror, as a gross violation of human rights and fundamental freedoms . . . and as a serious threat to world peace."[32]

A few resolutions that the General Assembly adopted in 1967 might be cited more fully. In one of them, by a vote of 89 to 2, with 12 abstentions, the General Assembly reiterated its condemnation of apartheid as a "crime against humanity" and "its conviction that the situation in South Africa constitutes a threat to international peace." The resolution went on to condemn those states ("particularly the main trading partners of South Africa," i.e. Britain, the United States, and France) whose "political, economic, and military collaboration" with South Africa encourage it to persist in its racial policies. It requested states to comply fully with Security Council resolutions on South Africa (among them the one to be noted below, calling for an arms embargo) and "to take urgent steps towards disengagement from South Africa." Further, the resolution asserted that "action under Chapter VII of the Charter . . . is essential in order to solve the problem of apartheid and that universally applied mandatory economic sanctions are the only means of achieving a peaceful solution."[33]

In another resolution adopted in 1967—by a vote of 82 to 7, with 21 abstentions—the General Assembly strongly condemned the colonial war waged by Portugal, "which constitutes a crime against humanity and a grave threat to international peace and security." It urged Portugal to recognize "the right of the peoples under its domination to self-determination and independence." Two years previously it had urged members to apply various diplomatic and economic sanctions against Portugal—for example, an arms ambargo, a "boycott of all trade with Portugal," a closure of ports to Portuguese vessels and a denial of landing and transit facilities to Portuguese aircraft. Now it recommended to the Security Council (as it had in 1966) that it make such sanctions mandatory.[34]

Numerous resolutions concern Southern Rhodesia, the more recent ones contrasting in an interesting way with those concerning South Africa. The prescription for South Africa, as noted above, is the application of economic sanctions, such sanctions being described as "the only means of achieving a peaceful solution." But with regard to Southern Rhodesia, the General Assembly in 1967 voted 92 to 2, with 18 abstentions, that economic sanctions have proved inadequate and that force should be used, the object being to overthrow the rebel regime and "to transfer power without further delay to the people of Zimbabwe on the basis of elections conducted according to the principle of 'one man, one vote.' "[35]

The General Assembly has also adopted numerous resolutions concerning South-West Africa. Since 1960 it has described the situation there as a "serious threat to international peace and security."[36] In 1963 it warned South Africa that any attempt to annex South-West Africa in whole or in part would be considered an act of aggression, and it urged all states to refrain from supplying various kinds of goods to South Africa because of its policies in the Territory.[37] In 1966 it declared that South Africa had failed to fulfil its obligations and had, in fact, disavowed the mandate; on this basis it decided "that the Mandate is therefore terminated, that South Africa has no other right to administer the Territory, and that henceforth South West Africa comes under the direct responsibility of the United Nations."[38] Later it established a Council for South-West Africa to govern the Territory pending its exercise of self-determination, and requested the Council to contact the authorities in South Africa to agree on procedures for the transfer of administrative control.[39]

The response of South Africa was to deny that the General Assembly had a legal right to terminate the mandate and to declare that it would "resist with all means at [its] disposal any attempt to endanger the safety of the country and the peoples committed to its care."[40] It denied the Council for South-West Africa permission to enter the Territory, after the Council had flown to Africa to assume its duties. The Soviet suggestion to the General Assembly was that it demand that the United States and the United Kingdom take it upon themselves to secure the withdrawal of South Africa from South-West Africa.[41] The British reaction was to regret that the United Nations had "not been prepared to confine itself to action which is clearly practical."[42] Later the delegate from Malawi commented as follows:

> The resolutions adopted in the Assembly have become steadily more violent in tone, more demanding in their requests on South Africa and, in the final analysis, more unrealistic. . . . Such was the at-

> mosphere of moral fervour engendered by the passionate stand of African nations that many Members must have felt that to cast a dissenting or abstaining vote would appear as if it were a vote for South Africa's policies.[43]

And so, he said, the Assembly was "stampeded" into adopting the resolution declaring the mandate over South-West Africa terminated.

The General Assembly itself condemned South Africa, declared that the continued presence of South African authorities in South-West Africa was "a flagrant violation of its territorial integrity and international status," recommended that members apply sanctions, and requested the Security Council to "take effective steps to enable the United Nations to fulfil the responsibilities it has assumed."[44]

### SECURITY COUNCIL ATTITUDES AND ACTIONS RELATING TO SOUTH AFRICA AND PORTUGAL

The Security Council and several of its individual members have responded only in part to appeals from the General Assembly. After the Sharpeville incident in 1960 the Security Council recognized "that the situation in the Union of South Africa is one that has led to international friction and if continued might endanger international peace," and it called upon South Africa "to initiate measures aimed at bringing about racial harmony based on equality in order to ensure that the present situation does not continue or recur, and to abandon its policies of *apartheid* and racial discrimination." But there was no invocation of Chapter VII.[45]

In 1963 the Security Council went farther, but still refused to act under Chapter VII. Among others, Adlai Stevenson took the view that it would be both "bad law and bad policy" to do so.

> It would be bad law because the extreme measures provided in Chapter VII were never intended and cannot reasonably be interpreted to apply to situations of this kind. The founders of the United Nations were very careful to reserve the right of the Organization to employ mandatory coercive measures in situations where there was an actuality of international violence or such a clear and present threat to the peace as to leave no reasonable alternative but resort to coercion. We do not have that kind of situation here.

He went on to say that it would be bad policy

> because the application of sanctions . . . is not likely to bring about the practical result that we seek, that is, the abandonment of apartheid. . . . Punitive measures would only provoke intransigence and harden the existing situation. Furthermore, the result of the adoption of such measures, particularly if compliance is not widespread and sincere, would create doubts about the validity of, and diminish respect for, the authority of the United Nations and the efficacy of the sanction process envisioned in the Charter.[46]

The British view was similar. In the absence of South African actions threatening the territorial integrity or political independence of another State, the British representative declared that the Security Council lacked the power to impose sanctions.[47]

Though refusing to invoke Chapter VII, the Security Council expressed the conviction "that the situation in South Africa is seriously disturbing international peace and security" and called upon all states "to cease forthwith the sale and shipment of arms, ammunition of all types and military vehicles to South Africa."[48] Subsequently it has adopted various other resolutions condemning South Africa or appealing for changes in policies and practices connected with apartheid. With respect to South-West Africa, it has "taken into account" the General Assembly resolution terminating South Africa's mandate, has called upon South Africa to discontinue "illegal trials" of South-West Africans accused of terrorism, and has censured South Africa for its defiance.[49] But it has not adopted steps, as the General Assembly requests, to enable the United Nations to assume jurisdiction over the Territory.

Though either voting for or permitting the adoption of the above resolutions, the United States, Britain, France, and a number of other states are obviously disinclined to get too much entangled in activities directed against South Africa. The center of such activities has been the Special Committee on the Policies of Apartheid of the Government of the Republic of South Africa, established by the General Assembly in 1962. Of the eleven states represented on the committee, all but one (Hungary) are located outside Europe and North America, and five come from Africa. The committee has been extreme in its reports and demands, doing little to build up confidence in its responsibility and judgment. In 1965 the General Assembly voted to add six additional states to the Committee so as to include those with "primary responsibility with regard to world trade," and "primary responsibility . . . for the maintenance of international peace and security," and so as to obtain equitable geographical distribution. But the President of the General Assembly, who was to appoint the new members, in the end had to admit failure. Of the nineteen states whom he approached on the matter, only the Soviet Union agreed unconditionally to serve. Two others agreed, but attached conditions that could not be met. All others, including the United States, Britain, and France, declined, leaving the Committee and the General Assembly in angry frustration, and no doubt contributing to the move referred to in the preceding chapter to involve the Commission on Human Rights and its members more directly in the campaign against the governments of southern Africa.

The stand of the Security Council with respect to Portugal has been somewhat similar to its stand with respect to South Africa. In 1961 it formally deplored "the large-scale killings and the severely repressive measures in Angola," and it expressed its conviction that "the continuance of the situation in Angola is an actual and potential cause of international friction and is likely to endanger the maintenance of international peace and security." It reaffirmed a General Assembly resolution calling upon Portugal to "consider urgently" the grant of self-determination to Angola. But it did not find a threat to the peace.[50] In the next several years it adopted other more or less similar resolutions. In that of November 1965, for example, it affirmed "that the situation resulting from the policies of Portugal both as regards the African population of its colonies and the neighboring States seriously disturbs international peace," and it went on to make a number of "urgent demands" relating to the abandonment of policies of repression and negotiations with representatives of political parties within and outside Portuguese territories in Africa concerning the exercise of the right of self-determination and the granting of independence.[51]

## SECURITY COUNCIL ATTITUDES AND ACTIONS RELATING TO SOUTHERN RHODESIA

The problem of Southern Rhodesia first came before the Security Council in 1963 with the break-up of the Federation of Rhodesia and Nyasaland. The crucial vote was on a draft resolution "recognizing that the present Government in Southern Rhodesia came to power as a result of an undemocratic and discriminatory constitution imposed on the population," and inviting Britain "not to transfer to its colony of Southern Rhodesia as at present governed any powers or attributes of sovereignty until the establishment of a government fully representative of all the inhabitants of the colony." Britain vetoed the resolution, the United States and France abstaining.[52] In the debate the British representative denied the allegation that developments pertaining to Southern Rhodesia constituted a threat to the peace: "Such a contention has no merit in law or in common sense."[53] And he rejected the contention "that the Security Council should in some way anticipate hypothetical troubles in an indefinite future."[54]

Southern Rhodesia's declaration of independence in November 1965 put Britain and others in a dilemma. Britain publicly declared against the use of force to topple the rebel regime, the justification being that the consequences and ramifications of a resort to force would be too difficult to predict and control; but the delegate of Ghana was

> forced to the conclusion that the United Kingdom Government is always ready to order its troops to shoot down colonial subjects when their skin is black or brown, but that the blood of white Rhodesian rebels is too sacred to be shed in the interests of majority rule.[55]

Wanting to rely on economic and diplomatic measures but needing the cooperation of other states in this connection, Britain resorted to the Security Council.

The first resolution of the Security Council was studiously ambiguous on the question whether Chapter VII was involved. The situation resulting from the proclamation of independence was said to be "extremely grave," and its "continuance in time" was said to be "a threat to international peace and security." The principal operative paragraph then called upon states to apply an arms embargo against Southern Rhodesia "and to do their utmost in order to break all economic relations with Southern Rhodesia, including an embargo on oil and petroleum products."[56] The wording suggests that voluntary action was contemplated, and the declared British view was that the resolution did not fall under Chapter VII.

But the measures recommended were not enough, and Britain returned to the Security Council in both April and December 1966. First it wanted —and got—authorization to use force if necessary to prevent the delivery of oil to Mozambique that was presumably destined for Southern Rhodesia. Then in December it finally asked that Chapter VII be invoked explicitly. Recalling the earlier resolution that the "continuance in time" of the situation resulting from the Rhodesian declaration of independence was a threat, the British Foreign Minister pointed out that the situation had continued for more than a year, and his assertion was that "the dangers to peace and stability in the whole region of Central and Southern Africa are acute."

> Here we have a small group of reckless men whose actions have provoked and are now serving to prolong a most critical situation, a situation fraught with great and growing danger of inter-racial strife and bloodshed throughout southern Africa—a danger which it is the duty of every one of us to do his utmost to avoid.[57]

In his view Southern Rhodesia was "a great moral issue. The only solution one can search for is a solution which is acceptable, which is seen to be acceptable . . . to the people of Rhodesia as a whole."[58]

Ambassador Goldberg agreed. There was in Southern Rhodesia "not a static but a deteriorating situation in which the danger to peace is obviously growing." He raised the question whether the situation justified the view that a threat to peace existed in the sense of Article 39 of the Charter, but he treated it as essentially a rhetorical question with the answer a foregone conclusion: we in the United States had "sadly learned over one hundred years ago that any attempt to institutionalize and legitimize a political principle of racial superiority in a new State was unacceptable. The effort to do so created an inflammatory situation. . . ." Goldberg supported mandatory sanctions "in the honest conviction that they are now necessary in order to drive home to the illegal regime that the international community will not tolerate the existence of a discriminatory system based on minority rule in defiance of the United Nations and its principles."[59] To him also Southern Rhodesia was "a basically moral issue."

The upshot was that the Security Council for the first time in its history declared that it was acting in accordance with Articles 39 and 41 of the Charter and went on to assert that "the present situation in Southern Rhodesia constitutes a threat to international peace and security." It then decided on mandatory sanctions of an economic sort. Among other things, all members of the United Nations were to prevent their nationals from participating in activities designed to bring about the delivery of oil and oil products to Southern Rhodesia. And members were reminded (South Africa and Portugal being the most obvious targets) that their failure or refusal to implement the resolution would be a violation of Article 25 of the Charter, binding members "to accept and carry out the decisions of the Security Council. . . ."[60] The Security Council rejected amendments inviting Britain "to prevent by all means the transport to Southern Rhodesia of oil or oil products" (which could well have meant military intervention in South Africa) and deploring Britain's refusal "to use every means including force to bring about the immediate downfall" of the Ian Smith regime.[61] One of the points on which Britain insisted was that the situation "must not be allowed to develop into a confrontation—economic or military—involving the whole of southern Africa."[62]

Again, however, the measures taken proved inadequate, not only because they were limited in extent but also because they were not fully applied. Despite warnings directed toward them, South Africa and Portugal obviously assisted Southern Rhodesia, and various other countries (e.g. Japan) allowed ingenious nationals to find ways of circumventing a number of the restrictions. In this situation—in March 1968—thirty-six African states, declaring that sanctions had failed, called for renewed consideration of the problem by the Security Council. They wanted sanctions extended in various ways, for example, the immediate severance of "all economic and other relations" with Southern Rhodesia—presumably including the severance of postal and other communications. They wanted a censure of South Africa and Portugal and a decision that "resolute and effective action" against these states would occur if they persisted in defying the Security Council. And they wanted the Security Council to urge the United Kingdom "to take urgently all necessary measures including the use of force" to overthrow the rebel regime.[63]

Prolonged negotiations ensued, mainly behind the scenes, leading to the unanimous adoption of a resolution that significantly extended the enforcement effort.[64] It called upon the United Kingdom "to take urgently all effective measures" to end the rebellion, without referring to the use of force. It sought to terminate virtually all economic (but not "other") relations with Southern Rhodesia, and requested states to go beyond the measures explicitly ordered. It called for reports from all members concerning the implementation of the sanctions and, more importantly, set up a supervisory committee authorized to examine the reports and to seek further relevant information from any state. The resolution contained warnings about the obligations of Article 25 without committing the Security Council to action in case vioations and evasions continued. It is perhaps worth noting that problems and temptations confront some governments controlled by blacks as well as some governments controlled by whites. Botswana reports that the economic consequences of the total application of the sanctions ordered would, for it, be "immediate and disastrous," and Malawi says that it could comply "only at the cost of severely imperiling its own economy, if not breaking it."[65]

## THE APPLICATION OF SANCTIONS: BAD LAW?

With regard to South Africa in 1963, as we have noted, Adlai Stevenson took the view that it would be both "bad law and bad policy" to act under Chapter VII. With regard to Southern Rhodesia in 1966, a different judgment was made. Given the ambiguities that pervade the problems of southern Africa, such differences are more or less to be expected.

The legal issues are tangled, all the more so because of the unique features in the situation of each of the accused governments. We will make no attempt here to argue these issues thoroughly, still less to explore the implications of all their unique aspects. But certain general observations can be made.

As indicated in Chapter 6 and elsewhere, the view here accepted is that the Charter, especially in Articles 55 and 56, imposes obligations that are enforceable in the same sense that any treaty obligation is enforceable. Article 2(7) does not bar international efforts to obtain implementation, whether under Chapter VI or Chapter VII. One of the difficulties is that Articles 55 and 56 are vague. But we noted in Chapter 6 that the obligation to *promote* respect for and observance of human rights without distinction as to race is at least an obligation to go in the direction of a non-discriminatory policy. If South Africa and Southern Rhodesia were in fact going in that direction, however slow their speed, their legal position would be much more nearly tenable. But they have been deliberately going in the opposite direction, actively denying human rights and hardening their policies of denial. Since they engage in illegal practices that are also highly provocative, sorely tempting others to take the law into their own hands and actually inducing them to prepare for and to take violent action, they give the United Nations a basis for a finding that they threaten the peace. Whether the finding should actually be made is much more a question of policy than a question of law.

It should hastily be added that lawful behavior might also be a threat to the peace. The point simply is that when behavior is not only inflammatory but also illegal the basis for the application of sanctions is easier to establish. And it should be noted explicitly that nothing in the Charter requires that, when sanctions are imposed, they must be directed against the state from which the threat most immediately comes. In the case of a breach of the peace or act of aggression, the usual presumption is that the guilty state is the one that fired the first shot or first sent armed forces into foreign territory. An analogous presumption is not so obvious or so strong in connection with a threat. The Security Council is free to find that the threat comes from the provocation, or simply from the situation that the provocation creates.

Ambassador Goldberg's explanations and justifications of his votes for mandatory sanctions against Southern Rhodesia add to the above considerations.

> When 94 percent of the people of Rhodesia are denied their rights because of their race, when their aspirations are inextricably interwoven with those of the entire continent, and when this situation has aroused the strongest emotions on every side—such a situation cannot under the plain provisions of the Charter be dismissed as an internal matter. I don't think anybody conversant with Africa today can deny for a moment the incendiary nature of this situation. Article 39 does not require the Security Council to hold its hand until the fire has broken into open flames.[66]

He thought that the judgment of the Security Council could "hardly be termed unreasonable. The attempt of 220,000 whites to rule 4 million nonwhites in a continent of nonwhite governments which have recently achieved independence involves great risks of violence."[67] He rejected the view that if a threat existed it came not from the whites of Rhodesia but from those who opposed them. The threat, as he saw it, stemmed from "the seizure of power by the Smith regime rather than the potential response to it. . . . The attempt of the Smith regime to alter the status quo in Rhodesia and create a new state committed to the violation of these world community standards is the real source of the threat to peace."[68]

If the principles and the reasoning applied to Southern Rhodesia justify a finding that it constitutes a threat to the peace, it is a very short step to the conclusion that South Africa does too.

The problem of Portugal is different from the problem of Southern Rhodesia and South Africa in that the principal accusation is a denial of self-determination rather than the practice and the reinforcement of racial discrimination. And, as we have noted in Chapter 5, it is not at all clear that a denial of self-determination is illegal. Though lawful behavior may be a threat to the peace, a greater question attends any contention that it is.

## THE APPLICATION OF SANCTIONS: BAD POLICY?

If the facts permit the conclusion that one situation or another in southern Africa involves a threat to the peace, the question remains whether, as a matter of policy, it is desirable or necessary actually to draw the conclusion and to act upon it. The answer depends, of course, on the vantage point from which the problem is viewed, i.e. the standard of judgment that is applied.

The United States has joined almost all other members of the United Nations in giving an affirmative answer in the case of Southern Rhodesia, the reasoning involved being suggested by two official statements. One was made by G. Mennen Williams, Assistant Secretary of State for African Affairs, who declared that "our entire posture in Africa rests squarely on the strong moral and material support we give African nations on issues of vital importance to them—and, obviously, the question of independence and majority rule in Southern Rhodesia is such an issue."[69] The implication is that one of our concerns was the favor of the African states, the importance of which is also a matter of judgment. Charles Burton Marshall, referring to new African members of the United Nations, warns against "the unwise practice of humoring them in exorbitant designs."[70] Though no official has publicly said so, a desire to support the British has no doubt also influenced decisions made in Washington.

Ambassador Goldberg made a somewhat broader statement of the factors influencing American policy.

> It is a basic interest of the United States to promote peace and stability in the world. . . . And experience demonstrates that in Africa today peace and stability are inseparable from orderly progress toward self-determination and equality for all the peoples of that continent. If the attempt to deny these rights to the African majority in Rhodesia were to succeed, this would inevitably strengthen the hand of violence, extremism, racism, and instability in the heart of Africa. The moderating and responsible participation by the United States in an international approach to the Rhodesian problem is essential to the resolution of that problem by peaceful means.[71]

An obvious question about the wisdom of the policy adopted is whether sanctions-short-of-force will be enough, and the record here is not encouraging, either in terms of general experience or in terms of the Rhodesian experience so far.[72] Even after the expansion of the sanctions program voted in May 1968, Ambassador Goldberg declared, "Based on the history of the program to date, we are under no illusions that even in the strengthened form it will produce a quick and clear-cut solution."[73] If failure has finally to be admitted, it is difficult to say what the consequences will be. At the very least, such faith as exists in the efficacy of sanctions-short-of-force will be seriously undermined. Though this might mean a shift toward sanctions that include force, the more likely implication is the abandonment for an indefinite period of serious thoughts of enforcing human rights through the United Nations. The corollary of this would be a tacit reaffirmation of the prerogatives of sovereignty and a setback in the movement to establish international accountability in the field of human rights. The whites in southern Africa, having survived a challenge, would presumably be relatively stronger for years to come and would no doubt persist in their gross violations of human rights. That the blacks of Africa would reconcile themselves permanently to discrimination and humiliation is very improbable, but it is also very uncertain when they would develop the power to vindicate their rights. Whatever faith they have in the determination of the United States, Britain, France, and other countries to act effectively against racial discrimination in the world would be substantially lost.

Questions of policy with regard to Southern Rhodesia are necessarily related to analogous questions with regard to South Africa and Portugal. The South African problem is especially difficult, and can best be discussed in terms of the demand that the Security Council should seek to "solve the problem of apartheid" through "universally applied mandatory economic sanctions."[74]

The ambiguity of the goal should be noted as a preliminary. The goal can be stated in a number of ways, and the statements vary in their connotations and implications. If the goal is to "solve the problem of apartheid," precisely what does this mean? Is it realistic to think that the problem might be "solved" in any visible future? According to Article 39, the goal should be stated differently; it should be "to maintain or restore international peace and security," which suggests not necessarily the "solution" of the problem but the reduction of the level of provocation—which raises the odd question what level of provocation should be regarded as tolerable. Still another way of stating the goal is that South Africa should be required to observe the terms of the Charter, that is, to "promote" human rights, which raises most of the questions discussed in this book. The Myrdal Committee, established in pursuance of a resolution adopted by the Security Council in 1963, stated the goal in a still different way. According to it,

> the first and basic principle [is] that all the people of South Africa should be brought into consultation and should thus be enabled to decide the future of their country at the national level.
>
> . . . We consider that all efforts should be directed to the establishment of a national convention fully representative of the whole population.
>
> . . . It is only on the road of free and democratic consultation and cooperation and conciliation that a way can be found towards a peaceful and constructive settlement. Only thus can all the people of South Africa be saved from catastrophe and the world from a conflagration of incalculable consequences.[75]

As a practical matter, the first goal would probably have to be to drive the Nationalists from power in South Africa. But who would replace them? Many forms of racial discrimination have been built into the culture of the South African whites over a period of several centuries. Most of the members of the major opposition party, the United party, are also racists, though perhaps objecting to some of the manifestations of apartheid and some of the ways of enforcing it. What organization, then, would be acceptable as the nucleus or dominant element of a new government? In principle, the national convention recommended by the Myrdal Committee might resolve the problem, but how would the composition of the convention be determined? If elections are held, what would the qualifications for voting be? Would South Africa have to be occupied by UN forces, and an interim UN government established? What countries would supply the occupying forces? on what basis? with what share of political control in the UN government? Mr. Lannung of Denmark once spoke of these problems, indicating that it would not be sufficient simply to obtain a declaration of good intentions from South African leaders, of whatever color, who endorsed the goal of "a truly democratic multiracial society with equal rights, liberties and privileges for all individuals."

> Guarantees would have to be given that those ideals would be upheld and assurances held out to allay the fear with which the white population regarded any change in the present conditions. The problems that would accompany a thorough change of heart, of policy and of society would be too heavy to be solved by the South African people alone. The United Nations might have to assist the people of South Africa in shaping the new society that must succeed apartheid.[76]

The only method for reaching the goal that the General Assembly recommends is "universally applied mandatory economic sanctions," which is surely disingenuous. Experience is Rhodesia and elsewhere warns against reliance on this method. A serious effort would have to include a blockade extending along more than 2000 miles of coast line,[77] and even an effective blockade would be unlikely to force the white South Africans to their knees. Serious splits among them are not to be expected. In all probability, increased outside pressures would unite an extremely high proportion of them solidly behind a government championing their racist cause. In such circumstances, as the record of wartime blockades shows, prolonged resistance to economic pressures is in general to be anticipated, and extensive special studies of the South African economy give no basis for anticipating anything else. Where the country is potentially most vulnerable, e.g. with respect to oil, the much-warned government has been taking precautionary measures.

Why, then, the demand for economic sanctions? Those making or ostensibly supporting the demand are apparently responding to one or more of a number of considerations. The first is the belief (whether naïve or calculated) that it is important to do something—perhaps to manifest support for moral principle and to gain the moral satisfaction that is thus obtained; perhaps to derive whatever advantages are to be gained at home or abroad from the pose and the propaganda of a champion of virtue; perhaps to forestall or undercut demands for even more extreme action. The second is that it is too much to expect a clear road to success when social and political problems are attacked, that such problems are never solved by those who dwell on the difficulties and the uncertainties, and that it is vital to carry on and intensify the struggle if only to learn better how to make it effective. The third is that it is important to get the United Nations—and, more particularly, certain of its members—committed to a program of vigorous action in the more or less deliberate expectation that they can be drawn on and on, perhaps into direct military intervention, until white supremacy in South Africa (and thus in all of southern Africa) is terminated. This statement suggests that economic sanctions are a kind of a lure and a trap, but an alternative is also quite possible: that economic sanctions might be adopted in full and open acknowledgment that military intervention is also likely to be necessary.[78] The fourth is more complex. On the one hand, it includes the expectation that economic sanctions will intensify the suffering of the blacks of South Africa, making them more inclined to rebel and giving them the courage of desperation in sabotage and guerrilla activities, shored up by the fact of outside aid and the hope of more. On the other hand, it includes the expectation that economic sanctions will put the United Nations and certain of its members in a position that virtually stops action on their part against those inside or outside South Africa who are willing to use armed force to achieve their goals. The underlying idea in the latter connection is that the support of liberals and humanitarians is valuable at least up to the point where the struggle becomes bloody, and that prior to reaching that point they must be so compromised and committed that they will be unable to interfere with those who are determined to go on. A commitment to mandatory universal sanctions would help do this, and so does a repeated endorsement of the idea that the struggle against apartheid is "legitimate" and that apartheid itself is a "crime against humanity."

In this light, it is understandable that the United States—along with France and Britain—should so far have resisted pressures for the application of sanctions against South Africa. The respectability of the position is attested to, among others, by Waldemar A. Nielsen, President of the African American Institute and a very vigorous critic of South Africa's policies. He thinks that sanctions "cannot be of use in changing the policy of apartheid," that they "might only make the white minority of South Africa even more determined to hold to its present course."[79] He thinks that the United States would violate "its own responsibilities as a world leader" and would be acting "contrary to the interests of its own citizens and of all mankind" if it were to vote in the Security Council for mandatory economic sanctions.[80]

American public opinion, actual and prospective, has considerable bearing on the question of the policy to pursue. So far the news media have provided little information about southern Africa, and few Americans have shown an interest in it—a situation which may or may not endure. Dean Acheson denounces the application of sanctions against Southern Rhodesia. As he sees it,

> The United States is engaged in an international conspiracy, instigated by Britain, and blessed by the United Nations, to overthrow the government of a country that has done us no harm and threatens no one. This is barefaced aggression, unprovoked and unjustified by a single legal or moral principle.[81]

He presumably would take a similar line if action were mounted against South Africa. Senator Thurmond thinks it "reprehensible" that the United States acted as it did on Rhodesia, and recommends that the country "bow gracefully out of any involvement in this issue and use its influence and prestige to reverse the United Nations action so far taken."[82] Representative Younger considers the vote for mandatory sanctions "a colossal mistake."[83] In contrast, Senator Robert F. Kennedy went to South Africa in 1966, making a speech in which in effect he exhorted the opponents of apartheid to have courage.[84] Senator Moss contemplates economic sanctions against South Africa, and Representative Fraser recommends them.[85] As a member of Congress, James Roosevelt once likewise recommended "strong sanctions" against South Africa and its suspension from the United Nations.[86] A Negro leader's speech in 1967 apparently started the process that led to the last-minute cancellation of the plan to have the aircraft carrier *Franklin D. Roosevelt* stop at Capetown on its way back to the United States from Vietnam.[87] SNCC was one of the few non-governmental organizations invited to send observers to the international seminar on apartheid held in Zambia in 1967 in cooperation with the United Nations. Martin Luther King held it to be "the shame of our nation" that it was "objectively an ally" of the monstrous government of South Africa "in its grim war with its own black people."[88] Senator Edward W. Brooke, reporting in April 1968 on a tour of Africa, also took the view that American policies concerning trade and investment in southern Africa imply complicity with the regimes in power there. "We must do all in our power," he said, "to end the intolerable situation in Southern Rhodesia, and that includes an absolute ban on United States trade with the territory." He did not speak specifically of sanctions against South Africa, but wanted the United States to "begin to disengage from its burgeoning economic ties to that country." He also wanted the United States to "begin to reduce its military relations with the Lisbon Government," unless that government made a "credible commitment to self-determination in Angola and Mozambique."[89]

One question is whether those lined up on opposite sides on domestic racial issues may extend their attitudes to cover the related foreign policy issues. In the eyes of the liberals and the Left, Vietnam has come to overshadow civil rights, and it is uncertain what issue may follow Vietnam; in the field of foreign affairs, southern Africa is an obvious candidate, offering the odd prospect that present Doves might turn into interventionist Hawks and vice versa. Whether this suggests that it may be good policy or bad policy to take strong action against racism and colonialism in southern Africa depends on considerations that we will not pursue.

The above attitudes, episodes, and possibilities fall far short of giving clear guidance. The policy of treating violations of human rights as threats to the peace and of seeking to solve the problem through mandatory sanctions is obviously very questionable. At the same time, the costs to the United States of a refusal to do anything about racism in southern Africa might well be large. Sooner or later many Americans would come to feel moral shame, as many Germans did after they learned of Dachau and Buchenwald. The moral posture of the United States would be impugned, the seriousness of its commitment to its own values questioned. For the United States to stand aloof in relation to the most egregious violations of human rights would suggest that it had little concern for such rights anywhere outside its own borders and would thus tend to undermine the whole movement for international action on human rights as it has developed since World War II. Moreover, it would in some degree alienate, and deprive the United States of diplomatic support from, governments in most of the black African republics, in much of Asia, and in some other parts of the world as well. It might even tend to jeopardize human rights within the United States, on the basis of the principle that indifference to their violation abroad would lead toward similar indifference to their violation at home. And it is a question whether aloofness would work as a policy any more than neutrality worked in the 1930's. The probability seems high that racial violence will increase in southern Africa, with massacres, guerrilla action, and even war as very distinct possibilities. Conceivably the United States could maintain its aloofness in the face of such events, but many features of the record of the past—and the growth of black power within the United States—make this seem quite unlikely. A policy of aloofness thus raises at least as many questions as a policy of support for mandatory sanctions.

In-between possibilities exist. One set of them follows, closely patterned after suggestions by Waldemar A. Nielsen.[90]

First, the United States might manifest stronger interest in human rights issues over the world, initiating proposals concerning them. The hope would be that it could thus promote a number of objectives simultaneously: the development of a world environment more congenial to the domestic political system that the American people want to maintain and develop, the demonstration of a genuine and general interest in human rights, pursued in good faith, and the introduction of a greater degree of realism into the consideration of the problems of southern Africa. This suggestion assumes that the problem of human rights should be treated as a global problem, that it is contrary to the spirit of the Charter to focus almost entirely on one or two types of violation in one part of the world, and that those inclined toward a restricted view should be induced to think in terms of principles of international accountability that are to be generally applied in connection with many types of violation and neglect in many parts of the world.

Second, though opposing the mandatory application of sanctions, the United States might in some degree disengage itself from South Africa. The General Assembly has recommended this, and Senator Brooke has taken up the term. The precise meaning of "disengage" would have to be worked out. Whereas mandatory sanctions suggest a commitment to inflict defeat on another state within a measureable future, and thus involve the prestige of the United Nations if not of the individual states championing the adoption of such sanctions, disengagement would suggest unilateral moral censure symbolized by policies that minimize complicity. As opposed to sanctions, disengagement would tacitly reflect an inability to prevent South Africa from pursuing its course, but would manifest a determination not to help it along. The United States has practiced various forms of disengagement in its policies toward the Soviet Union, Communist China, and Castro's Cuba, and could learn from its experiences in selecting the measures to apply to South Africa. The measures need not include a severance of diplomatic relations or a curtailment of travel. On the contrary, one object might well be to expand contact and communication on the assumption that the freest possible flow of information is desirable. Necessarily, however, most or all of the measures would be designed to induce or compel American concerns to forgo profits that might otherwise be made, and so would have to be based on a willingness within the government to face the political pressures that would come—especially if concerns from other countries take up the opportunities that are abandoned. The measures taken would have to go far beyond the existing ban on calls at South African ports by vessels of the U.S. Navy.

Third, the United States might do much more than it has been doing to contribute to educational programs for black Africans from countries lying both north and south of Zambesi, especially for those black Africans who show promise of future leadership; this is simply on the assumption that as a general rule the interests of the United States will be served if leaders abroad, whether in or out of governmental office, are knowledgeable. The educational programs might or might not be conducted within the United States. They presumably would not include a deliberate effort to train military or revolutionary leaders, or leaders in sabotage, though some of the participants would probably find themselves eventually in one or another of these categories.

Though educational programs for black Africans should no doubt take priority, the needs of whites in South Africa could well get attention too. It is especially important that the whites destined for future leadership have knowledge and experience of the outside world, that they should be directly exposed to moral currents and intellectual and political developments outside South Africa having to do with human rights and race relations.

George W. Ball stresses this consideration. He is scornful of policies so far pursued relating to apartheid. "The realistic hope of ameliorating the repulsive social practices of South Africa," he says, "is not by compulsion from without—the nation is too powerful for that—but by the encouragement of internal change. . . ." He thinks that a multi-racial South African society is pie in the sky, but he suggests taking up the idea of Bantustans, which the whites have themselves advanced. "We should encourage the government in every way to carry out its avowed objectives by greatly enlarging the Bantustans and making them economically viable."[91]

The suggestion—a possible fourth feature of American policy—is obviously highly debateable. On the one hand, it suggests an accommodation to racism, and would thus be opposed by many members of the United Nations, including many of those from Africa, and by the more militant black leaders within South Africa. Moreover, it directly attacks only the problem of the blacks who can be geographically set apart. On the other hand, Bantustans would provide their inhabitants with a measure of self-government, give them training and experience, and reduce the humiliation and indignity under which they now live. In various ways, too, e.g. by enhancing respect for the culture and achievement of the blacks and by reducing white fears of being numerically overwhelmed, Bantustans might contribute toward an alleviation of the position of the blacks left in the "white" area. The prospect is uncertain and the "solution" less than ideal. The question is whether the aphorism about half a loaf applies.

These lines of action will not solve the problem of apartheid or the other problems of southern Africa in any visible future. They would be interim measures, though they might need to be pursued for many years. What would follow from them remains unclear.

# 10

# Conditions of Implementation

Conditions of implementation are conditions favorable to achieving the standards or executing the commitments already accepted. They are conditions whose absence would seriously impede or even preclude the realization of goals or the meeting of obligations. Creating or improving conditions favorable to implementation is very largely a domestic task, but in some connections international action is also possible.

Conditions favoring the implementation of civil and political rights differ some from conditions favoring the implementation of economic and social rights. We will therefore deal with the two categories of rights in turn.

The subject is big and complex, even if confined to the problem of implementation within the United States, a much studied country; and it becomes far bigger and far more complex when considered on a global scale. To ask about conditions affecting the implementation of human rights is virtually to ask why political systems develop as they do and what the conditions of economic development are. Thus the object here cannot even be to summarize relevant knowledge, inadequate as it is, but only to point toward the relevant and to give some sense of the nature and magnitude of the problem.

## CONDITIONS RELATING TO CIVIL AND POLITICAL RIGHTS

Ideologies, political attitudes, and various features of government affect the problem of implementing civil and political rights, though almost all generalizations on the subject are hazardous.

The most obvious and probably the surest of the generalizations is that Nazism and the Nazi dictatorship were by their very nature antithetical to human rights, rejecting the idea that men are created equal, denying fair trials to many of those accused, and depriving millions of the right to life.

Communists claim to support human rights—claim, in fact, that human rights can be fully implemented only in the kind of society they aim to create—but communist dictatorships have varied in their records. Stalin's victims obviously did not enjoy civil and political rights any more than Hitler's. In rehabilitating a few out of the millions liquidated or sent to forced labor camps in earlier years, a number of communist governments admit their failings. We will not argue here the question of the extent to which the principle of a "dictatorship of the proletariat" and the continuing practices of communist regimes are compatible with the various rights set forth in the International Covenant on Civil and Political Rights, for example, the right to freedom of expression, the right of peaceful assembly, the right to freedom of association, the right "to take part in the conduct of public affairs, directly or through freely chosen representatives," and the right "to vote and to be elected at genuine periodic elections . . . guaranteeing the free expression of the will of the electors." The movements for liberalization in Hungary in 1956 and in Czechoslovakia in 1968 suggest that many communists themselves believed that rights such as these had been denied, and it is a question how long the Ulbricht regime in Eastern Germany would last if such rights were in fact implemented.

Non-communist dictatorships, i.e. the more or less personal dictatorships and the military dictatorships, vary considerably. Duvalier's regime in Haiti is guilty of egregious denials of civil and political rights. Ayub Khan of Pakistan had a better record, even if it was not pure. The military dictatorship in Greece frankly suspends the application of certain human rights, pleading the existence of a "public emergency threatening the life of the nation." The monarchy in Saudi Arabia does not hold elections, though its delegate in the United Nations sheds tears over the rejection of the principle of one man, one vote in Southern Rhodesia. One could go on down the list of dictatorships, no doubt finding human rights violated in some degree in all of them. The extent to which control is in military or civilian hands is not necessarily indicative of the extent of the violations, at least according to a survey by David H. Bayley; he finds "no clear pattern between military participation in politics and the resultant state of human rights. . . . Simple formulas equating uniforms with repression and business suits with freedom soon prove to be slender reeds."[1]

By definition, democracy as such (Western type) involves at least a limited respect for some rights of some human beings; but again generalizations are hazardous. For many decades the United States subscribed to the theory that all men are created equal, and operated as a democracy, while maintaining slavery. And for many more decades discrimination against women persisted. South Africa should probably be classified as a democracy today, but it is a democracy only for the whites; 80 per cent of the population are denied suffrage and many other human rights. Plainly some democracies make a distinction between those who count and those who do not; and rights go only or mainly to those who count. Given a sufficient degree of consensus among those who count, they can do the others in, and do it democratically.

The fact that democracies differ so much among themselves raises the question, what makes the difference? To shift and limit the question, what conditions make for and against respect for civil and political rights in democracies? Even within this limitation the question cannot be answered at all confidently. We have already discussed one of its aspects in Chapter 7, when we analyzed attitudes on the utility of bills of rights and formal legal or constitutional obligations. The conclusion was indecisive, and it is also indecisive when the question is approached from other angles.

John Roche has inquired into the tradition of freedom in the United States, and his analysis and arguments are relevant to the broader question of implementing civil and political rights. He advances two hypotheses.

> First, the individual liberty which was characteristic of early American society was a function of the openness and pluralism of that society rather than of any libertarian ideology.
>
> Second, the individual freedom of contemporary American society is largely a function of the impersonalization and bureaucratization of social relationships and of the formalization of these interactions in a meaningful, national legal conception—due process of law.[2]

Roche quotes Madison as saying that "in the extended republic of the United States, and among the great variety of interests, parties, and sects which it embraces, a coalition of a majority of the whole society could seldom take place on any other principles than those of justice and the general good." The line of thought, as Roche says, is both sophisticated and naïve—naïve in the sense that it does not take into account the problem of justice for those excluded from the system, namely the slaves. But in accordance with the line of thought, Roche contends that in the period of rural predominance individual freedom in America depended not so much on ideology, on moral or legal principle, as on "the strength of one's group, its ability to fight off attempts at domination," and on "the fragmentation of power among many groups, the absence of monolithic configurations." In contrast, he contends that in the period of urban predominance freedom depends upon the impersonalization of life: "it is possible to live differently and believe differently from one's neighbors without their knowing, much less caring, about the deviation." He attributes freedom to the absence of direct democracy, and to the tendency to transfer the powers of representative democracy from the local and state to the national level. Social control is exercised not so much on the basis of "wrath and its inevitable fellows, the tarpot, lash, and noose," as on the basis of the police power of government, guided and restrained by a nationally enforced commitment to due process of law. For liberty in urban America, "the symbolic institution . . . is the federal district judge informing the State of South Carolina that it cannot assert the sovereignty of numbers to deprive individual Negro citizens of their fundamental rights and liberties. American liberty, in short, has become the positive goal of national public policy, rather than a fortuitous consequence of fragmentation, pluralism, and social conflict."[3]

But how does it happen that liberty has become "the positive goal of national public policy?" Evidently it is not because people generally know the principles involved and are committed to them. Several studies relate to this question. One by Prothro and Grigg, based on a sample of voters in Ann Arbor and Tallahassee, confirmed the expectation that in these cities a general consensus exists on the idea of democracy and on the abstract principles of majority rule and minority rights; but it revealed sharp discord on ten more specific statements concerning concrete applications of those principles. For example, although respondents agreed on majority rule, they divided on the question whether a majority should have its way if it elected a Negro or a communist as mayor; and although they agreed on free speech, they divided on the question of permitting speeches against churches and religion, or for government ownership. As a group, the more highly educated were more consistently democratic in their responses than the less highly educated; in fact, "high education was the primary basis of agreement." But even the highly educated did not share a consensus; they came closer to a 50-50 split than to complete agreement on half of the specific statements presented to them. Despite such discord, the rights in question are generally respected in the communities studied. The findings led Prothro and Grigg to suggest that respect for rights may be due more to habitual patterns of behavior than to conscious agreement on principles.[4] But it is uncertain how the habitual patterns came to develop and what relationship their development has, if any, to Roche's argument concerning a nationally enforced commitment to due process of law.

A number of other studies relate to questions pertaining to respect for civil and political rights in the United States. Focusing on *Communism, Conformity, and Civil Liberties,* Stouffer found that in the United States "community leaders, on almost all questions, are more willing to respect the rights of the nonconformist than are the rank and file,"[5] which reinforces the natural expectation that their attitudes are of special significance in any effort to promote human rights.

Herbert McClosky, in "Consensus and Ideology in American Politics," makes numerous relevant statements.

> Democratic beliefs and habits are obviously not "natural" but must be learned; and they are learned more slowly by men and women whose lives are circumscribed by apathy, ignorance, provincialism and social or physical distance from the centers of intellectual activity. . . . Even in a highly developed democratic nation like the United States, millions of people continue to possess only the most rudimentary understanding of democratic ideology.[6]

Like Stouffer, McClosky finds that support for a democratic ideology in the United States, which includes support for at least some of the civil and political rights, is by and large stronger among the "political influentials" than among the "general electorate." His findings fit with Roche's argument; they refute the notion that "a passion for freedom, tolerance, justice and other democratic values springs spontaneously from the lower depths of the society, and that the plain, homespun uninitiated yeoman, worker and farmer are the natural hosts of democratic ideology."

> Usually the simpler the man, the lower his station in life, and the greater his objective need for equality, the more we have endowed him with a capacity for understanding democracy. We are thus inclined to give the nod to the farmer over the city man, the unlearned

> over the educated, the poor man over the man of wealth, the "people" over their leaders, the unsophisticated over the sophisticated. Yet every one of these intuitive expectations turns out, upon investigation, to be questionable or false.[7]

Interestingly enough, however, 46 per cent of both the "general electorate" and the "political influentials" agreed that "just as is true of fine race horses, some breeds of people are just naturally better than others"; and approximately the same percentage agreed that "when it comes to the things that count most, all races are certainly not equal." Moreover, on the question whether "the government should give a person work if he can't find another job," 47 per cent of the "general electorate" agreed as against only 24 per cent of the "political influentials."

Seymour Martin Lipset reports similar findings.

> The poorer strata everywhere are more liberal or leftist on economic issues; they favor more welfare state measures, higher wages, graduated income taxes, support of trade unions, and so forth. But when liberalism is defined in noneconomic terms—as support of civil liberties, internationalism, etc.—the correlation is reversed. The more well-to-do are more liberal, the poorer are more intolerant.[8]

Further, according to Lipset,

> The findings of public opinion surveys in thirteen different countries that the lower strata are less committed to democratic norms than the middle classes are reaffirmed by the research of more psychologically oriented investigators, who have studied the social correlates of the "authoritarian personality." Many studies in this area . . . show a consistent association between authoritarianism and lower-class status.[9]

Lipset's view on the importance of education is similar to that of Prothro and Grigg, quoted above. "The higher one's education, the more likely one is to believe in democratic values and support democratic practices. All the relevant studies indicate that education is far more significant than income or occupation. . . . If we cannot say that a 'high' level of education is a sufficient condition for democracy, the available evidence does suggest that it comes close to being a necessary one."[10] On a more general plane, Lipset makes an observation that surely has great significance to human rights over much of the world.

> The poorer a country, and the lower the absolute standard of living of the lower classes, the greater the pressure on the upper strata to treat the lower classes as beyond the pale of human society, as vulgar, as innately inferior, as a lower caste. The sharp difference in the style of living between those at the top and those at the bottom makes this psychologically necessary. Consequently, the upper strata also tend to regard political rights for the lower strata, particularly the right to share in power, as essentially absurd and immoral.[11]

This fits with a finding of Moskos and Bell, who focus on four of the Caribbean nations; their data tend to support the hypothesis that "feelings of social distance towards the subordinate socio-economic groups produce cynicism about political democracy."[12] Robert E. Scott makes a similar observation, saying that the ruling elites in Latin America "cannot conceive that the masses, those 'animals,' those Indians 'who have no souls,' should have the same political rights as a cultured aristocracy."[13] And a report of the Inter-American Juridical Committee says that "a consistent civic conscience with regard to the dignity of the individual is not prevalent today."[14]

Finally, one more study of the above types might be cited. Focusing on "Determinants of Support for Civil Liberties" in the United States, Selvin and Hagstrom report a series of correlations. Like others, they find that libertarianism increases with education. And they also find religious differences: "Almost half of the Jews (49 per cent) are highly libertarian, as against less than a third of the Protestants and Roman Catholics"; non-church-goers are more likely than church-goers to be libertarian. "In every section of the United States and on every issue the community leaders and the people with the most education (from whom the leaders are drawn) are more concerned about civil liberties and more tolerant of political dissent than is the general public."[15]

The studies described above do not give a clear answer to the question with which they were introduced: how it happens that liberty (and thus presumably civil and political rights in general) has become "the positive goal of national public policy." They suggest a combination of factors. Constitutional and institutional arrangements are among them—arrangements making it unlikely that any one coherent group can get complete control and make public policy conform to its conception of Truth. Education is among them, though it is unclear precisely what features of education are important. The absence of gross discrepancies in culture and ways of life is probably also among them. Respect for government, especially for the national government, is not specifically mentioned but can perhaps be inferred—a disposition to concede leadership to it and to accept the leadership that is forthcoming. Other conditions are no doubt relevant as well, and it is uncertain how a list based on studies of Gabon or South Africa or Bulgaria or Ecuador would differ from a list based on studies of the United States.

Conditions of implementation very different in character from those in point above should also be mentioned. The very operation of government depends on the availability of people with the kinds of values and the kinds of training that are required—in public administration, in the administration of justice, in the management of fiscal affairs, and so on. And suitable personnel must be available for varied kinds of activities outside government itself. For example, the report on the Seminar on Human Rights in Developing Countries, held in Kabul, Afghanistan, in 1964, speaks of agreement

> that one of the most basic prerequisites of the right to a fair trial was the existence of an adequate number of well-trained lawyers jealous of their independence, imbued with a sense of professional ethics, and fearless when faced with pressures of the government, political or economic groups or public opinion.[16]

Similarly, if freedom of the press is to be fully implemented, journalists with comparable qualities are essential. The fact is suggested by the statement of a Burmese delegate in the United Nations that in Burma

> the real restraint on freedom of information was imposed not by irksome laws but by the lack of training and the relatively unsettled ethical standards of journalists and other people concerned with the dissemination of information.[17]

Several of the studies cited above relating to civil and political rights in the United States produced conclusions on the importance of education. Its importance is emphasized in other connections too. For example, at the Kabul seminar mentioned above, "all speakers were agreed that the proclamation of the equality of men and women would have no real meaning unless at the same time there was an intensive campaign to raise the educational level of women in those countries where their education lagged behind that of men."[18]

Probable interrelationships between the civil and political, on the one hand, and the economic and social, on the other, should be emphasized. As Hernán Santa-Cruz says,

> The exercise of political rights is one of the most effective means of ensuring the effective protection of economic, social, and cultural rights. And conversely, full recognition and enjoyment of economic, social and cultural rights provides one of the best means of ensuring the effective protection of political rights.[19]

Surely economic conditions affect the implementation of civil and political rights. Quincy Wright attributes crucial significance to them, as well as to circumstances having to do with foreign relationships: "Democracy and liberalism have developed only within states which have enjoyed moderate prosperity and education and which have been secure from external attack because of geographical isolation, a stable balance of power, or a rule of law. . . . Freedom from fear and freedom from want are the prerequisites to freedom of religion and freedom of opinion."[20] David H. Bayley, examining *Public Liberties in the New States,* agrees that moderate prosperity is important to civil and political rights.[21] The United States is inclined to emphasize a right to property as a basis for the development and protection of other rights, and many see the existence of a middle class as crucial. Communists, of course, go farthest in stressing the importance of the material base, although from their point of view the private ownership of property is an enemy rather than a promoter of freedom. According to the communist view, the "real exercise" of all human rights and fundamental freedoms "depends above all on the socio-economic structure of society."[22] The line, and its vagueness, are familiar. "Democracy is built into the very nature of Socialism and is determined by its economic system—abolition of private property in the means of production. Socialist property, and labor emancipated from exploitation, are the principal conditions for the true freedom of the individual."[23]

Along a different line, David H. Bayley notes that in many countries discrimination exists as the product of impersonal circumstance.

> In many of the new states large sections of the populace are unable to compete for positions in government service or even to compete effectively for national office because they have a language skill only in a local, restricted dialect. This may be called "structural discrimination." It is discrimination in the sense that opportunities are uniformly limited for a group by circumstances beyond their control.[24]

This is at least suggestive of the kinds of conditions that affect the implementation of civil and political rights. Quite obviously, neither the ratification of an international convention nor direct efforts to implement it are likely to have much effect unless the conditions of implementation are in some degree present. In recognition of this fact (and as part of the "action program" suggested by the United States in 1953), the United Nations—in cooperation with host countries—has been sponsoring seminars such as the one held in Kabul in 1964. John Humphrey describes the seminars as "one of the most dynamic and useful features of the human rights program."[25] UNESCO's activities on behalf of education at all levels are in point. Among other things, UNESCO awards fellowships enabling journalists in developing countries to undertake advanced study abroad, and it has assisted in the establishment of regional training centers aimed at raising standards in journalism.[26] Needs of these sorts are endless.

### CONDITIONS RELATING TO ECONOMIC AND SOCIAL RIGHTS

The conditions of implementing economic and social rights are known even less clearly than the conditions of implementing civil and political rights. Again a mass of material is relevant, but theories are neither well developed nor reliable.

Organizational and institutional arrangements are obviously among the relevant conditions; and these arrangements are important in a number of fields of activity.

Political and governmental institutions are among the most important. For the implementation of economic and social rights these institutions must be reasonably efficient, responsible, and stable. They must shape policy, and enact and administer law; and this means, among other things, that they must build roads, run schools, collect taxes, manage the currency, develop statistical records, and so on. For such purposes they must be able to recruit and retain capable and suitably trained personnel, and they must have effective control over people and territory. Moreover, leadership in politics and government must be in the hands of those who, whether because of their own genuine preference or because of the pressures and demands that they face, believe that economic and social rights should be promoted and implemented. The notion of promoting and implementing economic and social rights through governmental action assumes a level of political development that many states have obviously achieved, especially in the Western world, but that many others are still striving for with varying degrees of success.

Serious disagreement is unlikely on the underlying theme of the above paragraph—that governments must govern if economic and social rights are to be achieved. In contrast, disagreement is sharp on questions pertaining to the effect of ideologies and forms of government. Communists emphasize the idea of economic and social *rights*, and claim that such rights cannot really be achieved under "bourgeois democracy." But it is not at all clear that societies under communist dictatorship actually produce benefits more effectively than others are able to do. A paper on "Human Rights and Representative Democracy," prepared in the Secretariat of the Inter-American Commission on Human Rights, takes an opposite line. It speaks of a need

> to re-emphasize that far from being secondary rights, the civil and political rights are the forerunners of the economic and social rights; that democratic governments must be rooted in a firm recognition of these rights and liberties; and that without civil and political rights, all men are dependent on the volatile benevolence of those persons who seize power, no matter how socially conscious their government pretends to be.[27]

"Rights," says Carl Friedrich, "depend for their effectualization upon the marshalling of appropriate power." And he quotes Martin Luther King as saying, "We know through painful experience that freedom is never voluntarily given by the oppressor; it must be demanded by the oppressed."[28] Governments vary in the extent to which they permit the oppressed to voice demands and the champions of rights to marshall appropriate power. The dictatorships of Hitler and Stalin were so brutal and ruthless that those deprived of rights were substantially helpless. Duvalier's dictatorship is in this category today. It is the very nature of dictatorship that limits of some sort be imposed on the marshalling of any power that is regarded as adverse. Democracies are in general more permissive, and appropriate power is much more commonly marshalled in them. But those who lack rights in democracies sometimes also lack the knowledge and the motivation to marshall the power that is potentially theirs, and sometimes the democracy is in fact an oligarchy of class or color, content (if not determined) to maintain a system of privilege. In the OAS, a report on the work of the Inter-American Juridical Committee deplores "the fact that the Charter of Social Guarantees . . . has remained no more than a list of desires and hopes, an ideal," and it goes on to say why this has happened:

> This is because of the unfortunate existence of the problem in various Latin American countries, of the preponderant position of the economically powerful classes, whose members exercise decisive influence on the respective governments.[29]

The situation in South Africa is more extreme, the white government making very determined efforts to prevent the non-whites from developing demands and from marshalling power to press for their effectualization.

An implication of this should be noted explicitly: democratic institutions permit a marshalling of power against as well as in favor of the recognition and implementation of social and economic rights. Senator Bricker and the ABA Committee on Peace and Law Through the United Nations demonstrated this very effectively in the early 1950's. And the absence of organized opposition is sometimes as important as the presence of organized support if economic and social rights are to be granted.

Other sorts of institutions, in addition to the political and governmental, are also important conditions of the implementation of economic and social rights. Educational institutions are necessary not only to implement the right to education itself, but also to provide the various kinds of training on which the implementation of other rights depends. A college of medicine, for example, may be among the conditions of the implementation of a right to health; and colleges of law, engineering, agriculture, and so on, play similar roles. Institutions of a commercial and financial sort are necessary, as are trade union organizations and associations of trade unions.

Resources of various sorts are interrelated with organizational and institutional arrangements as conditions of the implementation of economic and social rights. Human resources are among them—people with the necessary qualities. Their level of health and education is important, their motivations and values, their awareness of possibilities, and their determination to realize them. The attitudes of the elites in the society are particularly important, as the section on civil and political rights suggests. On the one hand, those who deny equality in the civil and political realm are likely to deny it also in the economic and social realm. Slaves do not have economic and social rights, any more than they have civil and political rights. And apartheid means a denial of rights in both categories. On the other hand, those who support equality of civil and political rights are likely also to support the principle of equality of opportunity in the economic and social field, whether or not they believe it is the proper function of government to see to it that economic and social "rights" are implemented.

The importance of human resources to the implementation of economic and social rights is suggested by contrasts between the more advanced and the underdeveloped and primitive countries. The peoples that enjoy economic and social rights most fully (or, if not "rights," then benefits) are those with good health, high levels of education, training and skills, high degrees of motivation, substantial freedom from beliefs that prevent or seriously impede vigorous participation in productive activity, and confidence or hope that a better life can be achieved. Conversely, those who enjoy these rights minimally, if at all, may or may not have good health, probably lack education or the relevant training and skills, probably lack a vision of progress and hope that it can be achieved, and may be caught up in religious or other beliefs that impose limits on what they want or are able to achieve.

Material resources are of course important too, both natural and man-made; and these resources are distributed very unevenly over the globe. To take advantage of those that nature provides and to increase those that stem from human labor is obviously necessary to the full realization of economic and social rights. To be meaningful, freedom of the press, for example, depends on all the factors that make the publication of newspapers possible: the trees from which newsprint is manufactured, the transportation system that delivers the trees to the paper mill and that delivers the newsprint to the printing plant, the domestic and international communication system through which news dispatches flow, the electric power that runs the printing press, and so on and on. The Food and Agriculture Organization can appropriately claim that it is contributing to the freedom of the press when it assists members to grow the trees from which newsprint is made, and so can those who bring about a reduction in the costs of cable and telegraph facilities.

Just as international tension and war affect the implementation of civil and political rights, so do they affect the implementation of economic and social rights, though the effect does not necessarily go in the same direction. Quincy Wright's view is that economic and social rights

> may, under some circumstances, be advanced by socialistic activity of governments, and such activity may sometimes be facilitated by restraints upon individual liberty of speech, economic enterprise, and other civil liberties. Governmental activity of this kind may be less resisted in times of war or high tension. . . . Thus, the relationship to war of advances in economic and social rights may be the opposite of advance in civil liberties.[30]

Qualified as it is, the statement is no doubt true. At the same time, the possibility is obvious that war may be so destructive in material and nonmaterial ways (either or both) that it impedes rather than facilitates the implementation of economic and social rights.

Thus it is obvious that the conditions of implementing economic and social rights have a great deal in common with the conditions of development, both political and economic. And this suggests that the growing literature on the problem of the development of underdeveloped societies is relevant to the problem of identifying and bringing into existence conditions making for the implementation of economic and social rights. However, a review of that literature will not be attempted here.[31]

# V

# Conclusion

# 11

# Conclusion

The preceding chapters are addressed to three questions: What are human rights? What international obligations relating to human rights have states accepted, and what issues are raised, especially in the United States, by the possibility of accepting more? What kinds of international methods are or might be employed to promote or protect human rights over the world?

The first of these questions concerns the relationship of the individual and the state—an age-old question in a new form; it concerns the limits and the obligations that the state should accept in its treatment of individuals, both in the realm of the civil and the political and in the realm of the economic, social, and cultural. The second and third questions concern the relationship of the individual and the state, on the one side, with the international community on the other; they ask about the respective roles of the state and the international community in promoting and protecting human rights. The treatment of these questions has been guided and influenced by another concerning the foreign policies of the United States and the immediately related domestic policies—the policies that are or perhaps should be pursued relating to international action on human rights.

Now the purpose is to give a summary review, to check on some of the appraisals and prognoses that others have advanced, and to consider questions of policy that are posed.

## WHAT ARE HUMAN RIGHTS?

Votes in the United Nations and other international organizations indicate a substantial degree of consensus on the question, what are human rights, when the answer is confined to general principles.

Members of the United Nations agreed almost unanimously in 1948 on the text of the Universal Declaration, and they agreed again in 1966 on the two Covenants. They have adopted a Convention on Genocide, a Convention on the Political Rights of Women, and a Convention on the Elimination of All Forms of Racial Discrimination; and they have adopted numerous special declarations. Members of the ILO have adopted an even greater number of conventions and declarations having to do with labor, e.g. one dealing with the right to organize and to engage in collective bargaining. Members of UNESCO have adopted a Convention against Discrimination in Education. Members of WHO endorse a statement of rights relating to health. And so on. Regional agreements also exist, for example, the American Declaration of the Rights and Duties of Man and, above all, the European Convention on Human Rights.

Agreement on principles is significant, and might well become far more significant. At the same time, even in connection with the documents approved, agreement is incomplete. Like the United States Constitution, these documents are open to interpretation, and the fact that two states have voted for the same words may or may not mean that they agree on the meaning to be assigned to them. The rather general reluctance of states to ratify conventions, even after voting for them, is at least in part explained by fear that they might be held to a meaning they did not intend. The United States and the Soviet Union both endorse the idea of free speech and free press, but they obviously give the terms different meanings. Both accept the freedom of workers to organize into trade unions, but delegates of the United States in the ILO are chronically troubled over the question whether those who claim to represent Soviet labor do so in any meaningful sense. The parties to the first protocol of the European Convention on Human Rights, including Greece, agree to the holding of "free elections," but it is not yet entirely clear whether they all agree on the meaning of the term. None of this is surprising. Agreement on the United States Constitution has been accompanied by disagreement on its meaning from the very first, and new meanings are still being found in it.

In a very few areas, sharp differences have appeared, even on questions of principle, and in still others no serious effort to achieve agreement has occurred. The right to property is affirmed in the Universal Declaration of Human Rights, but not in either of the Covenants; not that any state rejects all private right to the ownership of property, but simply that agreement on any general statement of the right has been impossible to achieve. Similarly, though the General Assembly endorses the right of self-determination by overwhelming votes, disagreements about the meaning of the term are so great as to amount to disagreements about the principle.

The question when life begins is among those on which no very serious effort has yet been made to achieve agreement. More broadly, though all states subscribe to a right to life, they do not try to specify when it either begins or ends. An inter-American draft convention specifies that it begins "at the moment of conception," a view to which Japan, the Soviet Union, and a number of other states are not likely to subscribe. Apparently no international document attempts to define death. Many private references occur to the "human right" to regulate the size of the family or to regulate conception by artificial methods, but international documents are silent on the question. Though widespread agreement exists on a right to freedom of movement within countries, and freedom to choose a place of residence, no right is recognized to enter a country other than one's own. Understandably, states have not made agreements with each other guaranteeing their citizens a right of conscientious objection in war, though it is not at all far-fetched to say that the right to life should have as a counterpart a right not to be required to kill. Discrimination is now condemned when it is based on race, sex, language, or religion, but not when it derives from differences of opportunity due to family or social circumstance. No serious attack has yet been made on the question of the proportion of the available resources that must be allocated to the implementation of each of the various economic and social rights. To put this point differently, no serious attack has yet been made on such questions as the amount and the quality of education required, given the total resources of the state, if the right to education is to be suitably implemented, or the quality or extent of social security or health care.

Thus inadequacies and gaps exist in the answers so far accepted to the question, what are human rights. Nevertheless, agreement is extensive and significant, providing a basis for the elaboration of specific obligations and for their implementation.

## THE ACCEPTANCE OF INTERNATIONAL OBLIGATIONS

Articles 55 and 56 of the Charter require members to cooperate with the United Nations in promoting respect for human rights. It is generally agreed that the articles impose obligations, but just what the obligations are remains uncertain. The Universal Declaration, the numerous other declarations, the Covenants, and the various conventions that the General Assembly has adopted can no doubt be taken to suggest the list of rights that must be promoted, but the very fact that the Covenants and conventions are recommended for ratification reflects an unwillingness to take the stand that states have already accepted the obligations involved. In general, the United Nations has not sought the enforcement of Articles 55 and 56 against specific states in concrete circumstances. The principal exception to this relates to Southern Rhodesia and South Africa, who undoubtedly violate the requirement to promote human rights "without distinction as to race." Moreover, action against these states is also based on the charge that they, or situations that they create, threaten the peace.

Many states have accepted obligations in the field of human rights in addition to those of the Charter. Most notable among them are the parties to the European Convention on Human Rights, who have quite deliberately placed their respect for civil and political rights under international supervision. Moreover, many of these states and others all over the world have ratified a large number of the specialized conventions—conventions recommended by the General Assembly, the ILO, and UNESCO. A rather extensive network of treaty obligations in the field of human rights—especially in the portion of the field relating to labor—is in process of development.

The acceptance of international obligations in the field of human rights since World War II is significant, in fact, potentially revolutionary. It marks a sharp departure from the long established principle that the treatment that a state meted out to its own citizens was not, save in very exceptional circumstances, a matter of international concern, and it marks a reversal of the stand taken by those who drafted the Covenant of the League of Nations. Further, the willingness of many states to go beyond the Charter in spelling out the obligations more specifically or in adding to them is also notable.

At the same time, the extent to which states have given specific meaning to the Charter provisions, and the extent to which they have gone beyond the Charter in accepting obligations should not be exaggerated. In truth, the emphasis should probably be on their failure to do more. We will note shortly the fact that members of the UN seek international action to implement the obligations of the Charter in only rather limited ways and circumstances. They are also very obviously reluctant about accepting additional obligations, as their failure to ratify the Covenants attests. A number of factors, no doubt varying from country to country, account for the reluctance. Some governments have what they regard as more urgent matters to attend to and do not want to divert time or energy to the question of accepting international obligations in the field of human rights. Some object in principle to one or more provisions of instruments recommended to them. For example, as a matter of practical domestic politics, the United States can scarcely ratify, say, the Covenant on Civil and Political Rights, even though it already in practice accepts most of the principles involved; it would be sure to face difficulty over Article 50, specifying that the provisions of the Covenant "shall extend to all parts of federal States without any limitations or exceptions," and it would probably face difficulty over Article 20 requiring the outlawry of "propaganda for war" and "any advocacy of national, racial or religious hatred that constitutes incitement to discrimination, hostility or violence." Many governments face such severe domestic problems—perhaps to create or maintain unity in the face of divisive forces, or perhaps to avert economic collapse or to stimulate economic development—that they do not want to limit their freedom of action—for example, in the realm of freedom of speech, or in the realm of judicial safeguards. Especially where respect for human rights is not already deeply imbedded in the national tradition, or where human rights are in effect the privileges of the well-to-do, reluctance about accepting international obligations is likely to be found, if for no other reason than that the oligarchy or the political elite sees no advantage in taking a different view. Endorse a declaration? Why not? But make a commitment that might lead to international pressures and international embarrassment, or even to domestic change? Why?

The above reasons for a reluctance to accept additional international obligations is sometimes expressed as a desire to maintain the prerogatives of sovereignty—a desire which also springs from emotions existing independently of reasons. Nationalists generally want to avoid international accountability for domestic practices, or at least to keep it at a minimum.

And if nationalists like former Senator Bricker, or like the members of the Committee on Peace and Law Through the United Nations of the ABA, think that they see in government officials some weakening of nationalistic resolve, they can appeal to chauvinistic pride and play on patriotic sensitivities about the foreigner and about foreign interference in what has traditionally been, in all countries, a matter of domestic jurisdiction.

In this light, the fact that states have not gone farther and faster in accepting international obligations in the field of human rights should not be surprising.

The appeal to sovereignty is, in a sense, misguided. The statement that a political entity is sovereign is simply a statement that it has a right to exercise jurisdiction within the limits of international law and international treaties. Treaties or conventions that provide for additional limits are not incompatible with sovereignty, but simply reduce the field within which it applies. States ratifying the UN Covenants would thereby restrict to some extent the freedom of action they now have, but would still be sovereign nevertheless.

## IMPLEMENTATION THROUGH INTERNATIONAL ACTION

The obligation of the United Nations to "promote" respect for human rights can be satisfied by a wide variety of possible actions. Merely to put questions pertaining to the subject on the agendas of various UN agencies, and to discuss them, can be classified as an effort to promote, and so can the request for reports, the making of studies, and the adoption of declarations and conventions.

Such activities are very inconclusive in themselves, and do not necessarily indicate progress.[1] In truth, in the United Nations additional studies have at times been commissioned mainly as an excuse for delay, and considerable reason has been given for the rather negative appraisals that we will note in a moment, if not also for cynicism.

Nevertheless, activities in these categories are obviously essential if the promotion of human rights is to occur. They lay the foundation for more significant measures. They contribute to a greater understanding of the problems and the possibilities. They keep reminding both governments and peoples of the relevant obligations, and keep informing delegates and peoples that some governments actually assure the rights and freedoms being discussed. Especially as long as a number of governments both champion human rights in international organizations and respect them at home, governments that act otherwise are put into a more or less invidious position.

> Even governments that suppress individual rights feel compelled to pay them the homage of hypocrisy, and those who preach, even if they do not yet practice, inevitably keep alive the aspirations and hopes and demands of their citizens. Peoples demand rights which others enjoy; governments are pressed to accord rights which others grant. All governments, moreover, seek friendship and political influence, whether in the United Nations or in ideological or regional groupings; instability and repression at home are not conducive to continued influence and leadership, whether in Africa or in the Communist Bloc. The threat of complaint and criticism—in the United Nations, in a regional organization, before organizations like the International Commission of Jurists, or in the world press—is a deterrent of significance.[2]

The story is told of the owner of a latifundia in Latin America who repeatedly served as a delegate to the United Nations and who bemusedly indicated in private that some time he might come to believe that the principles he championed in New York should actually be implemented at home.

Just as the parties to the European Convention have gone farthest in committing themselves to international legal obligations, so have they gone farthest in accepting international supervision of their measures of implementation. They have done what most defenders of sovereignty find abhorrent, that is, they have granted their own citizens a right to petition to an international agency for a redress of grievances. Moreover, the system has worked with little public notice and little difficulty, as if it were a part of a normal and natural order. No noteworthy international tensions have been created, and no other adverse effects have been apparent, though the assurance of justice for individuals has clearly been enhanced.

> The Rome Convention has shown that it is possible to reconcile two requirements which were once fairly generally regarded as incompatible, i.e., that it is possible to protect, through an independent authority (preferably judicial but not exclusively so), the fundamental rights of man on an international or transnational scale, without paralysing the machinery of the State or impairing its function of upholding law and order and national security. It has also

> been seen that the system is all the more effective in that it has been kept outside the field of politics.[3]

Intergovernmental complaints, such as the one now pending relating to denials of human rights by the military dictatorship in Greece, are necessarily political, and they obviously do not contribute in the short run to friendly relationships, but even such complaints have not caused any great crisis and if they have any effect in the long run it will surely be to reinforce human rights, democracy, and peace.

The Inter-American Commission on Human Rights has provided the most spectacular example of international supervision by its activities in the Dominican Republic. But the circumstances were unique, and it is still uncertain what role the Inter-American Commission may in the longer run play.

UN efforts to implement human rights vis-à-vis specific countries have revolved pretty much around the cold war, racism, and colonialism, raising a question about the extent to which the efforts have been motivated by a genuine concern for human rights as such and the extent to which they have been motivated by ulterior concerns. More significantly, the record raises a question about the prospect that more balanced and even-handed implementation can be achieved.

It is mainly on contemplation of this problem that the negative appraisals referred to above have been made. Thus Louis Henkin asserts that

> Human rights proved not a common interest but a political football. Except for the early drafting of the Declaration, the Cold War inevitably turned United Nations activity from cooperation in promoting human rights to exploitation of human rights issues for Cold War purposes.[4]

Moses Moskowitz, speaking of a more recent period, comes to an analogous conclusion. He says,

> An air of embarrassing unreality has been hanging over the debates on human rights in the United Nations. All the drama of words, all the moving eloquence, and all attempts to give these debates a sense of higher purpose have proved a poor substitute for clarity of policy, for decency of motives, and for strength of commitment. Clearly, the United Nations has lost sight of the appeal of human rights as the supreme testimony of human solidarity and overlooked their potency as a mighty weapon in the struggle for peace and justice, at home and abroad.

And Moskowitz goes on to assert that "but for the concerted drive against the policy of apartheid, the question of human rights would likely have long ago disappeared from the active agenda of the United Nations." He believes that hostility toward South Africa's racial policies has provided a political motive force which a more general effort on behalf of human rights "could not even remotely command."[5] In his view, international concern with the rights and freedom of man "has been reduced to a marginal interest tangential to the main purposes of the United Nations and outside the mainstream of international activity."[6] Harlan Cleveland, as Assistant Secretary of State for International Organization Affairs, implicity took a somewhat similar position when he said that the great issue of the next twenty years in the United Nations might well be "how—and indeed whether—to bring to life the human rights provisions of the Charter."[7] Louis Henkin despairs of bringing them to life, at least in the sense of taking direct measures of implementation.

> The principal hope for human rights lies in continuing international peace, in reduced international tensions, in internal stability, in developing political institutions, and in rising standards of living. For the most part, human rights can only be promoted indirectly, by promoting welfare in national societies and a peaceful, cooperative international society in which human rights can strike root and grow.[8]

The outcome of the application of sanctions against Southern Rhodesia and the course of the struggle against apartheid may or may not have much to do with the soundness of these judgments. On the one hand, if the Afro-Asian states get the support of the United Nations with regard to racism and colonialism, matters in which they have special concern, without being obliged to take a wider view of the problem of human rights, the broader area of potential activity may well be neglected or ignored for a long time to come. On the other hand, if those who appeal to the human rights provisions of the Charter in the name of racial equality and self-determination are obliged to accept the wider implications of equality, freedom, and the dignity of man, more change might come, and within a shorter span of time. The fate of the proposal to establish a High Commissioner's Office for Human Rights, and the actual functioning of that Office, if established, is likely to be highly significant. A High Commissioner who is both aggressive and prudent might do a great deal to promote the even-handed, global implementation of human rights. Similarly, what happens to the United Nations program is likely to be affected by what happens to the comparable programs of the OAS and of the states of Western Europe; if the states involved in the programs continue to make them successful, they will presumably press through the United Nations for comparable global achievements. Finally, it is obvious that the policies of individual powers—above all of the Soviet Union and the United States —will necessarily have a profound effect on UN policies and actions. It is to the question of United States policy that we now turn.

## IMPLICATIONS FOR THE UNITED STATES

Quincy Wright advises liberals as follows on "Policies for Strengthening the United Nations."

> In the field of foreign policy the liberal is beset by particular difficulties because he believes, on the one hand, in the independence of nations and the self-determination of peoples, and, on the other hand, in respect for human rights based upon the values of individual freedom, democracy, constitutionalism, and social progress. He is, therefore, at the same time, an advocate of peaceful coexistence and mutual toleration among the nations and peoples of the world, with their vast differences in value systems, religions, ideologies, and forms of government, economy, and society; and a militant crusader for the American interpretation of freedom, democracy, constitutionalism and progress.
>
> Emphasis on the first would seem to tolerate tyranny, regimentation, and oppression, contrary to democratic values, but persisting in many nations, while the second would seem to require non-recognitions, propagandas, interventions maintaining high international tensions and cold war, threatening hot war likely to destroy mankind.[9]

Wright's analysis makes a policy dilemma obvious. At the one extreme the stress could be on independence and on the freedom of every state to treat those under its jurisdiction as it sees fit. But surely the clock cannot thus be turned back. The many states so aroused about racism in southern Africa are very unlikely to go into reverse and to resign themselves to the view that, after all, Portugal and South Africa should have the prerogatives of sovereignty as they existed in Hitler's time. Still less are they likely to apply the spirit of such an abnegation to the problems of Southern Rhodesia and South-West Africa. It is probably too late even to treat racism in southern Africa as a problem *sui generis* and remove it from the human rights category. Further, quite apart from the problem of racism in southern Africa, it must be remembered that a great many states have accepted not only the limitations of the Charter but also the limitations of numerous special conventions, further eroding the rule of sovereign exclusiveness as it once existed. Even in the absence of formal obligation, a tendency has been growing over the years to manifest greater concern for the fate of human beings abroad, above all where large groups are involved. As Louis Henkin says, "Governments may continue to claim that how they treat their own inhabitants is of concern to them alone; increasingly it is a losing claim with little hope that it can prevail in politics if not in law."[10]

Even if the old prerogatives of sovereignty could be restored, it would probably not be in the national interest to have it done. The overriding interest of the United States is in a world environment favorable to the kind of domestic system that the American people want to maintain and develop, and respect for human rights is one of the major characteristics of such an environment. Nothing more favorable to the interests of the United States can be imagined than a situation in which all governments placed great stress on the implementation of the rights spelled out in the Universal Declaration and in the Covenants. It is one of the paradoxes of the time that a state whose own tradition and practices put so much stress on human rights and whose interests would so clearly be served by their promotion over the world has been so inhibited about championing them in the United Nations and in other international agencies. Perhaps Article 28 of the Universal Declaration is worth recalling: "everyone is entitled to a social and international order in which the rights and freedoms set forth in this Declaration can be fully realized." If anything, a serious effort to implement this right would call for much greater limitations on the freedom of states than have already been accepted.

Of course, the idea of keeping the prerogatives of sovereignty intact, and even of regaining some that have been lost, has a kind of chauvinistic appeal. The issue raised is fundamental. Is ultimate value to be placed on the preservation of sovereignty as it exists or existed at some specified date? Or is ultimate value to be placed on the welfare of individuals—whether all or some of them? And if the answer is that the welfare of individuals is the goal, then the question of the desirable prerogatives of sovereignty becomes a question of means. And no one who contemplates the wars and threats of war of the present century, and the prospect of utter catastrophe in some future war, is entitled to conclude that the continuation of all the prerogatives of sovereignty is a reliable means of assuring maximum welfare. It is uncertain, of course, what would follow greater stress on human rights, on international accountability for policies affecting them, and therefore on limiting the realm of sovereignty still more, but that such a course could have adverse effects on human welfare, and specifically on American welfare, can scarcely be imagined.

The domestic example of the United States no doubt exerts some influence abroad, but it does not do nearly as much as might be done either to counteract adverse developments or to promote favorable developments. In theory, other states might go ahead with the development of an international program for the promotion and protection of human rights even if the United States played no more than a marginal role. In fact, the parties to the European Convention have done this. But their example is not likely to be generally followed, at least as long as the United States holds back. José A. Cabranes puts the point very well so far as the inter-American system is concerned, and the principle that he asserts is applicable in the United Nations as well.

> Without the support and adherence of the United States there can be no reasonable expectation that a human rights convention operating within the framework of the Inter-American system will ever be widely ratified. The Latin Americans would doubtless feel that it was an unflattering and paternalistic assessment of their national institutions to be asked to surrender a substantial degree of their national sovereignty while the United States remains unwilling to do likewise.[11]

Cabranes further comments on the fact that the Inter-American Commission on Human Rights has shown no inclination to undertake an inquiry into alleged violations of civil rights in the United States.

> In view of the rebuff that it might receive if it sought to do so, . . . this reluctance is well considered. But it raises the fundamental question of the extent to which an international body of this kind, avowedly concerned with the promotion and protection of human rights in all of the American republics, can indulge the United States' traditional reluctance to accept any international responsibility for alleged deprivations of the rights of its nationals.

> If the United States' constitutional and political inhibitions are to be indulged, in the interest of the Commission's effective operation in less-well-endowed parts of the Western Hemisphere, the Commission will ultimately be required to acknowledge that it exists only to oversee the conduct of the OAS' Hispanic-American members. Alternatively, if there is to be any pretense at an even-handed administration of its mandate, the Commission may feel obliged to confine its intervention to situations in which the national system of government and law enforcement has completely broken down.[12]

At the end of Chapter 8 we quoted a statement by the U.S. delegate to the UN Commission on Human Rights that the United States would welcome it if the Commission examined violations of human rights within its territory, provided the same was done in respect of violations occurring elsewhere. But just what he meant, and whether he really meant it, is a question. As long as the Senate Committee on Foreign Relations, and the Senate itself, are so obviously influenced by Senator Bricker's principles and limit themselves to what the ABA will approve, and as long as the President and Secretary of State attach little urgency to the issue, others are entitled to considerable doubt on the question whether the United States is serious about the pronouncement that its delegate made. The fact that Congress, though considering the question, failed to make any provision for commemorating the International Human Rights Year (1968) did little to bolster hope that the United States might resume the leadership dropped in 1953.

The policies of the United States on human rights have been so hesitant as to give little need for a reminder of Quincy Wright's statement concerning the possible implications of a crusade for global ideological uniformity. Conducted in the manner of a Napoleon, a Hitler, or a Stalin, such a crusade would by definition be disastrous. But many possible choices lie between a Brickerite insistence on national sovereignty and a Hitlerite insistence on reorganizing the world (or any part of it) on ideological lines. Representative Donald M. Fraser made a sensible statement of the problem when he said that "as members of the human race we have to have a basic regard for individual dignity and freedom whether our concern stems from the Soviet Union, South Africa, or wherever it is." And he said further that "the sole question that remains to be answered is how do you go about expressing your concern in a way that doesn't draw you in over your head, and which is compatible with your capabilities, and doesn't lead to worse evils than you try to correct."[13] This prescription would rule out war for human rights and any other line of action that involved serious risk of war, such as a blockade of South Africa. But it does not necessarily rule out sanctions-short-of-force, above all if they are deliberately designed to symbolize disapproval of the violation of human rights rather than a determination to defeat or overthrow a guilty government. Granting the possibility of exceptional situations, such as that of Southern Rhodesia, both American interests and human rights will surely be best served if the promotion of human rights occurs primarily through the methods of example, education, and persuasion, through the exercise of the gentler pressures, and through the development of the underlying conditions that contribute indirectly to the achievement of the goals sought. A policy developed along these lines would surely include active leadership in formulating declarations and conventions spelling rights out and the acceptance of some degree of international accountability in connection with their implementation.

# Notes

CHAPTER 2

1. OEA/Ser.E/XI.1. Doc. 8. 5 November 1959.
2. *Seminar on Human Rights in Developing Countries*. Kabul, Afghanistan, 12-25 May 1964. Organized by the United Nations in Cooperation with the Government of Afghanistan (New York: United Nations, 1964), p. 15, pars. 54-58. (Hereafter cited as: *Kabul Seminar on Human Rights in Developing Countries.*)
3. *Department of State Bulletin*, 59 (September 2, 1968), 259.
4. Cf., OEA/Ser.L/V/II.15. Doc. 26. 15 November 1966. Pp. 3-4.
5. Cf., *Congressional Record*, Vol. 113, No. 36 (March 7, 1967), S3217.
6. Cf., E/CN.4/SR.958. 20 February 1968. Provisional. And: UN Commission on Human Rights, Report on the Twenty-fourth Session. 5 February-12 March 1968. P. 53, par. 124. (Hereafter cited as: UNCHR, *Report on Twenty-fourth Session.*)
7. GA/Res/59 (I). 14 December 1946.
8. GA/Res/424 (V). 14 December 1950.
9. Cf., ECOSOC. 31st Sess. Annexes. Agenda item 10. Part II. Doc. A/3443, "Report on Developments in the Field of Freedom of Information Since 1954." 16 February 1961. Esp. p. 53, par. 316. And *1962 Seminar on Freedom of Information*, New Delhi, India. 20 February-5 March 1962. Organized by the United Nations in Cooperation with the Government of India (New York: United Nations, 1963), pp. 12-16.
10. S. I. Benn and R. S. Peters, *The Principles of Political Thought* (New York: Free Press, 1965), pp. 263-276.
11. GAOR. VII. Annexes, Vol. I, Agenda item 29, p. 30.
12. ECOSOC. OR. 2nd Yr., 5th Sess., Annex 6d, Doc. E/AC.7/30. 1 August 1947. P. 332.

13. ECOSOC. OR. 2nd Yr., 5th Sess., Sup. No. 5. Doc. E/441, pp. 7-8.
14. ECOSOC. OR. 2nd Yr., 5th Sess., Annex 6d, Doc. E/AC.7/30. 1 August 1947. P. 331.
15. GAOR. VII. Annexes, Vol. I, Agenda item 29, p. 31.
16. ECOSOC. OR. 3rd Yr., 7th Sess. 221st Mtg. 27 August 1948. P. 755.
17. GAOR. XIV. 3rd Cttee, 972nd Mtg. 1 December 1959. P. 311.
18. ECOSOC. OR. 27th Sess. 1062nd Mtg. 20 April 1959. P. 97.
19. GAOR. XIV. 3rd Cttee. 975th Mtg. 3 December 1959. P. 324.
20. *Seminar on Human Rights in Developing Countries*. Dakar, Senegal, 8-22 February 1966. Organized by the United Nations in Cooperation with the Government of Senegal (New York: United Nations, 1966), p. 30, par. 132. (Hereafter cited as: *Dakar Seminar on Human Rights in Developing Countries*.)
21. *1962 Seminar on Freedom of Information*, pp. 17-19.
22. GAOR. XIV. 3rd Cttee. 973rd Mtg. 2 December 1959. P. 316.
23. GAOR. XVI. 3rd Cttee. 1074th Mtg. 16 October 1961. P. 71.
24. GAOR. XV. 3rd Cttee. 1029th Mtg. 21 November 1960. Pp. 234-235, pars. 10-11.
25. GAOR. XIV. 3rd Cttee. 971st Mtg. 30 November 1959. P. 301.
26. GAOR. XV. 3rd Cttee. 1035th Mtg. 25 November 1960. P. 265.
27. GAOR. XV. 3rd Cttee. 1031st Mtg. 22 November 1960. P. 240.
28. ECOSOC. 31st Sess. Annexes. Agenda item 10. Part II. Doc. A/3443, "Report on Developments in the Field of Freedom of Information Since 1954." 16 February 1961. P. 10, par. 48.
29. GA. XXII. A/6658. 27 June 1967.
30. ECOSOC. OR. 3rd Yr., 7th Sess. 221st Mtg. 27 August 1948.
31. GA/Res/2106A (XX). 21 December 1965.
32. *Department of State Bulletin*, 54 (February 7, 1966), 214, 215.
33. Cf., Egon Schwelb, "The International Convention on the Elimination of All Forms of Racial Discrimination," *International and Comparative Law Quarterly*, 15 (October 1966), 1021-1025.
34. Edmond Rabbath, "La théorie des droits de l'homme dans le droit musulman," *Revue internationale de droit comparé*, 11 (October-December 1959), 682.
35. Morris B. Abram, "Fight for Human Rights," *National Jewish Monthly*, 81 (June 1967), 12.
36. N. J. Coulson, "The State and the Individual in Islamic Law," *International and Comparative Law Quarterly*, 6 (January 1957), 49-60.
37. *Dakar Seminar on Human Rights in Developing Countries*, p. 26, par. 113.
38. David H. Bayley, *Public Liberties in the New States* (Chicago: Rand McNally, 1964), pp. 3, 29, 53.
39. Cf., UN. *Study of the Right of Everyone to Be Free from Arbitrary Arrest, Detention, and Exile* (New York, 1964). E/CN.4/826/Rev.1. And Evan Luard, ed., *The International Protection of Human Rights* (New York: Praeger, 1967), p. 312.

40. GA/Res/2312 (XXII). 14 December 1967.
41. GA/Res/2263 (XXII). 7 November 1967.
42. C. W. W. Greenidge, *Slavery* (New York: Macmillan, 1958), pp. 37, 56.
43. Report of the Twentieth Session of the Sub-Commission on Prevention of Discrimination and Protection of Minorities . . . 1967. E/CN.4/947, E/CN.4/Sub.2/286. 4 December 1967. P. 44, par. 98.
44. Greenidge, *op. cit.*, pp. 94-104.

CHAPTER 3

1. GA/Res/103 (I). 19 November 1946.
2. C. Wilfred Jenks, *Human Rights and International Labour Standards* (New York: Praeger, 1960), pp. 75-76.
3. GA/Res/1904 (XVIII). 20 November 1963.
4. GA/Res/2263 (XXII). 7 November 1967.
5. Cf., Egon Schwelb, "The International Convention on the Elimination of All Forms of Racial Discrimination," *International and Comparative Law Quarterly*, 15 (October 1966), 1057-1058.
6. Cf., S. I. Benn and R. S. Peters, *The Principles of Political Thought* (New York: Free Press, 1965), p. 129.
7. Article 1, International Convention on the Elimination of All Forms of Racial Discrimination.
8. UN. *Protection of Minorities. Special Protective Measures of an International Character for Ethnic, Religious or Linguistic Groups* (New York, 1967). Sales No.: 67.XIV.3. Pp. 27-32. S. A. de Smith, "Fundamental Rights in the New Commonwealth–I," *International and Comparative Law Quarterly*, 10 (January 1961), 99.
9. GAOR. II. 1st Cttee. Annex 8, pp. 558-559. "Report of the Union of South Africa in Connection with the Recommendation of the General Assembly of 8 December 1946."
10. R. F. Alfred Hoernlé, *South African Native Policy and the Liberal Spirit* (Johannesburg: Witwatersrand University Press, 1945), p. 133. Colin de B. Webb, "The Foreign Policy of the Union of South Africa," in Joseph E. Black and Kenneth W. Thpmpson, *Foreign Policies in a World of Change* (New York: Harper & Row, 1963), p. 427.
11. Ronald Segal, ed., *Sanctions Against South Africa* (Baltimore: Penguin, 1964), p. 16.
12. For an excellent summary exposition of South African legislation and practices relating to apartheid, see: UN Commission on Human Rights, "Study of Apartheid and Racial Discrimination in Southern Africa," Chapter 1 (E/CN.4/949. 22 November 1967).
13. Republic of South Africa. Parliament. *Debates of the House of Assembly* (Hansard), Vol. 5 (25 January 1963), col. 242. (Cited hereafter as: South Africa, *Hansard*.)
14. Quoted in GAOR. XIX. Annexes. Annex No. 12. P. 70.

15. South Africa, *Hansard*, Vol. 107 (23 March 1961), col. 3509.
16. South Africa. Commission for the Socio-Economic Development of the Bantu Areas. *Summary of the Report of the Commission*. U.G. 61/1955. (Pretoria, 1955). P. 103.
17. OAS. Second Special Inter-American Conference. Rio de Janeiro, Brazil, November 17-30, 1965. *Final Act*. OEA/Ser.C/I.13. Resolution XXV. P. 37.
18. Hilgard Muller. GAOR. XIX. Plenary Mtgs. 21 December 1964. P. 3, pars. 23-24.
19. Douglas Brown, *Against the World. Attitudes of White South Africa* (Garden City, N.Y.: Doubleday, 1968), pp. 90-91.
20. Charles A. W. Manning, "In Defense of Apartheid," *Foreign Affairs*, 43 (October 1964), 140. Cf., K. L. Roskam, *Apartheid and Discrimination* (Leyden: Sythoff, 1960), pp. 133-134.
21. Hilgard Muller. GAOR. XIX. Plenary Meetings. 21 December 1964. P. 3, par. 21.
22. GA. XXII. A/6688. 11 August 1967. Annex, p. 7.
23. Mr. Jooste. GAOR. XVIII. 1236th. Mtg. 10 October 1963. P. 3.
24. Prime Minister Verwoerd. South Africa, *Hansard*, Vol. 107 (10 April 1961), col. 4175.
25. *Ibid.*, Vol. 98 (15 September 1958), cols. 3803-3804.
26. *Ibid.*, Vol. 99 (27 January 1959), col. 49; and Vol. 101 (20 May 1959), col. 6236.
27. Anthony Sampson, "Old Fallacies with a New Look: Ignoring the Africans," in: *South Africa, Two Views of Separate Development* (New York: Oxford, 1960), pp. 43-49, 54-55, 76.
28. South Africa, *Hansard*, Vol. 99 (27 January 1959), col. 62.
29. *Ibid.*, Vol. 107 (10 April 1961), col. 4195.
30. *Ibid.*, Vol. 99 (27 January 1959), col. 66.
31. *Ibid.*, Vol. 101 (20 May 1959), col. 6217. S. Pienaar, "Safeguarding the Nations of South Africa," in: *South Africa: Two Views of Separate Development*, pp. 25-26.
32. South Africa, *Hansard*, Vol. 101 (20 May 1959), col. 6218.
33. GA. XXII. A/6688. 11 August 1967. Annex, p. 25.
34. See, for example, the testimony of Richard Logan: U.S. Congress. House of Representatives. Committee on Foreign Affairs. *United States-South African Relations*. Hearings before the Subcommittee on Africa. 89th Cong., 2d Sess. March 1966, I, pp. 166-170.
35. GA/Res/616B (VII). 5 December 1952.
36. GA/Res/1598 (XV). 13 April 1961.
37. GA/Res/2074 (XX). 17 December 1965. Cf., GA/Res/2202A (XXI). 16 December 1966.
38. GAOR. II. 1st Cttee. Annex 8, p. 557. "Report of the Union of South Africa in Connexion with the Recommendation of the General Assembly of 8 December 1946."

39. International Court of Justice. *Pleadings, Oral Arguments, Documents. South West Africa Cases.* 1966. Vol. V, p. 131, par. 22. (Hereafter cited as: ICJ. *Pleadings. South West Africa Cases 1966.*)
40. *Ibid.*, Vol. IV, pp. 71, 427.
41. *Ibid.*, Vol. VI, p. 12.
42. J. C. Smuts, *Jan Christian Smuts, A Biography* (New York: William Morrow, 1952), p. 406.
43. Eric H. Louw, *The Case for South Africa* (New York: Macfadden Books, 1963), p. 135.
44. Prime Minister Verwoerd. South Africa, *Hansard,* Vol. 107 (10 April 1961), col. 4193.
45. Quoted in the "Report of the Special Committee on the Policies of Apartheid of the Government of the Republic of South Africa," GA. XX. A/4947. 16 August 1965. P. 77.
46. State of the Union Message, January 1940.
47. *Journal Officiel des Communautés Européennes,* Vol. 10, No. 103 (2 June 1967), 2058-67. Cf., A. H. Robertson, *Human Rights in Europe* (New York: Oceana, 1963), pp. 36-37. Council of Europe, *Consultative Assembly Debates,* Session 2, Ninth Sitting (16 August 1950), p. 268 and pp. 281-282.
48. GAOR. XVI. 3rd Cttee. 1096th Mtg. 8 November 1961. P. 179.
49. *Seminar on Human Rights in Developing Countries.* Dakar Senegal. 8-22 February 1966. Organized by the United Nations in Cooperation with the Government of Senegal (New York: United Nations, 1966), p. 35, par. 155. (Hereafter cited as: *Dakar Seminar on Human Rights in Developing Countries.*)
50. Hernán Santa Cruz, *Study of Discrimination in the Matter of Political Rights* (New York: United Nations, 1962), p. 98.
51. *Ibid.*, pp. 13-14. GAOR. III, Pt. 1. 3rd Cttee. Pp. 33, 452.
52. OAS. *Final Act of the Ninth International Conference of American States.* Bogotá, Colombia. March 20-May 2, 1948 (Washington: Pan American Union, 1948), p. 263. Article 20.
53. OAS. Fourth Meeting of Consultation of Ministers of Foreign Affairs, March 26-April 7, 1951. *Final Act.* Conferences and Organizations Series, Number 13. Washington: Pan American Union, 1951. P. 10.
54. OAS. Fifth Meeting of Consultation of Ministers of Foreign Affairs. Santiago, Chile. August 12-18, 1959. *Final Act.* OEA/Ser. C/II.5. Washington: Pan American Union, 1960. P. 5.
55. OAS. Eighth Meeting of Consultation of Ministers of Foreign Affairs. Punta del Este, Uruguay. January 22-31, 1962. *Final Act.* OEA/Ser. C/II.8. Washington: Pan American Union, 1962. P. 9.
56. *Department of State Bulletin,* 45 (October 23, 1961), 677.
57. *Ibid.*, 54 (May 9, 1966), 728.
58. Cf., Jerome Slater, *The OAS and United States Foreign Policy* (Columbus: Ohio State University Press, 1967), pp. 239-250.

59. OAS. Inter-American Juridical Committee. *Study on the Juridical Relationship between Respect for Human Rights and the Exercise of Democracy.* CIJ-52. Washington: Pan American Union, 1960, pp. 10-11. For an interesting discussion of conceptions of democracy, see David H. Bayley, *Public Liberties in the New States* (Chicago: Rand McNally, 1964), pp. 8-11, 71. Cf., Benn and Peters, *op. cit.*, p. 418.
60. OAS. Second Special Inter-American Conference. Rio de Janeiro, Brazil. November 17-30, 1965. *Final Act.* OEA/Ser. C/I.13. Washington: Pan American Union, 1965. Resolution XXVI, pp. 38-39.
61. OAS. Eighth Meeting of Consultation of Ministers of Foreign Affairs. Punta del Este, Uruguay. January 22-31, 1962. *Final Act.* OEA/Ser. C/II.8. Washington: Pan American Union, 1962. P. 14.
62. Sir William Ivor Jennings, *The Approach to Self-Government* (Cambridge: At the University Press, 1956), p. 65. W. J. M. Mackenzie, *Free Elections* (London: Allen & Unwin, 1958), p. 27.
63. Santa Cruz, *Study of Discrimination in the Matter of Political Rights,* p. 31.
64. GA. XXII. A/6807. Memorandum by the Secretary-General, "Constitutions, Electoral Laws and Other Legal Instruments Relating to the Political Rights of Women."
65. T. E. Smith, *Elections in Developing Countries* (New York: St. Martin's Press, 1960), p. 87.
66. ECOSOC. Commission on Human Rights. Sub-Commission on Prevention of Discrimination and Protection of Minorities. 20th Sess. *Special Study of Racial Discrimination in the Political, Economic, Social and Cultural Spheres* (Report Submitted by the Special Rapporteur, Mr. Hernán Santa-Cruz. E/CN.4/Sub.2/276. 24 July 1967. Mimeo. Pp. 40-41.
67. Cf., ICJ. *Pleadings. South West Africa Cases 1966,* Vol. IV, p. 451.
68. South Africa, *Hansard,* Vol. 107 (23 March 1961), col. 3507.
69. Henry A. Fagan, *Coexistence in South Africa* (Cape Town: Juta, 1963), pp. 45-46.
70. SCOR. 19th Year. Sup. for April, May, June 1964. Doc. S/5658, 20 April 1964, Annex, p. 25.
71. SC/Res/191 (1964). 18 June 1964.
72. G. Mennen Williams, "United States Policy in Africa," *Department of State Bulletin,* 54 (April 12, 1965), 543.
73. Cf., R. B. Ballinger, "UN Action on Human Rights in South Africa," in Evan Luard, ed., *The International Protection of Human Rights* (New York: Praeger, 1967), p. 282.
74. Quoted by Fagan, *op. cit.*, pp. 61-62.
75. GAOR. XVII. 4th Cttee. 1366th Mtg. 30 October 1962. Pp. 238-239. Leo Baron, "Rhodesia: Taking Stock. The 1961 Constitution and the Tiger Proposals," *World Today,* 23 (September 1967), 370-371.
76. GA/Res/1747 (XVI). 28 June 1962.
77. GA/Res/2022 (XX). 5 November 1965.

78. GA/Res/2382 (XXIII). 7 November 1968.
79. Maurice Zinkin, in George L. Abernethy, ed., *The Idea of Equality* (Richmond, Virginia: John Knox Press, 1959), p. 333.
80. "General Principles on Freedom and Non-Discrimination in the Matter of Political Rights," in Santa Cruz, *Study of Discrimination in the Matter of Political Rights,* Annex, p. 97.
81. A. H. Robertson, "The European Convention on Human Rights," in Luard, *op. cit.*, p. 116.

CHAPTER 4

1. Quoted by Sanford A. Lakoff, *Equality in Political Philosophy* (Cambridge: Harvard University Press, 1965), p. 99.
2. Frank Maloy Anderson, *The Constitution and Other Select Documents Illustrative of the History of France,* 1789-1907 (2d ed.; New York: Russell & Russell, 1908, reissued 1967), p. 59.
3. Sandford Fawcett, "A British View of the Covenant," *Law and Contemporary Problems,* 14 (Summer 1949), 439.
4. Maurice Cranston, "Human Rights, Real and Supposed," in D. D. Raphael, ed., *Political Theory and the Rights of Man* (Bloomington: Indiana University Press, 1967), p. 43.
5. *Ibid.*, p. 53. Cf., Maurice Cranston, *What Are Human Rights?* (New York: Basic Books, 1962), pp. 40-41.
6. Richard Wollheim, "Equality," *Proceedings of the Aristotelian Society,* Vol. LVI (1955-1956), pp. 294-295.
7. Frank E. Holman, "International Proposals Affecting So-Called Human Rights," *Law and Contemporary Problems,* 14 (Summer 1949), 480-481.
8. *Congressional Record,* Vol. 97, Pt. 6 (July 17, 1951), p. 8257.
9. U.S. Congress. Senate. Committee on Interior and Insular Affairs. *Approving Puerto Rican Constitution.* Hearings . . . on S. J. Res. 151. 82nd Cong., 2d Sess. 1952. P. 50. Testimony of Jaime Benitez, Chancellor of the University of Puerto Rico.
10. *Congressional Record,* Vol. 98, Pt. 4 (May 13, 1952), p. 5120.
11. *Ibid.*, Vol. 98, Pt. 5 (May 28, 1952), p. 6179.
12. *Ibid.*, p. 6182.
13. *Ibid.*, p. 6169.
14. U.S. Congress. Senate. *Senate Reports.* Report No. 1720, from the Committee on Interior and Insular Affairs, to Accompany S. J. Res. 151. *Approving the Constitution of the Commonwealth of Puerto Rico.* 82d Cong., 2d Sess. 1952. Pp. 1-2.
15. D. D. Raphael, "Human Rights, Old and New," in Raphael, ed., *Political Theory and the Rights of Man,* p. 65.
16. S. I. Benn and R. S. Peters, *The Principles of Political Thought* (New York: Free Press, 1964), p. 167.

17. Charles Malik, "Human Rights and the United Nations," *United Nations Bulletin*, 13 (September 1, 1952), 253.
18. GA/Res/308 (IV). 25 November 1949.
19. Text in: A. H. Robertson, *Human Rights in Europe* (New York: Oceana, 1963), p. 244.
20. Cranston, "Human Rights, Real and Supposed," *loc. cit.*, p. 50.
21. GA/Res/128 (III). 17 November 1947.
22. Cf., C. Wilfred Jenks, "The International Protection of Trade Union Rights," in Evan Luard, ed., *The International Protection of Human Rights* (New York: Praeger, 1967), pp. 214, 216.
23. C. Wilfred Jenks, *Human Rights and International Labour Standards* (New York: Praeger, 1960), pp. 51, 55.
24. *Ibid.*, p. 51. Jenks, "The International Protection of Trade Union Rights," *loc. cit.*, pp. 214-215.
25. U.S. Congress. House. 82nd Congress, 1st Sess. House Document No. 176, pp. 6, 28-32.
26. Jenks, "The International Protection of Trade Union Rights," *loc. cit.*, p. 231.
27. Robertson, *op. cit.*, pp. 12, 35-36.
28. 68 S. Ct. 469, fn. 9.
29. Jenks, *Human Rights and International Labour Standards*, p. 107.
30. *Ibid.*, p. 111.
31. GA/Res/317 (IV). 2 December 1949.
32. GA/Res/1713 (XVII). 7 November 1962; GA/Res/2018 (XX). 1 November 1965.
33. GA/Res/2263 (XXII). 7 November 1967.
34. GA. XXII. A/C.3/SR.1469. 6 October 1967. Pp. 3-4.
35. GA/Res/1386 (XIV). 20 November 1959.
36. GA/Res/2037 (XX). 7 December 1965.
37. United Nations. *Seminar on Human Rights in Developing Countries*. Dakar, Senegal. 8-22 February 1966. Organized by the United Nations in Cooperation with the Government of Senegal (New York: United Nations, 1966). Pars. 90-92.
38. Cf., ECOSOC. OR. Thirteenth Session. Sup. No. 9. Commission on Human Rights. *Report of the Seventh Session* (16 April-19 May 1951), p. 12. ECOSOC. OR. Fourteenth Session. Sup. No. 4. Commission on Human Rights. *Report of the Eighth Session*, 14 April to 14 June 1952, pp. 22-23. ECOSOC. OR. Eighteenth Session. Sup. No. 7. Commission on Human Rights. *Report of the Tenth Session*. 23 February 16 April 1954, pp. 7-8.
39. Robertson, *op. cit.*, pp. 31-32.
40. *Department of State Bulletin*, 19 (December 19, 1948), 751.
41. Benjamin V. Cohen, "Human Rights Under the United Nations Charter," *Law and Contemporary Problems*, 14 (Summer 1949), 432.
42. United Nations. *Repertory of Practice of United Nations Organs*. Vol. III, Articles 55-72 of the Charter (New York, 1955), p. 36.

43. James Simsarian, "United Nations Action on Human Rights in 1948," *Department of State Bulletin*, 20 (January 2, 1949), 21. Charles Malik, *loc. cit.*, p. 251.
44. Cf., James Simsarian, "Economic, Social, and Cultural Provisions of the Human Rights Covenant. Revisions of the 1951 Session of the Commission on Human Rights," *Department of State Bulletin*, 24 (June 25, 1951), 1005-1006.
45. Ernst B. Haas, *Beyond the Nation-State* (Stanford: Stanford University Press, 1964), pp. 233-238.
46. *Final Act of the Ninth International Conference of American States.* Bogotá, Colombia. March 30-May 2, 1948. (Washington: Pan American Union, 1948), pp. 31, 36, 38.
47. Hadley Cantril, *The Pattern of Human Concerns* (New Brunswick, N. J.: Rutgers University Press, 1965), p. 36.

CHAPTER 5

1. GA/Res/420 (V). 4 December 1950. Cf., Louis K. Hyde, *The United States and the United Nations, Promoting the Public Welfare* (New York: Manhattan, 1960), p. 176.
2. GA/Res/545 (VI). 5 February 1952.
3. GAOR. X. Annexes. Agenda item 28-I, p. 39.
4. GA/Res/1514 (XV). 14 December 1960. Cf., David A. Kay, "The Politics of Decolonization: The New Nations and the United Nations Political Process," *International Organization*, 21 (Autumn 1961), 793.
5. Harlan Cleveland, "Reflections on the Pacific Community," *Department of State Bulletin*, 48 (April 22, 1963), 616.
6. Cf., J. Wayne Fredericks, "Our Policy Toward Africa," *Department of State Bulletin*, 49 (August 19, 1963), 286.
7. GAOR. XXI. 1966. Annexes. Vol. III, Agenda item 87, p. 91, par. 459. And see A/AC.125/L.44, part VI.
8. Rosalyn Higgins, *The Development of International Law Through the Political Organs of the United Nations* (New York: Oxford University Press, 1963), p. 103.
9. GAOR. XXI. 1966. Annexes. Vol. III, Agenda item 87, p. 91, par. 457.
10. *Ibid.*, p. 94, par. 480.
11. GA. XXIII. A/PV.1679. 3 October 1968. Provisional, p. 31. Cf., *The New York Times*, September 27, 1968, 3:1.
12. Franklin D. Roosevelt, *The Public Papers and Addresses of Franklin D. Roosevelt*, compiled . . . by Samuel I. Rosenman. 1943 Volume. *The Tide Turns* (New York: Harper, 1950), p. 78.
13. U.S. President. *Public Papers of the Presidents of the United States. Lyndon B. Johnson*. 1965. Book I. January 1 to May 31, 1965 (Washington, 1966). Paper No. 221, p. 472.
14. OAS. Inter-American Peace Committee. *Report to the Eighth Meeting*

of *Consultation of Ministers of Foreign Affairs.* 1962. OEA/Ser.1/III. CIP/1/62. (Washington: Pan American Union, 1962), p. 46.

15. OAS. *First Symposium on Representative Democracy.* Santo Domingo, Dominican Republic, 17-22 December 1962. *Final Report.* (Washington: Pan American Union, February, 1963), p. 11.
16. Higgins, *op. cit.*, pp. 104-105.
17. GA/Res/2262 (XXII). 3 November 1967.
18. SCOR. 18th. Year. Sup. for October, November, and December, 1963. Doc. S/5488. 31 October 1963.
19. U.S. President. *Public Papers of the Presidents of the United States. Harry S Truman.* January 1 to December 31, 1946. (Washington, 1962), p. 43. State of the Union Message, January 21, 1946.
20. UN *Yearbook on Human Rights for 1954*, p. 397.
21. *Department of State Bulletin,* 34 (April 2, 1956), 543. Cf., Vernon McKay, *Africa in World Politics* (New York: Harper & Row, 1963), pp. 320-325.
22. *Department of State Bulletin,* 49 (December 16, 1963). 946.
23. Fredericks, *loc. cit.*, p. 286.
24. *Congressional Record,* Vol. 109, Pt. 3 (March 7, 1963), pp. 3,695, 3,696.
25. Cleveland, *loc. cit.*, p. 616.
26. GA/Res/637A (XVII). 16 December 1962.
27. Maurice Cranston, *What Are Human Rights?* (New York: Basic Books, 1962), pp. 68-69.
28. Philip M. Allen, "Self-Determination in the Western Indian Ocean," *International Conciliation,* No. 560 (November, 1966), pp. 40-48.
29. S/PV.1268. 23 November 1965. P. 5, par. 24. SC/Res/218 (1965). 23 November 1965.
30. SCOR. 18th Yr. 1080th Mtg. 6 December 1963. P. 7.
31. GAOR. XXI. 1966. Annexes. Vol. III, Agenda item 87, p. 91, par. 459.
32. A/AC.125/L.44, part VI.
33. Patricia Wohlgemuth Blair, *The Ministate Dilemma* (New York: Carnegie Endowment for International Peace, Occasional Paper No. 6, October, 1967), pp. 3-6.
34. GAOR. XV. 947th Plenary Mtg. 14 December 1960. P. 1283.
35. Alfred Cobban, *National Self-Determination* (Chicago: University of Chicago Press, 1944), pp. 12-22.
36. GAOR. X. 3rd Cttee. 642nd Mtg. 24 October 1955. Pp. 90-91.
37. GAOR. X. 3rd Cttee. 669th Mtg. 23 November 1955. P. 255.
38. GAOR. X. 3rd Cttee. 642nd Mtg. 24 October 1955. P. 94.
39. GAOR. X. 3rd Cttee. 649th Mtg. 1 November 1955. P. 124.
40. Boutros Boutros-Ghali, "The Addis Ababa Charter," *International Conciliation,* No. 546 (January, 1964), p. 55.
41. Doudou Thiam, *The Foreign Policy of African States* (London: Phoenix House, 1965), pp. 44, 76-77.
42. GAOR. XVI. 1065 Plenary Mtg. 27 November 1961. P. 848, par. 157.

43. S/PV.1088. 5 February 1964. Pars. 70-71.
44. SC/Res/169 (1961). 24 November 1961.
45. UN. Office of Public Information. *A New Course in South Africa*. Report of the Group of Experts Established in Pursuance of the Security Council Resolution of 4 December 1963. (New York: United Nations, Sales No. 64.I.13, 1964), p. 7.
46. *Department of State Bulletin*, 27 (December 8, 1952), 919.
47. Richard N. Gardner, "The United Nations in Crisis: Cuba and the Congo," *Department of State Bulletin*, 48 (April 1, 1963), 479.
48. G. Mennen Williams, "United States Policy in Africa," *Department of State Bulletin*, 52 (April 12, 1965), 545. G. Mennen Williams, "Congo Realities and United States Policy," *Department of State Bulletin*, 52 (May 24, 1965), 798.
49. Cf., GAOR. XVI. Annexes. Agenda Items 88 and 22 (a). P. 18. Letter of 25 November 1961 from the Representative of the U.S.A. to the President of the General Assembly. See also Cobban, *op. cit.*, pp. 101-122; and Richard Pipes, " 'Solving' the Nationality Problem," *Problems of Communism*, 16 (September-October, 1967), 125-131.
50. Higgins, *op. cit.*, pp. 104-105.
51. Walker Connor, "Self-Determination. The New Phase," *World Politics*, 20 (October 1967), 52.
52. S. K. Panter-Brick, "The Right of Self-Determination: Its Application to Nigeria," *International Affairs*, 44 (April 1968), 254-266.
53. Connor, *loc. cit.*, p. 52.
54. Rupert Emerson, *Self-Determination Revisited in the Era of Decolonization* (Cambridge: Harvard University, Center for International Affairs, Occasional Papers in International Affairs, No. 9, December, 1964), pp. 45-53.
55. Higgins, *op. cit.*, pp. 104-105.
56. GAOR. XVI. Special Political Cttee. 289th Mtg. 15 November 1961. P. 149.
57. In addition to the article by Walker Connor, cited above, see John H. Spencer, "Africa at the United Nations: Some Observations," in William John Hanna, ed., *Independent Black Africa. The Politics of Freedom* (Chicago: Rand McNally, 1964), pp. 542-554.
58. GAOR. XIX. 1308th Plenary Mtg. 21 December 1964. P. 3, pars. 24-26.
59. GA. XXII. A/6688. 11 August 1967. Annex, p. 7.
60. Republic of South Africa. *Report of the Commission of Enquiry into South West Africa Affairs*. 1962-1963. R. P. No. 12/1964. Pp. 55-79, 515; esp. pars. 185-190, 222, 1555. Cf., p. 427, pars. 1431-1434.
61. GA. XXII. A/PV.1632. 14 December 1967. P. 83-85.
62. GA. XXII. A/7045/Add.9. 19 February 1968. P. 36.
63. South African Institute of Race Relations. *A Survey of Race Relations in South Africa, 1966* (Johannesburg, 1967), p. 147.
64. GA. XIX. Annex 12, p. 25, par. 79.

65. GA. XXII. A/PV.1632. 14 December 1967. P. 3.
66. GA. XXII. A/PV.1624. 11 December 1967. P. 13.
67. GA. XXII. Agenda Item 23. A/6700. Part II. 2 October 1967. Pp. 208ff, par. 744. And GA. XXII. A/6700/Add.2. 31 October 1967. Agenda Item 64(a).
68. Inis L. Claude, Jr., *National Minorities, An International Problem* (Cambridge: Harvard University Press, 1955), p. 46.
69. GAOR. XVI. 3rd Cttee. 1103rd Mtg. 14 November 1961. Pp. 213-214, par. 12.
70. ECOSOC. OR. 18th Sess. Sup. No. 7. Commission on Human Rights. Report of 10th Sess., 23 February-16 April 1954, p. 48, par. 420.
71. GAOR. III. Pt. 1. 3rd Cttee. 161st Mtg. 27 November 1948. P. 726.
72. OAS. Second Special Inter-American Conference. Rio de Janeiro, Brazil, November 17-30, 1965. *Final Act* (Washington: Pan American Union, 1965. (OEA/Ser.C/I.13). Resolution XXV, p. 37.
73. ECOSOC. OR. 18th Sess. Sup. No. 7. Commission on Human Rights. Report of 10th Sess., 23 February-16 April 1954, p. 49, par. 420.
74. Claude, *op. cit.*, p. 161.
75. Cf., United Nations. *Protection of Minorities. Special Protective Measures of an International Character for Ethnic, Religious or Linquistic Groups* (Sales No. 66.XIV.3; New York, 1967), pp. 7-46.
76. *Ibid.*, p. 19.
77. GAOR. XV. Special Political Cttee. 176th Mtg. 18 October 1960. P. 9.
78. GAOR. XV. Special Political Cttee. 177th Mtg. 19 October 1960. P. 13.
79. GAOR. XV. Special Political Cttee. 181st Mtg. 24 October 1960. P. 31.
80. ECOSOC. OR. 14th Sess. Sup. No. 4. Commission on Human Rights. Report of 8th Sess. 14 April to 14 June 1952. P. 8.
81. GA/Res/3158 (XXI). 25 November 1966.
82. Cf., Mrs. Oswald B. Lord, "Principles Involved in Human Rights Covenants," *Department of State Bulletin*, 31 (December 6, 1954), 877. And Mrs. Oswald B. Lord, "Self-Determination Article in Human Rights Covenants," *Department of State Bulletin*, 34 (January 9, 1956), 70-71. James N. Hyde, "Permanent Sovereignty over Natural Wealth and Resources." *American Journal of International Law*, 50 (October 1956), 854-867. George W. Haight, "Human Rights Covenants," *Proceedings* of the American Society of International Law, Sixty-Second Annual Meeting, April 25-27, 1968, p. 99, and comments by John Carey, p. 104.

### CHAPTER 6

1. United Nations. *Repertory of Practice of United Nations Organs,* I (1955), pp. 144-146, par. 414, and I, Sup. No. 2 (1964), pp. 171-172, par. 162. Hersh Lauterpacht, *International Law and Human Rights* (New York: Praeger, 1950), p. 154, n. 20. Raghubir Chakravarti, *Human Rights and the United Nations* (Calcutta: Progressive Publishers, 1958), pp. 45-46.

2. GA/Res/1248 (XIII). 30 October 1958. Cf., GA/Res 616B (VII). 5 December 1952. And cf., Lauterpacht, *op. cit.*, p. 153.
3. GAOR. I. Part 2. Joint Committee of the First and Sixth Committees, pp. 3-4.
4. Rosalyn Higgins, *The Development of International Law Through the Political Organs of the United Nations* (New York: Oxford University Press, 1963), p. 119.
5. Cf., D. H. N. Johnson, "The Effect of Resolutions of the General Assembly of the United Nations," *British Yearbook of International Law*, 1955-1956, esp. pp. 107, 121-122.
6. International Court of Justice. *Reports of Judgments, Advisory Opinions and Orders. 1966. South West Africa Cases.* P. 144. (Hereafter cited as: ICJ, *Reports*, 1966.)
7. International Court of Justice. *Pleadings, Oral Arguments, Documents. 1966. South West Africa Cases.* Vol. IV, p. 493. (Hereafter cited as: ICJ, *Pleadings*, 1966.)
8. *Ibid.*, Vol. V, p. 140.
9. *Ibid.*, Vol. V, p. 127.
10. ICJ, *Reports*, 1966, p. 438.
11. *Ibid.*, p. 464.
12. *Ibid.*, pp. 296, 300, 314.
13. *Ibid.*, p. 289.
14. *Repertory of Practice of United Nations Organs*, III (1955), p. 117. Cf., C. Wilfred Jenks, *The Common Law of Mankind* (London: Stevens, 1958), pp. 283-287.
15. Chakravarti, *op. cit.*, p. 19.
16. Lauterpacht, *op. cit.*, p. 168.
17. GAOR. VII. 381st Plenary Meeting. 17 October 1952. Pp. 54-57, pars. 15-41.
18. GA/Res/39 (I). 12 December 1946.
19. GA/Res/285 (III). 25 April 1949.
20. *Repertory of Practice of United Nations Organs*, I. Sup. No. 2 (1964), pp. 144-156.
21. GAOR. VII. 401st Plenary Meeting. 5 December 1952. P. 335, par. 117.
22. Cf. GAOR. VII. First Cttee. 538th Mtg. 6 December 1952. Pp. 201-202, pars. 52-56, speech of Selwyn Lloyd; and GAOR. VII. 401st Plenary Mtg. 5 December 1952. P. 334, pars. 106-110.
23. GAOR. VII. 381st Plenary Mtg. 17 October 1952. P. 61.
24. GAOR. XV. Special Political Cttee. 242nd Mtg. 5 April 1961. P. 77, par. 13.
25. *Repertory of Practice of United Nations Organs*, I (1955), p. 102, par. 211.
26. UN Commission on Human Rights. XXIV. E/CN.4/SR.949. 12 February 1968. Provisional.
27. GAOR. VII. Ad Hoc Political Committee. 17th Mtg. 15 November 1952.

Pp. 90-91, pars. 10-13. GAOR. VII. 401st Plenary Mtg. 5 December 1952. P. 332, par. 89.

28. Cf., Rupert Emerson, *Africa and United States Policy* (Englewood Cliffs: Prentice-Hall, 1967), p. 89.
29. *New York Times*, March 7, 1968, 12: 1. U. S. Mission to the UN, Press Release USUN-30 (68) Corr. 1, March 11, 1968.
30. Richard N. Gardner, *Department of State Bulletin*, 50 (January 6, 1964), 23.
31. *Congressional Record*, Vol. 97, Pt. 8 (August 23, 1951), 10537.
32. *Ibid.*, Vol. 97, Pt. 8 (August 30, 1951), 10795.
33. GAOR. III. Part 1. 3rd Cttee. 91st Mtg. 2 October 1948. P. 48. Mr. Chang.
34. For summary reviews of the positions taken, see Chakravarti, *op. cit.*, pp. 67-73; and Commission to Study the Organization of Peace, Eighteenth Report, *The United Nations and Human Rights* (Dobbs Ferry, N. Y.: Oceana, 1968), pp. 60-72.
35. GAOR. III. Part 1. 182nd Plenary Mtg. 10 December 1948. P. 111. Mr. Andrews.
36. GAOR. III. Part 1. 3rd Cttee. 89th Mtg. 30 September 1948. Pp. 34-35. Mrs. Newlands.
37. GAOR. III. Part 1. 3rd Cttee. 92nd Mtg. 2 October 1948. P. 61; and GAOR. III. Part 1. 180th Plenary Mtg. 9 December 1948. P. 866.
38. GAOR. III. Part 1. 3rd Cttee. 93rd Mtg. 4 October 1948. P. 64.
39. Commission to Study the Organization of Peace, Eighteenth Report, pp. 71-72.
40. Quoted in United Nations, International Conference on Human Rights, *Methods Used by the United Nations in the Field of Human Rights*, Study Prepared by the Secretary-General (A/CONF. 32/6, 20 June 1967), p. 114, par. 364.
41. Cf., Egon Schwelb, *Human Rights and the International Community* (Chicago: Quadrangle Books, 1964), esp. pp. 46-55.
42. GA/Res/285 (III). 25 April 1949.
43. GAOR. V. 4th Cttee. 187th Mtg. 25 November 1950. P. 287, par. 24.
44. GA/Res/1514 (XV). 14 December 1960.
45. GA/Res/1654 (XVI). 27 November 1961.
46. GA/Res/1904 (XVIII). 20 November 1963.
47. GAOR. XVIII. 1261st Plenary Mtg. 20 November 1963. P. 7.
48. U.S. Congress. Senate. Committee on Foreign Relations. *Human Rights Conventions*. Hearings before a Subcommittee. 90th Cong., 1st Sess. 1967. P. 46.
49. *Department of State Bulletin*, 59 (September 2, 1968), 258.
50. Schwelb, *op. cit.*, p. 70.
51. Sir Humphrey Waldock, "Human Rights in Contemporary International Law and the Significance of the European Convention," in British Institute of International and Comparative Law, International Law Series No.

5, *The European Convention on Human Rights* (Supplementary Publication No. 11 [1965], *The International and Comparative Law Quarterly*), p. 15. Cf., John P. Humphrey, "The UN Charter and the Universal Declaration of Human Rights," in Evan Luard, ed., *The International Protection of Human Rights* (New York: Praeger, 1967), p. 53.

52. OAS. Final Act of the Ninth International Conference of American States. Bogotá, Colombia. March 20-May 2, 1948 (Washington: Pan American Union, 1948), pp. 87-88.

CHAPTER 7

1. U.S. President. *Public Papers of the Presidents of the United States. Harry S Truman. Containing the Public Messages, Speeches, and Statements of the President. January 1 to December 31, 1950* (Washington, 1965), p. 495. Address of June 27, 1950. (Hereafter cited as: *Public Papers of the Presidents, Truman*, 1950).
2. John Foster Dulles, "The Future of the United Nations," *International Conciliation*, No. 445 (November 1948), p. 585.
3. U.S. Congress. Senate. Committee on Foreign Relations. *The Genocide Convention*. Hearings before a Subcommittee. 81st Cong., 2d Sess. on Executive O. 1950. P. 240. (Hereafter cited as: Senate Hearings, *Genocide Convention*, 1950.)
4. *Department of State Bulletin*, 19 (December 19, 1948), 755.
5. *Ibid*., 23 (September 4, 1950), 379.
6. Senate Hearings, *Genocide Convention*, 1950, p. 19.
7. Richard N. Gardner, *In Pursuit of World Order. U. S. Foreign Policy and International Organizations* (New York: Praeger, 1964), p. 250.
8. Address of March 21, 1967, *Congressional Record*, Vol. 113, No. 83 (May 25, 1967), S7450. Six conventions on human rights have been sent to the Senate and await approval: Freedom of Association (ILO), Genocide (UN), Forced Labor (ILO), Political Rights of Women (UN), Employment Policy (ILO), and Political Rights of Women (OAS). The United States has signed the Convention on the Elimination of All Forms of Racial Discrimination (UN) and the Convention on Consent to Marriage (UN), but the President has not referred them to the Senate. The President has also refrained from sending to the Senate various other conventions not requiring signature, e.g. the Convention on Discrimination in Education (UNESCO).
9. U.S. Congress. Senate. Committee on Foreign Relations. *Human Rights Conventions*. Hearing. 90th Cong., 1st Sess., on Executive J, Executive K, and Executive L. 1967. Part 2. Pp. 9, 64-65. (Hereafter cited as: Senate Hearings, *Human Rights Conventions*, 1967, II.)
10. John P. Humphrey, "International Protection of Human Rights," *Annals of the American Academy of Political and Social Science*, 255 (January 1948), 21.

11. Senate Hearings, *Human Rights Conventions,* 1967, II, 75.
12. *Ibid.,* p. 76.
13. *Ibid.,* p. 64. For an extended examination of the question whether the acceptance of international obligations in the field of human rights is beyond the scope of the treaty or other federal power, see Myres S. McDougal and Gertrude C. K. Leighton, *Studies in World Public Order* (New Haven: Yale University Press, 1960), pp. 373-392. And Louis Henkin, "The Constitution, Treaties, and International Human Rights," *University of Pennsylvania Law Review,* 116 (April 1968), 1012-1032.
14. Senate Hearings, *Human Rights Conventions,* 1967, II, 76.
15. *Ibid.,* pp. 64-65.
16. *Ibid.,* p. 8.
17. U.S. Congress. Senate. Committee on the Judiciary. *Treaties and Executive Agreements.* Hearings before a Subcommittee . . . on S. J. Res. 130. 82nd Cong., 2d Sess. 1952. P. 165. (Hereafter cited as: Senate Hearings, *Treaties and Executive Agreements,* 1952.). Cf., Senator Bricker, "Freedom of the Press and the United Nations," *Congressional Record,* Vol. 98, Pt. 10 (May 27, 1952), A3261.
18. *Congressional Record,* Vol. 98, Pt. 8 (February 14, 1952), A839.
19. *Ibid.,* Vol. 97, Pt. 8 (August 16, 1951), 10129.
20. *Ibid.,* Vol. 98, Pt. 1 (February 7, 1952), 912.
21. *Ibid.,* Vol. 97, Pt. 6 (July 17, 1951), 8257; Vol. 98, Pt. 8 (February 14, 1952), A839.
22. *Ibid.,* Vol. 98, Pt. 10 (May 14, 1952), A2953.
23. U.S. Congress. Senate. Committee on the Judiciary. *Treaties and Executive Agreements.* Hearings before a Subcommittee on Constitutional Amendments. S. J. 1. 84th Cong., 1st Sess. 1955. P. 210. (Hereafter cited as: Senate Hearings, *Treaties and Executive Agreements,* 1955.)
24. *Ibid.,* p. 526.
25. *Congressional Record,* Vol. 102, Pt. 5 (April 16, 1956), 6341.
26. Louis K. Hyde, *The United States and the United Nations, Promoting the Public Welfare* (New York: Manhattan Publishing Co., 1960), pp. 168-170.
27. Patricia R. Harris, "U. N. Adopts International Covenants on Human Rights," *Department of State Bulletin,* 56 (January 16, 1967), 104-105.
28. Frank E. Holman, "International Proposals Affecting So-Called Human Rights," *Law and Contemporary Problems,* 14 (Summer 1949), 483.
29. U.S. Congress. Senate. Committee on the Judiciary. *Treaties and Executive Agreements.* Hearings before a Subcommittee on S. J. Res. 1 and S. J. Res. 43. 83rd Cong., 1st Sess. 1953. P. 116. (Hereafter cited as: Senate Hearings, *Treaties and Executive Agreements,* 1953).
30. Hyde, *op. cit.,* p. 184.
31. Senate Hearings, *Human Rights Conventions,* 1967, II, 81-82.
32. *Congressional Record,* Vol. 95, Pt. 13 (March 24, 1949), A1928.
33. A. H. Robertson, *Human Rights in Europe* (New York: Oceana, 1963), p. 4.

34. Pierre-Henri Teitgen, quoted by Robertson, *op. cit.*, p. 6.
35. *Congressional Record,* Vol. 97, Pt. 6 (July 17, 1951), p. 8254.
36. Senate Hearings, *Treaties and Executive Agreements,* 1955, pp. 13-14.
37. U.S. Congress. Senate. Committee on Foreign Relations. *Japanese Peace Treaty and Other Treaties Relating to Security in the Pacific.* Hearings. 82nd Cong., 2d Sess. 1952. P. 153.
38. Senate Hearings, *Treaties and Executive Agreements,* 1953, p. 825.
39. U.S. Department of State. *Foreign Relations of the United States. Diplomatic Papers* 1938. Volume V. *The American Republics* (Washington, 1956), p. 74.
40. *Congressional Record,* Vol. 98, Pt. 2 (March 18, 1952), p. 2469.
41. Senate Hearings, *Treaties and Executive Agreements,* 1953, p. 1219.
42. Senate Hearings, *Treaties and Executive Agreements,* 1955, p. 659.
43. *Ibid.*, pp. 676, 678-679.
44. Senate Hearings, *Human Rights Conventions,* 1967, II, 69.
45. Sherman Kent, "The Declaration of the Rights of Man and Citizen," in R. M. MacIver, ed., *Great Expressions of Human Rights* (New York: Harper, 1950), p. 176.
46. Quoted by S. A. de Smith, "Fundamental Rights in the Commonwealth—Part I," *International and Comparative Law Quarterly,* 10 (January, 1961) 87, n. 19.
47. Jacques Lambert, *Latin America: Social Structure and Political Institutions* (Berkeley: University of California Press, 1967), p. 273.
48. *Ibid.*, pp. 273, 275, 277, 279.
49. Indian Statutory Commission, *Report,* Vol. II, Cmd. 3569 (1930), p. 23.
50. Sir William Ivor Jennings, *The Approach to Self-Government* (Cambridge: At the University Press, 1956), pp. 99, 101, 102, 108, 110.
51. S. I. Benn and R. S. Peters, *The Principles of Political Thought* (New York: Free Press, 1965), p. 411.
52. Council of Europe. *European Convention on Human Rights. Collected Texts* (Strasbourg, September 1966), Section 5 (c).
53. David H. Bayley, *Public Liberties in the New States* (Chicago: Rand McNally, 1964), pp. 21-22.
54. United Kingdom. Colonial Office. *Nigeria. Report of the Commission Appointed to Enquire into the Fears of Minorities and the Means of Allaying Them.* Cmnd. 505. 1958. P. 97, par. 38.
55. Cf., UN. International Conference on Human Rights, 1968. Measures Taken Within the United Nations in the Field of Human Rights. Study prepared by the Secretary-General. A/CONF.32/5. 20 June 1967. Pars. 47-57.
56. UN Commission on Human Rights. XXIV. Periodic Reports on Human Rights. E/CN.4/907/Rev.2. 3 January 1968. And *International Year for Human Rights Newsletter,* Number 3 (December 1967), 44-50. *UNESCO Chronicle,* 14 (June 1968), 221. In the case of the convention on Discrimination in Education, two of the 41 ratifications occurred in 1968.

Cf., A/CONF.32/15. 28 March 1968. "Acceptance of Human Rights Treaties."

57. OAS. Final Act of the Ninth International Conference of American States, Bogotá, Colombia, March 20-May 2, 1948 (Washington: Pan American Union, 1948), p. 45. Resolution XXXI.
58. OAS. Inter-American Juridical Committee. *Strengthening and Effective Exercise of Democracy*. Report . . . CIJ-42 (Washington: Pan American Union, January 1959), p. 7.
59. OAS. Fifth Meeting of Consultation of Ministers of Foreign Affairs. Santiago, Chile, August 12-18, 1959. *Final Act*. OEA/Ser. C.II.5 (Washington: Pan American Union, 1960), Resolution VIII, pp. 10-11.
60. OAS. Inter-American Juridical Committee. *Strengthening and Effective Exercise of Democracy*, p. 7.
61. OAS. Eleventh Inter-American Conference, Quito, Ecuador, 1960. *Study on the Juridical Relationship Between Respect for Human Rights and the Exercise of Democracy*. OEA/Ser. E/XI.1. Document 16. 24 November 1959 (Washington: Pan American Union, 1959). P. 5.
62. OEA/Ser.G/V. C-d-1631. 2 October 1968.
63. OAS. Inter-American Commission on Human Rights. "Report of the OAS to the International Conference on Human Rights, 1968." OEA/Ser.L/V/1.5. 18 December 1967. P. 83.
64. C. Wilfred Jenks, *Human Rights and International Labor Standards* (New York: Praeger, 1960), pp. 131-132.
65. Quincy Wright, "Freedom and Human Rights under International Law," in M. R. Konvitz and C. Rossiter, eds., *Aspects of Liberty* (Ithaca: Cornell University Press, 1958), p. 195. Cf., Quincy Wright, "Human Rights and the World Order," *International Conciliation*, No. 389 (April 1943), 245, 250.
66. "The ILO–Front Line for Workers," *American Federationist*, 68 (November 1961), 17. Cf., Bayley, *op. cit.*, p. 22.
67. *Congressional Record*, Vol. 99, Pt. 2 (April 8, 1953), 2813.
68. *Ibid.*, Vol. 101, Pt. 6 (May 31, 1955), 7237.
69. *Ibid.*, Vol. 103, Pt. 3 (March 5, 1957), 3167-3168.
70. *Ibid.*, Vol. 104, Pt. 9 (June 24, 1958), 11993-11994.
71. Francis O. Wilcox, "The United Nations: Its Role in a Changing World," *Department of State Bulletin*, 41 (September 28, 1959), 442.
72. ILO. International Labor Conference. *Record of Proceedings*, 40th Sess. (1957), p. 346.
73. Senate Hearings, *Treaties and Executive Agreements*, 1952, p. 246.
74. U.S. Congress. House of Representatives. Committee on Education and Labor. *International Labor Organization, 1964*. Hearings before the Ad Hoc Subcommittee on the ILO. 88th Cong. 2d Sess. P. 11. (Hereafter cited as: House ILO Hearings, 1964.) Cf., Ernst B. Haas, *Beyond the Nation-State. Functionalism and International Organization* (Stanford: Stanford University Press, 1964), pp. 233-236.

75. U.S. Congress. House of Representatives. Committee on Education and Labor. *International Labor Organization.* Hearings before the Ad Hoc Subcommittee . . . on U.S. Participation in the ILO. 88th Cong., 1st Sess. P. 43. (Hereafter cited as: House ILO Hearings, 1963).
76. Bert Seidman, "Labor Standards and Human Rights," *American Federationist,* 68 (January 1961), 11.
77. House ILO Hearings, 1963, p. 45.
78. *Congressional Record,* Vol. 109, Pt. 17 (November 27, 1963), 22907; and Vol. 110, Pt. 3 (February 24, 1964), 3407.
79. *Ibid.*, Vol. 111, Pt. 5 (March 25, 1964), 5882.
80. U.S. Congress. Senate. Committee on Foreign Relations. *Human Rights Conventions.* Hearings before a Subcommittee. 90th Cong., 1st Sess. 1967. Pp. 91, 97. (Hereafter cited as: Senate Hearings, *Human Rights Conventions,* 1967, I.)
81. *Congressional Record,* Vol. 113, No. 3 (January 12, 1967), S204.
82. Senate Hearings, *Human Rights Conventions,* 1967, II, p. 88.
83. Address of March 21, 1967. *Congressional Record,* Vol. 113, No. 83 (May 25, 1967), S7449-7451.
84. *Ibid.*, p. S7449.
85. Senate Hearings, *Human Rights Conventions,* 1967, II, p. 88.
86. *Ibid.*, p. 114.
87. *Ibid.*, p. 88.
88. *Congressional Record,* Vol. 113, No. 83 (May 25, 1967), S7450.
89. Senate Hearings, *Human Rights Conventions,* 1967, I, p. 40.
90. *Ibid.*, pp. 119-120.
91. *Public Papers of the Presidents, Truman,* 1950, p. 495.
92. Senate Hearings, *Treaties and Executive Agreements,* 1952, p. 198.
93. U.S. Congress. House. Committee on Foreign Affairs. *U.S. Observance of International Human Rights Year,* 1968. Hearings before the Subcommittee on International Organizations and Movements. 89th Cong., 2d Sess. 1966. P. 32.
94. Senate Hearings, *Human Rights Conventions,* 1967, I, p. 30.
95. *Ibid.*, p. 121.
96. U.S. President. *Public Papers of the Presidents of the United States. Harry S Truman* . . . January 1 to December 31, 1947 (Washington, 1963), pp. 324-325.
97. *Department of State Bulletin,* 21 (October 31, 1949), 644.
98. *Ibid.*, 19 (October 3, 1948), 432.

## CHAPTER 8

1. UN. General Assembly. International Conference on Human Rights, 1968. *Methods Used by the United Nations in the Field of Human Rights.* A/CONF.32/6. 20 June 1967. P. 36, par. 85. (Hereafter cited as: *Methods Used by the United Nations.*)

2. John C. Dreier, *The Organization of the American States and the Hemisphere Crisis* (New York: Harper & Row, 1962), pp. 104-105.
3. OAS. *Report of the OAS to the International Conference on Human Rights, 1968.* OEA/Ser.L/V/1.5. 18 December 1967. Pp. 43-44.
4. Inter-American Institute of International Legal Studies, *The Inter-American System, Its Development and Strengthening* (Dobbs Ferry, N.Y.: Oceana, 1966), p. 45, fn. 12. (Hereafter cited as *The Inter-American System.*)
5. OAS. Second Special Inter-American Conference. Rio de Janeiro, Brazil, November 17-30, 1965. *Final Act.* OEA/Ser.C/I.13. Res. XXII, p. 33. Cf., OAS. Inter-American Commission on Human Rights. *Report Submitted . . . to the Second Special Inter-American Conference.* OEA/Ser. L/V/II.11. Doc. 5, Rev. 2. 15 October 1965.
6. John Carey, "Procedures for International Protection of Human Rights," *Iowa Law Review,* 53 (October 1967), 320-321.
7. Moses Moskowitz, *The Politics and Dynamics of Human Rights* (Dobbs Ferry, N.Y.: Oceana, 1968), p. 96.
8. Quoted by Louis B. Sohn, "Supplementary Paper. A Short History of United Nations Documents on Human Rights," in Commission to Study the Organization of Peace, Eighteenth Report, *The United Nations and Human Rights* (Dobbs Ferry, N.Y.: Oceana, 1968), p. 80.
9. *Ibid.*, p. 79.
10. *Ibid.*, p. 84.
11. UN. Commission on Human Rights. Sub-Commission on Prevention of Discrimination and Protection of Minorities. *Report of the Nineteenth Session . . . .* 4-23 January 1967. E/CN.4/930. Pp. 77, 82-83, pars. 248, 263-270. *New York Times,* January 21, 1967, 6: 2.
12. UN. ECOSOC. Official Records: 39th Session. Sup. No. 8. Commission on Human Rights. *Report on the Twenty-First Session,* 22 March-15 April 1965. E/4024. P. 148.
13. UN. ECOSOC. Official Records: 41st Session. Sup. No. 8. Commission on Human Rights. *Report on the Twenty-Second Session.* 8 March-5 April 1966. P. 113, par. 453. (Hereafter cited as: UNCHR. XXII. Report.) Cf., William Korey, "The Key to Human Rights—Implementation," *International Conciliation,* No. 570 (November 1968), pp. 24-28.
14. E. A. Landy, *The Effectiveness of International Supervision. Thirty Years of I.L.O. Experience* (Dobbs Ferry, N.Y.: Oceana, 1966), pp. 155, 159-163.
15. *Ibid.*, p. 15.
16. *Ibid.*, pp. 180, 186.
17. *Ibid.*, p. 66.
18. UN. ECOSOC. Fortieth Session, Agenda item 9. E/4144. 29 December 1965. "Report of the International Labor Organization." P. 12.
19. C. Wilfred Jenks, *Human Rights and International Labor Standards* (New York: Praeger, 1960), p. 21; see also pp. 138-193.

20. Ernst B. Haas, *Beyond the Nation-State. Functionalism and International Organization* (Stanford: Stanford University Press, 1964), p. 258.
21. Landy, *op. cit.*, p. 203.
22. Egon Schwelb, "The International Convention on the Elimination of All Forms of Racial Discrimination," *International and Comparative Law Quarterly*, 15 (October 1966), 1034-1037.
23. José A. Cabranes, "Human Rights and Non-Intervention in the Inter-American System," *Michigan Law Review*, 65 (April 1967), 1181-1182, n. 83.
24. GA/Res/1133 (XI). September 14, 1957.
25. *Methods Used by the United Nations*, p. 157, pars. 502ff.
26. UN. ECOSOC. Official Records. First Year, Second Session. Commission on Human Rights. Report. Doc. E/38, p. 230.
27. UN. ECOSOC. Official Records. Fourth Session. 1947. Sup. No. 3. Commission on Human Rights. Report. Doc. E/259, p. 6, par. 22.
28. Hersh Lauterpacht, *International Law and Human Rights* (New York: Praeger, 1950), pp. 229-236, 259.
29. Cf., Morris B. Abram, "Fight for Human Rights," *National Jewish Monthly*, 81 (June 1967), 12.
30. GA/Res/2144. (XXI). 26 October 1966.
31. ECOSOC. Res/1102 (XL). 4 March 1966.
32. UNCHR. Res/8 (XXIII). 16 March 1967.
33. UNCHR. Res/2 (XXIII). 6 March 1967.
34. Cf., UNCHR. Res/3 (XXIV). 16 February 1968; and Res/14 (XXIV). 8 March 1968.
35. UNCHR. XXII. Report, p. 7. And Hoare, *loc. cit.*, p. 67.
36. UNCHR. XXII. Report, p. 7.
37. GA/Res/2443. (XXIII). 19 December 1968.
38. UN. Commission on Human Rights. Sub-Commission on Prevention of Discrimination and Protection of Minorities. *Report of the Twentieth Session* . . . 25 September-12 October 1967. E/CN.4/947. 4 December 1967. P. 40, par. 95.
39. E/CN.4/SR.965, 23 February 1968. E/CN.4/SR.969, 27 February 1968.
40. UN. ECOSOC. Official Records. Forty-Fourth Session. Sup. No. 4. Commission on Human Rights. *Report on the Twenty-Fourth Session.* 5 February-12 March 1968. P. 71, par. 174. (Hereafter cited as: UNCHR. XXIV. Report.)
41. E/CN.4/SR.970. 28 February 1968.
42. Korey, *op cit.*, p. 24.
43. Resolution 2 (XXI) of the Sub-Commission on Prevention of Discrimination and Protection of Minorities. E/CN.4/Sub.2/L.503/Add.2.
44. Haas, *op. cit.*, pp. 361-370.
45. Haas, *op cit.*, p. 402. Haas devotes an entire chapter to an examination of the activity of the Committee on Freedom of Association, presenting

a valuable analysis. See also Jenks, *Human Rights and International Labor Standards*, p. 62.

46. UN. General Assembly. XXII. A/6699/Add.1. 14 September 1967. P. 5, par. 7.
47. C. Wilfred Jenks, "The International Protection of Trade Union Rights," in Luard, ed., *op. cit.*, p. 232. Landy, *op. cit.*, pp. 145-146.
48. José A. Cabranes, "The Protection of Human Rights by the Organization of the American States," *American Journal of International Law*, 62 (October 1968), 889-908. Durward V. Sandifer, "The Inter-American Commission on Human Rights in the Dominican Republic, June 1965 to June 1966," OEA/Ser.L/V/II.14. Doc. 13. 15 April 1966. Thirteenth Session. P. 27. Ann Van Wynen Thomas and A. J. Thomas, Jr., "The Inter-American Commission on Human Rights," *Southwestern Law Journal*, 20 (June 1966), 286-287.
49. OAS. Inter-American Peace Committee. *Report . . . on the Case Presented by Venezuela*. June 6, 1950 [1960]. App. D, pp. 14-15. U.S. Department of State. Bureau of Public Affairs. Historical Office. *Inter-American Efforts to Relieve International Tensions in the Western Hemisphere* 1959-1960. Publication 7409, July 1962, p. 203.
50. OAS. Inter-American Commission on Human Rights. Report on the Work Accomplished During its First Special Session, January 3 to 23, 1963. OEA/Ser.L./V/II.6. Doc. 18. April 25, 1963. P. 11.
51. Sandifer, "The Inter-American Commission on Human Rights in the Dominican Republic, June 1965 to June 1966," pp. 2-3. Carlos A. Dunshee de Abranches, "Special Protection of Human Rights in the Dominican Republic," in Washington World Conference, *World Peace through Law* (St. Paul, Minn.: West Publishing Co., 1967), pp. 343-349. Anna P. Schreiber and Philippe S. E. Schreiber, "The Inter-American Commission on Human Rights in the Dominican Crisis," *International Organization*, 22 (Spring 1968), 508-528. John Carey, ed., *The Dominican Republic Crisis 1965* (Dobbs Ferry, N.Y.: Oceana, 1967).
52. OAS. *Report of the OAS to the International Conference on Human Rights*, 1968. OEA/Ser.L/V/1.5. 18 December 1967. P. 54.
53. *OAS Chronicle*, 1 (October 1965), 27.
54. Sandifer, "The Inter-American Commission on Human Rights in the Dominican Republic, June 1965 to June 1966," p. 23. Thomas and Thomas, "The Inter-American Commission on Human Rights," *Southwestern Law Journal*, 20 (June 1966), 306.
55. OAS. *Report of the OAS to the International Conference on Human Rights*, 1968. OEA/Ser.L/V/1.5. 18 December 1967. L. Ronald Scheman, "The Inter-American Commission on Human Rights," *American Journal of International Law*, 59 (April 1965), 343.
56. A. H. Robertson, *Human Rights in Europe* (Dobbs Ferry, N.Y.: Oceana, 1963), pp. 59-60.
57. *Yearbook of the European Convention on Human Rights*, 1963, pp. 740-800.

58. *Journal Officiel des Communautés Européenes*, Vol. 10, No. 103 (2 juin 1967), p. 2058.
59. *Forward in Europe*, October-November 1967, p. 3. Thomas Buergenthal, "Proceedings against Greece under the European Convention on Human Rights," *American Journal of International Law*, 62 (April 1968), 441.
60. *Human Rights Journal*, Vol. I, No. 1 (March 1968), p. 129.
61. Council of Europe. Consultative Assembly. Nineteenth Ordinary Session. Texts Adopted. Resolution 361 (31 January 1968).
62. Egon Schwelb, "The International Convention on the Elimination of All Forms of Racial Discrimination," *International and Comparative Law Quarterly*, 15 (October 1966), 1037-1041.
63. Moses Moskowitz, *Human Rights and World Order. The Struggle for Human Rights in the United Nations* (Dobbs Ferry, N.Y.: Oceana, 1958), pp. 113-135.
64. UN. ECOSOC. Official Records. Third Year. Sixth Session. Sup. No. 1. Annex C of Doc. E/600. December 17, 1947. P. 41.
65. Quoted by Lauterpacht, *op. cit.*, p. 307.
66. *Yearbook on Human Rights*, 1948-1949, p. 541.
67. UN. ECOSOC. Official Records. Third Year. Sixth Session. Sup. No. 1. Annex C of Doc. E/600. December 17, 1947, P. 41.
68. James Pomeroy Hendrick, "Progress Report on Human Rights," *Department of State Bulletin*, 19 (August 8, 1948), 163.
69. Richard N. Gardner, *In Pursuit of World Order. U.S. Foreign Policy and International Organizations* (New York: Praeger, 1964), p. 256.
70. Moskowitz, *Politics and Dynamics of Human Rights*, p. 103. Cf., Moskowitz, *Human Rights and World Order*, p. 113.
71. *Methods Used by the United Nations*, p. 163, par. 526.
72. Cf., Egon Schwelb, "The United Nations and Human Rights," *Howard Law Journal*, 11 (Spring 1965), 367-368. John Carey, "The United Nations' Double Standard on Human Rights Complaints," *American Journal of International Law*, 60 (October 1966), 796-797.
73. *Forward in Europe*, December 1967, p. 16.
74. A. B. McNulty, "The European Convention on Human Rights: Its Sanctions and Practice," in British Institute of International and Comparative Law, International Law Series No. 5, *The European Convention on Human Rights* (Supplementary Publication No. 11 [1965], *The International and Comparative Law Quarterly*), pp. 77-78.
75. OAS., *Report of the OAS to the International Conference on Human Rights*, 1968. OEA/Ser.L/V/1.5. 18 December 1967. P. 45. Thomas and Thomas, "The Inter-American Commission on Human Rights," *Southwestern Law Journal*, 20 (June 1966), 292-293. Schreiber and Schreiber, *loc. cit.*, p. 525.
76. OEA/Ser.G/V. C-d-1631. 2 October 1968.
77. ECOSOC. Res/1237 (XLII). 6 June 1967.
78. ECOSOC. Official Records. Fourteenth Session. Sup. No. 4. Commis-

sion on Human Rights. Report of the Eighth Session (14 April to 14 June 1952). Pp. 58-61.

79. Cf., R. ST.J. Macdonald, "The United Nations High Commissioner for Human Rights," *Canadian Yearbook of International Law*, V (1967), 84-117.
80. ECOSOC. Official Records. Third Year. Sixth Session. Sup. No. 1. Commission on Human Rights. Report on the Second Session, 2-17 December 1947. Document E/600. P. 48.
81. ECOSOC. Official Records. Fourth Year. Ninth Session. Sup. No. 10. Commission on Human Rights. Report on the Fifth Session. 9 May to 20 June 1949. Doc. E/1371. Pp. 36-45. Cf., Lauterpacht, *op. cit.*, pp. 308, 386-387.
82. J. E. S. Fawcett, "The Protection of Human Rights on a Universal Basis: Recent Experience and Proposals," in A. H. Robertson, ed., *Human Rights in National and International Law* (Dobbs Ferry, N.Y.: Oceana, 1968), p. 294.
83. OEA/Ser.G/V. C-d-1631. 2 October 1968.
84. John Carey, "Procedures for International Protection of Human Rights," *Iowa Law Review*, 53 (October 1967), 297.
85. *Ibid.*, p. 295. Cf., Luis Kutner, "World Habeas Corpus: A Legal Ligament for Political Diversity," in The Washington World Conference, *World Peace Through Law*, pp. 362-374.
86. Karel Vasak, "Regionalization of the International Protection of Human Rights and Fundamental Freedoms," in The Washington World Conference, *World Peace Through Law*, pp. 356-362.
87. E/CN.4/SR.969. 27 February 1968.
88. José A. Cabranes, "Human Rights and Non-Intervention in the Inter-American System," *Michigan Law Review*, 65 (April 1967), 1181.

### CHAPTER 9

1. John Huston, "Human Rights Enforcement Issues of the United Nations Conference on International Organization," *Iowa Law Review*, 53 (October 1967), 277-278.
2. SCOR. 1st Year. 1st Series, No. 2. 34th Mtg. 17 April 1946. Pp. 155, 159, 167.
3. SCOR. 1st Year. 1st Series. 46th Mtg. 17 June 1946. P. 357; cf., 34th Mtg. 17 April 1946. P. 168.
4. SCOR. 1st Year. 1st Series. Special Sup. "Report of the Sub-Committee on the Spanish Question." 31 May 1946. Doc S/75. P. 10, par. 27.
5. *Ibid.*, pp. 11-12.
6. GA/Res/39 (I). 12 December 1946.
7. *Department of State Bulletin*, 22 (January 30, 1950), 158.
8. *Ibid.*, 13 (November 25, 1945), 864-866.
9. *Ibid.*, 13 (December 2, 1945), 892.

10. Cf., John C. Dreier, *The Organization of the American States and the Hemisphere Crisis* (New York: Harper & Row, 1962), pp. 94-95. Jerome Slater, *The OAS and United States Foreign Policy* (Columbus: Ohio State University Press, 1967), pp. 240-242.
11. Charles G. Fenwick, "The Problem of the Recognition of De Facto Governments," *Inter-American Juridical Yearbook, 1948* (Washington: Pan American Union, 1949), p. 31.
12. *Ibid.*, pp. 33-34.
13. OAS.. Eleventh Inter-American Conference, Quito, Ecuador, 1960. Study on the Juridical Relationship Between Respect for Human Rights and the Exercise of Democracy. OEA/Ser.E/XI.1. Doc. 16. 24 November 1959.
14. Department of State. Bureau of Public Affairs. Historical Office. *Inter-American Efforts to Relieve International Tensions in the Western Hemisphere* 1959-1960. Publication 7409. July 1962. P. 200.
15. *Ibid.*, pp. 205-206.
16. OAS. Inter-American Peace Committee. Report to the Eighth Meeting of Consultation of Ministers of Foreign Affairs 1962. OEA/Ser.1/III. CIP/1/62. P. 46.
17. OAS. Eighth Meeting of Consultation of Ministers of Foreign Affairs. Punta del Este, Uruguay. January 22-31, 1962. Final Act. OEA/Ser.C/II. 8. P. 14.
18. OAS. Second Special Inter-American Conference. Rio de Janeiro, Brazil, November 17-30, 1965. *Final Act.* OEA/Ser.C/I.13. Resolution XXVI.
19. UN. General Assembly. XXII A/PV.1627. 12 December 1967. Pp. 17, 18-20.
20. UN. General Assembly. XXII. A/PV.1647. 2 May 1968.
21. Quoted by Amelia C. Leiss, "A Summation," in Amelia C. Leiss, *Apartheid and United Nations Collective Measures: An Analysis* (New York: Carnegie Endowment for International Peace, 1965), p. 162.
22. Lord Caradon. General Assembly. XXII. A/PV.1631. 14 December 1967. P. 68.
23. Moses Moskowitz, *The Politics and Dynamics of Human Rights* (Dobbs Ferry, N. Y.: Oceana, 1968), p. 186.
24. Summit Conference of Independent African States, Addis Ababa, May 1963, *Proceedings.* Resolution on Decolonization.
25. *Congressional Record.* Vol. 114, No. 71 (April 29, 1968), S4566.
26. *The New York Times*, June 30, 1968, 13:1.
27. UN. General Assembly. XXII. A/6864/Add.1. 26 October 1967. Agenda Item 34(a). P. 70, par. 279. *Ibid.*, A/6864. 18 October 1967. Agenda Item 35(a). Pars. 81, 296. *The New York Times*, April 28, 1968, 12:1.
28. UN. General Assembly. XXII. A/PV.1647. 2 May 1968. Provisional. P. 17.
29. S/8843. 11 October 1968. P. 27, par. 98.
30. A/AC.125/L.48.
31. UN. General Assembly. XXII. A/6864. 19 October 1967. Agenda Item 35(a). P. 54, par. 134.

32. UN. ECOSOC. Official Records: 44th Session. Sup. No. 4. Commission on Human Rights. Report on the Twenty-Fourth Session. 5 February-12 March 1968. P. 161. Resolution 15 (XXIV). (Hereafter cited as: UNCHR. XXIV. Report.)
33. GA/Res/2307 (XXII). 13 December 1967.
34. GA/Res/2270 (XXII). 17 November 1967.
35. GA/Res/2262 (XXII). 8 November 1967.
36. GA/Res/1568 (XV). 18 December 1960.
37. GA/Res/1899 (XVIIII). 13 November 1963.
38. GA/Res/2145 (XXI). 27 October 1966.
39. GA/Res/2248 (S-V). 19 May 1967.
40. UN. General Assembly. XXII. A/6897. 10 November 1967. Agenda Item 64(b). Report of UN Council for South-West Africa. Annex 2.
41. UN. General Assembly. XXII. A/PV.1627. 12 December 1967. Provisional. P. 97.
42. UN. General Assembly. XXII. A/PV.1567. 26 September 1967. Provisional. P. 51.
43. UN. General Assembly. XXII. A/PV. 1664. 28 May 1968. Pp. 8-10, 11. Provisional.
44. GA/Res/2325 (XXII). 21 December 1967.
45. S/Res/134 (1960). 1 April 1960.
46. SCOR. 18th Year. 1052nd Mtg. 2 August 1963. P. 16, pars. 65-66.
47. SCOR. 18th Year. 1054th Mtg. 6 August 1963. P. 19, par. 85.
48. S/Res/181 (1963). 7 August 1963.
49. S/Res/245. 25 January 1968. S/Res/246. 14 March 1968.
50. S/Res/163 (1961). 9 June 1961.
51. S/Res/218 (1965). 23 November 1965.
52. S/5425/Rev.1. 11 September 1963.
53. SCOR. 18th Year. 1064th Mtg. 9 September 1963. P. 2, par. 4.
54. SCOR. 18th Year. 1066th Mtg. 10 September 1963. P. 12, par. 76.
55. SC. Provisional. 20th Year. S/PV/1257. 12 November 1965. For an exposition of the British view see General Assembly. XXII. A/C.4/SR.1702. 31 October 1967. P. 2.
56. S/Res/217 (1965). 20 November 1965.
57. SC. Provisional. 21st Year. S/PV.1331. 8 December 1966.
58. SC. Provisional 21st Year. S/PV.1332. 9 December 1966.
59. SC. Provisional. 21st Year. S/PV.1333. 12 December 1966.
60. S/Res/232 (1966). 16 December 1966.
61. SC. Provisional. 21st Year. S/PV.1340. 16 December 1966.
62. SC. Provisional. 21st Year. S/PV.1331. 8 December 1966.
63. S/8545. 16 April 1968.
64. S/Res/253 (1968). 29 May 1968.
65. S/8786. 28 August 1968. Annex II, pp. 7, 50.
66. *Department of State Bulletin*, 54 (May 23, 1966), 800.

67. *Ibid.*, 56 (January 23, 1967), 143.
68. *Ibid.*
69. *Ibid.*, 54 (January 3, 1966), 14.
70. Charles Burton Marshall, *Crisis Over Rhodesia, A Skeptical View* (Baltimore: Johns Hopkins, 1967), p. 73.
71. *Department of State Bulletin*, 56 (January 20, 1967), 291.
72. Johan Galtung, "On the Effects of International Economic Sanctions. With Examples from the Case of Rhodesia," *World Politics*, 19 (April 1967), 378-416. George Alfred Mudge, "Domestic Policies and UN Activities: The Cases of Rhodesia and the Republic of South Africa," *International Organization*, 21 (Winter 1967), 55-78.
73. Press Release USUN-83 (68). May 29, 1968.
74. GA/Res/2307 (XXII). 13 December 1967.
75. S/5658. 20 April 1964. Annex, p. 25.
76. GAOR. XVIII. Special Political Cttee. 380th Mtg. 9 October 1963. P. 16. Cf., Amelia C. Leiss, "Efforts to Alter the Future: Military Measures," in Leiss, *op. cit.*, pp. 152, 155-164.
77. SCOR. 20th Year. Special Sup. No. 2. P. 298.
78. Cf., Philip Mason, "South Africa and the World: Some Maxims and Axioms," *Foreign Affairs*, 43 (October 1964), 159, 163-164.
79. U.S. Congress. House of Representatives. Committee on Foreign Affairs. *United States-South African Relations*. Hearings before the Subcommittee on Africa. 89th Cong., 2d Sess. 1966. Part I, p. 92.
80. Waldemar A. Nielsen, *African Battleline: American Policy Choices in Southern Africa* (New York and Evanston: Harper & Row, 1965), p. 86.
81. Dean Acheson, "The Arrogance of International Lawyers," *The International Lawyer*, 2 (July 1968), 593. Cf., "The Acheson-Goldberg Correspondence on Rhodesia," *Africa Report*, 12 (January 1967), 56-57.
82. *Congressional Record*, Vol. 113, No. 11 (January 26, 1967), S1016.
83. *Ibid.*, Vol. 113, No. 14 (February 1, 1967), H887.
84. *Ibid.*, Vol. 112, No. 137 (August 18, 1966), 18956.
85. *Ibid.*, Vol. 111, Pt. 5 (March 29, 1965), 6217-6218; Vol. 111, Pt. 5 (March 24, 1965), 5803-5804.
86. *Ibid.*, Vol. 109, Pt. 10 (July 31, 1963), 13829.
87. *Ibid.*, Vol. 113, No. 27 (February 21, 1967), H1627-1628; Vol. 113, No. 15 (February 2, 1967), H917; Vol. 113, No. 18 (February 7, 1967), A501; Vol. 113, No. 19 (February 8, 1967), A552.
88. Quoted by Rupert Emerson, *Africa and United States Policy* (Englewood Cliffs, N. J.: Prentice-Hall, 1967), p. 108.
89. *Congressional Record*, Vol. 114, No. 71 (April 29, 1968), S4566.
90. Nielsen, *op. cit.*, pp. 86-97.
91. George W. Ball, *The Discipline of Power* (Boston: Little, Brown, 1968), pp. 256-259. Cf., Gwendolen M. Carter, Thomas Karis, and Newell M. Stultz, *South Africa's Transkei. The Politics of Domestic Colonialism* (Evanston: Northwestern University Press, 1967), esp. pp. 175-184.

CHAPTER 10

1. David H. Bayley, *Public Liberties in the New States* (Chicago: Rand McNally, 1964), p. 2.
2. John P. Roche, "American Liberty: An Examination of the 'Tradition' of Freedom," in Milton R. Konvitz and Clinton Rossiter, eds., *Aspects of Liberty* (Ithaca: Cornell University Press, 1958), p. 133.
3. *Ibid.*, esp. pp. 145, 162.
4. James W. Prothro and Charles M. Grigg, "Fundamental Principles of Democracy: Bases of Agreement and Disagreement," *Journal of Politics*, 22 (May 1960), 276-294.
5. Samuel A. Stouffer, *Communism, Conformity, and Civil Liberties. A Cross-section of the Nation Speaks its Mind* (Garden City, N.Y.: Doubleday, 1955), pp. 27, 49, 57.
6. Herbert McClosky, "Consensus and Ideology in American Politics," *American Political Science Review*, 58 (June 1964), 375.
7. *Ibid.*
8. Seymour Martin Lipset, *Political Man: The Social Bases of Politics* (Garden City, N.Y.: Doubleday Anchor, 1963), p. 92.
9. *Ibid.*, pp. 95-96. Cf., Theodore W. Adorno *et al.*, *The Authoritarian Personality* (New York: Harper, 1950). Richard Christie and Peggy Cook, "A Guide to Published Literature Relating to the Authoritarian Personality," *Journal of Psychology*, 45 (April 1958), 171-199. William J. Goode, "Family Patterns and Human Rights," *International Social Science Journal*, Vol. 18, No. 1, 1966, pp. 41-54.
10. Lipset, *op. cit.*, pp. 39-40.
11. *Ibid.*, p. 51.
12. Charles C. Moskos, Jr., and Wendell Bell, "Attitudes towards Democracy among Leaders in Four Emergent Nations," *Studies in Comparative International Development* (St. Louis: Washington University, Social Science Institute, 1965), Vol. I, 1965, No. 14, p. 224.
13. Robert E. Scott, "Political Elites and Political Modernization: The Crisis of Transition," in Seymour Martin Lipset and Aldo Solari, *Elites in Latin America* (New York: Oxford University Press, 1967), p. 126.
14. OAS. Inter-American Juridical Committee. Strengthening and Effective Exercise of Democracy. Report prepared in accordance with Resolution VII of the Fouth Meeting of Consultation of Ministers of Foreign Affairs. CIJ-42 (Washington: Pan American Union, 1959 [1960?], p. 2.
15. Hanan C. Selvin and Warren O. Hagstrom, "Determinants of Support for Civil Liberties," *British Journal of Sociology*, 11 (March 1960), 51-73.
16. UN. Seminar on Human Rights in Developing Countries. Kabul, Afghanistan. 12-25 May 1964. Organized by the United Nations in Cooperation with the Government of Afghanistan. P. 19, par. 78.
17. GAOR. XV. Third Cttee. 1033rd Mtg. 24 November 1960. P. 251.

18. UN. Seminar on Human Rights in Developing Countries. Kabul, Afghanistan. 12-25 May 1964. P. 28, par. 127.
19. Hernán Santa Cruz, Special Reporter of the Sub-Commission on Prevention of Discrimination and Protection of Minorities, *Study of Discrimination in the Matter of Political Rights*. E/CN.4/Sub.2/213/Rev.1. P. 15.
20. Quincy Wright, "Policies for Strengthening the United Nations," in James Roosevelt, ed., *The Liberal Papers* (Garden City, N.Y.: Doubleday Anchor, 1962), pp. 319-320.
21. Bayley, *op cit.*, p. 126.
22. Y. Arkadyev, "International Human Rights Year," *International Affairs* (Moscow), No. 4 (April 1968), p. 8.
23. L. Onikov, "Socialism and Democracy," *International Affairs* (Moscow), No. 6 (June 1968), p. 9.
24. Bayley, *op. cit.*, p. 94.
25. John P. Humphrey, "The UN Charter and the Universal Declaration of Human Rights," in Evan Luard, ed., *The International Protection of Human Rights* (New York: Praeger, 1967), p. 46.
26. UN. ECOSOC. Official Records: 31st Session. Annexes. Agenda item 10 (Part II). Doc. E/3443. "Report on Developments in the Field of Freedom of Information Since 1954." P. 37.
27. Durward V. Sandifer and L. Ronald Scheman, *The Foundations of Freedom. The Interrelationships between Democracy and Human Rights* (New York: Praeger, 1966), p. 122.
28. Carl J. Friedrich, "Rights, Liberties, Freedoms: A Reappraisal," *American Political Science Review*, 57 (December 1963), 849.
29. Dr. José Joaquin Caicedo Castilla, *The Work of the Inter-American Juridical Committee* (Washington: Pan American Union, June 1964), p. 29.
30. Wright, "Freedom and Human Rights under International Law," *loc. cit.*, p. 196.
31. Cf., Samuel P. Huntington, *Political Order in Changing Societies* (New Haven: Yale University Press, 1968). Charles W. Anderson, *Politics and Economic Change in Latin America. The Governing of Restless Nations* (Princeton: Van Nostrand, 1967).

### CHAPTER 11

1. Cf., Franklin H. Williams' address in the "Symposium on the International Law of Human Rights," *Howard Law Journal*, 11 (Spring 1965), 383.
2. Louis Henkin, "The United Nations and Human Rights," *International Organization*, 19 (Summer 1965), 514.
3. Jean-Flavien Lalive, in A. H. Robertson, ed., *Human Rights in National and International Law* (Dobbs Ferry, N.Y.: Oceana, 1968), pp. 332-333.
4. Henkin, *loc. cit.*, p. 511.

5. Moses Moskowitz, *The Politics and Dynamics of Human Rights* (Dobbs Ferry, N.Y.: Oceana, 1968), pp. 88-89.
6. *Ibid.*, p. 92.
7. *Department of State Bulletin*, 52 (January 4, 1965), 10.
8. Henkin, *loc. cit.*, p. 514.
9. Quincy Wright, "Policies for Strengthening the United Nations," in James Roosevelt, ed., *The Liberal Papers* (Garden City, N.Y.: Doubleday Anchor, 1962), p. 316.
10. Henkin, *loc. cit.*, p. 506.
11. José A. Cabranes, "Human Rights and Non-Intervention in the Inter-American System," *Michigan Law Review*, 65 (April 1967), 1179.
12. *Ibid.*, p. 1181.
13. U.S. Congress. House. Committee on Foreign Affairs. *United States-South African Relations.* Hearings before the Sub-committèe on Africa. 89th Cong., 2d Sess. 1966. Part II, p. 340.

# Index